Acclaim for "Falling Uphill"

[Stoll] did something most of us would not do: He decided to ride his bicycle around the world. His impulse isn't as strange as it might sound. Humans have always sought answers to life's perplexing questions by undertaking long and arduous journeys.
  ~ San Francisco Chronicle

It was an exhausting yet exhilarating trip filled with both human kindness and treachery, with nature's beauty, challenge and danger.
  ~ Milwaukee Journal Sentinel

I've found an author whose book sucked me in and made me contemplate brushing off the old passport and booking the first cheap flight anywhere. ~ Beth I.

A book that makes me itch to get on the road again.... What surprised me was the style; not just another travelogue from A to B, but a whole philosophy of life and cycling. The best read since I read "Zen and the Art of Motorcycle Maintenance" over 10 years ago! ~ Andy G.

Scott's accomplishments and struggles reveal the beautiful and ugly sides of human nature, and his story gives us hope that we can all follow our dreams, no matter how foolish or impossible they seem. ~ Kate M.

A masterpiece on humanity. Thanks for not quitting so we can read about it and at the same time enrich our own lives. ~ Dick and Ingrid A.

The more I read, the more I remember my own journeys, my own stories, my own difficulties struggling with great questions. ~ Patrick M.

I recognize the struggles you described, not so much because I traveled as far or as rough as you, but the struggle a lot of us have to be more appreciative of our lot in life, and to see the world with new eyes everyday. ~ Chris D.

I found it very enlightening and profound. Through the author's words and experiences, I've had many self-realizations. See! He did make a difference. ~ Gerald H.

Scott's courage is a tremendous inspiration to would-be adventurers everywhere! ~ Michelle H.

What a great way to see the earth and its people. What a gift to share. ~ Bruce L.

Thanks for the chance to peek at the world through your eyes. ~ Jan

FALLING UPHILL

25,742 miles, 1461 days,
50 countries, 6 continents
& 4 moments of enlightenment
on a bicycle.

Scott Stoll

Falling Uphill
25,742 miles, 1461 days, 50 countries, 6 continents
& 4 moments of enlightenment on a bicycle.

Published by The Argonauts. First edition 2008. Printed in the United States.

Cover photo of "American Bull" by artist Dwayne Wilcox, as photographed by Scott Stoll, copyright permission courtesy of Sandy Conard (owner). Center cover photo and Guatemalan chicken bus courtesy of Dennis Snader. Additional thanks to Edwin, Debbie, Matt and everyone else that played impromptu photographers or models upon my request and whom I believe wish to remain anonymous.

Some names, places and events have been combined and/or changed to protect the identity of those involved and/or provide artistic clarity, but do not significantly alter the story's emotional authenticity as experienced by the author.

For up to date information on this title page, please visit:
http://www.theargonauts.com/falling-uphill/copyright.shtml

Ordering information:
Falling Uphill is available at special bulk discounts upon request.
www.theArgonauts.com
or: http://www.theargonauts.com/falling-uphill/how-to-order.shtml

Library of Congress Control Number: 2008909714

ISBN: 978-0-61523-045-0

The gentle reader will never, never know what a consummate ass he can become until he goes abroad.

~ Mark Twain

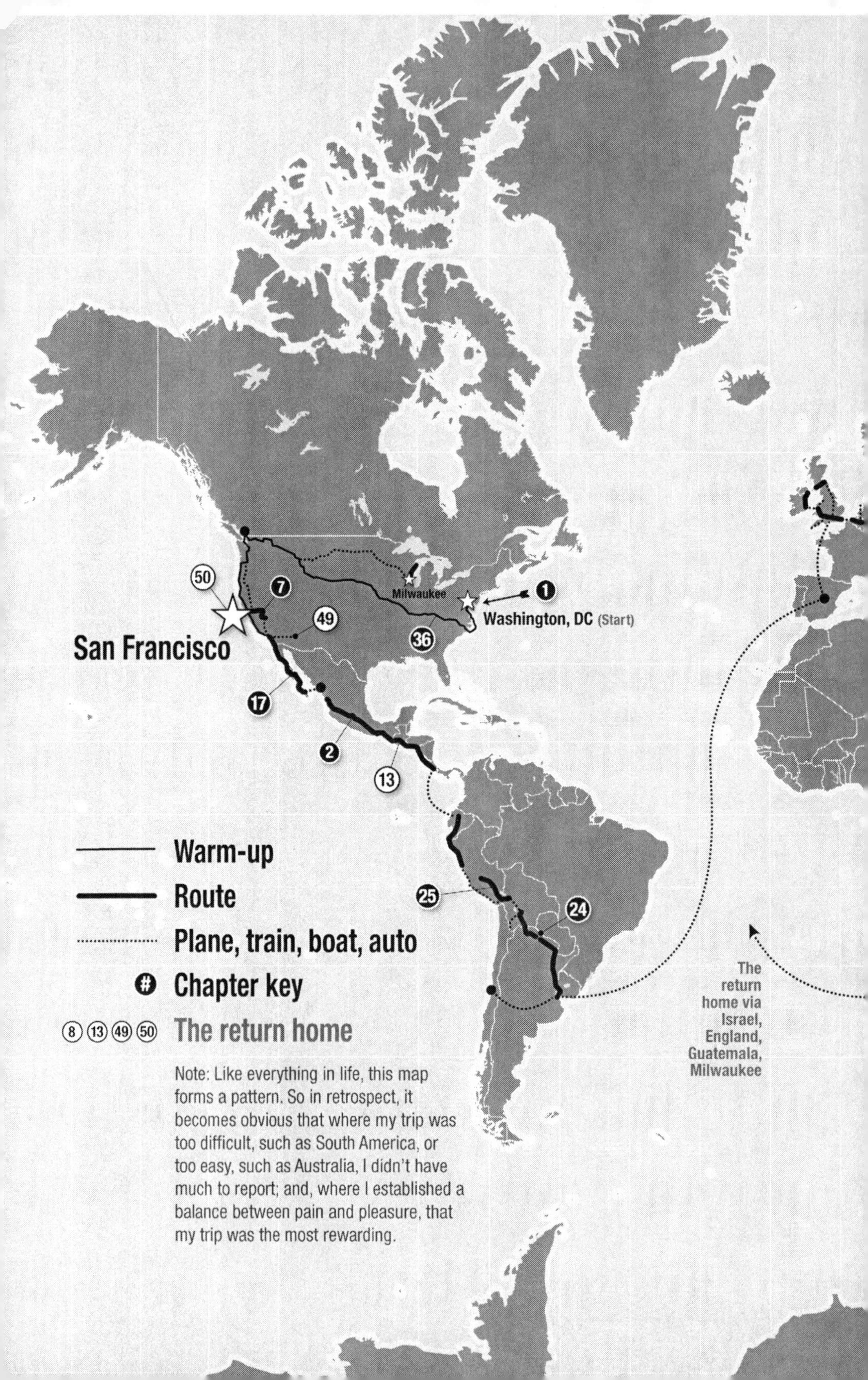

50

7

50

San Francisco

49

Milwaukee

Washington, DC (Start)

36

17

2

13

25

24

Warm-up

Route

Plane, train, boat, auto

8 **Chapter key**

8 13 49 50 **The return home**

Note: Like everything in life, this map
forms a pattern. So in retrospect, it
becomes obvious that where my trip was
too difficult, such as South America, or
too easy, such as Australia, I didn't have
much to report; and, where I established a
balance between pain and pleasure, that
my trip was the most rewarding.

The
return
home via
Israel,
England,
Guatemala,
Milwaukee

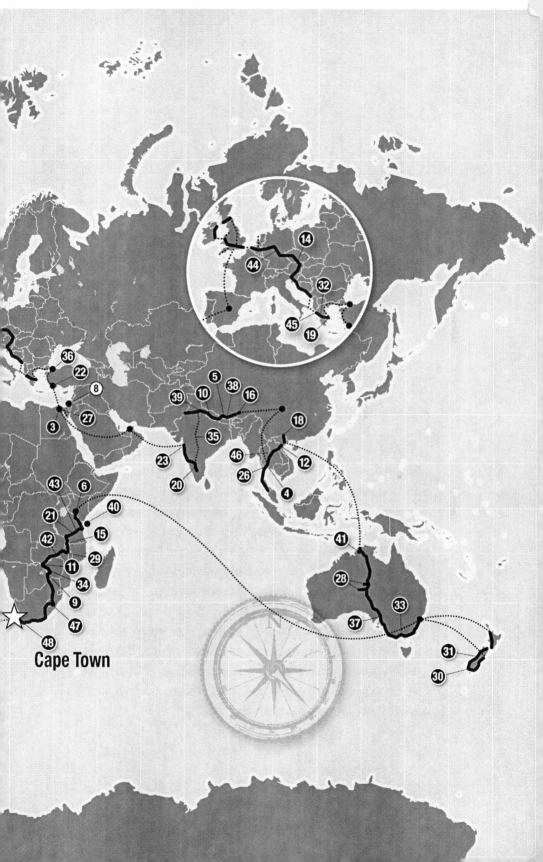

Cape Town

Acknowledgements

It truly took me years to absorb the lessons I learned while I traveled, and one of the toughest lessons I learned was the lesson of coming home, not only to my country, but to myself. I feel I owe everyone a debt of gratitude for helping make my journey of self-discovery and my book possible. Specifically, thanks to my family and Dennis for setting my wheels in motion, and the tens of thousands of people that I met along the way who kept them spinning, your kindness and hospitality have been a tribute to humanity. Thanks to my armchair fans, many days I was inspired to keep going for everyone who said they never could. I even feel thankful for those people who fueled my passion by saying that I couldn't do it, and I was a fool for trying. Finally, thanks to all my future readers that will help bring Falling Uphill to life. I hope you find my adventures and misadventures entertaining, inspiring and somewhat enlightening.

May the winds be with you. ~ Scott

Table of contents

PART III: Oneness

Epilogue

Preface

During my long years of meditative cycling, despite moments of agony, months of chronic pain, illness, injury and overexposure, I realized my journey was many times more joyful than painful; however, ironically, I discovered it was the misadventures that forged my character and revealed my truer self, like suffering from heat exhaustion and realizing everything I owned was worth one glass of water, and if I had one wish before I died it would be to say goodbye to the ones I loved, and like standing on mountain tops in foreign cultures, realizing my entire knowledge base (belief system) didn't work anymore, and that it was possible, if not desirable, to survive with a totally different concept of reality.

As the Earth spun under my wheels, the miles began to burn the self-pity out of my mind and body. I slowly realized that I'd trained myself to be comfortably numb—or should I say?—that my culture conditioned me to be numb, feel helpless and wallow in my suffering; conversely, my culture also demanded force and encouraged the attitude that you're either running with the wolves—taking what you want before someone else does, thinking you're smarter, faster and better—or you're hiding among the sheep—playing follow the leader, hoping to be sent to pasture rather than slaughter.

My travels sparked new ideas: conceivably life can be a cooperative endeavor rather than competitive. Perhaps our cultural concepts like, "life is a bitch and then you die," are illusions; and, stumbling and suffering through mistakes one-by-one to learn life's lessons and grow was only half the formula, or less than half? What if the spiritual cliché, "enjoy the moment," was the other half?

Much later than I want to admit, after I burned through several cycling companions (many people would join my journey for sections), I began to experience the beauty of the world and its people, especially the kindness of strangers, who would often give me their last morsel of food, or exert great effort just to say hello. Somewhere in India, I stopped looking for *the answer*—as if there was one big answer that would solve all my problems—and learned to cherish the never-ending mysteries of life and self as they unfolded.

One mystery was that everywhere I went, sometimes dozens of times per day, people asked me the same questions. Most had never read a newspaper or watched television; some had never seen a foreigner, heard of America, or even knew in which country they lived. The frequency and the order of the questions gave me insight to human nature—that we all are hoping to travel from a path of struggle and survival, through a quest for meaning and happiness, and ultimately seeking peace and enlightenment.

This book is a collection of short stories written so that the reader may relive the various "good" and "bad" experiences of cycling around the world. I begin with stories that illustrate the most common questions asked throughout my journey, like the seemingly mundane, "What do you eat?" (A question that implies the majority of the world's inhabitants haven't met their basic needs, or haven't overcome their fear of survival despite their abundance.) I end with less common, yet spiritually profound questions, like, "Are you happy?" (A question that implies happiness is a relatively rare commodity, which everyone is seeking; and, I suspect people wanted verification that if they followed their dreams, they could also find happiness.) However, the book may be read in any order, including chronologically by following the chapter key on the map. The first two chapters, the *how* and the *why,* are not the most common questions, though I think they're the most relevant questions. They belong in the section about questing, or what you might call emotional survival, but they serve as a nice introduction.

I offer one of the lessons I learned upfront to the reader as a caveat: this book is full of my observations and interpretations and misinterpretations; I'm not an authority of any kind and you should judge me only by what I can exemplify, not theorize—I don't think anyone wants theories as much as they want experiences; therefore, this book is meant primarily for your enjoyment. That being said, I'm sure as you combine your life experiences with mine, you will make some delightful discoveries. Though, frankly, if you're seeking a magical solution to life, I suggest you drop all your books, get on a bicycle and go find it.

Author's note: When I say "bicycle" I often mean the literal and metaphorical vehicle of the spiritual journey.

Introduction

*Better to sink in boundless deeps, than float on vulgar shoals;
and give me, ye gods, an utter wreck, if wreck I do.*

~ Herman Melville

1 ○ Why are you riding a bicycle around the world?

Lounging on a couch that smells like old newspapers, I drink bitter ice beer because it has the highest alcohol to expense ratio. The shades are drawn and the hypnotic, blue flicker of mind-numbing television floods the apartment. This is my home remedy for depression. A week ago, just before Christmas, my girlfriend dumped me. Her words echo in my mind, "I love you, but I don't like you."

With a rattle and a puff of mildew and pet dander, the front door swings open. "What are you doing home?" my best friend, Samuel, asks. Five months ago, we had moved to Washington, DC, with dreams of shedding our Midwestern, corn-fed roots. We planned to climb the social ladder by dating rich, famous and powerful women, and to climb the corporate ladder by working harder, faster and smarter than everyone else.

"I got fired today," I say despondently.

"What happened?"

"I went into my boss's office to wish him a happy New Year and he said, 'I've been in this business for thirty years, and—I have to be honest—for your own good—I've never seen an art director as bad as you.'"

"Is that true?" Samuel asks.

"Everyone seems to think so. Just before I left he said, 'Don't bother to ask me for a recommendation.'"

"Did you tell him about Mary Ann? That chick was sexually harassing you. I told you to watch your back. You can't trust anyone."

"No. I think she was taking credit for my work and bad-mouthing me—playing me against my boss," I sigh and look to Samuel for sympathy, but he hangs his head sheepishly and looks at me with worried eyes. "What? Why are you looking at me like that?"

"There's something I need to tell you...."

I sip my beer, waiting, as he fidgets, as if afraid of my reaction.

"Well? Just say it."

"I eloped."

"What? Since when were you engaged? I thought you didn't even like her," I say, my voice edged with betrayal.

"I've been thinking about that a lot. I made a list. She's almost everything I want." He takes a deep breath. "There's something else.... I'm moving to Omaha."

"Nebraska! Isn't that the corn something-or-other state? I thought we were escaping the Midwest."

"I'm leaving this weekend."

"Who's going to pay rent?"

"I'll try to help, but you'll have to find somebody else. I'm sorry." He walks into the bedroom, shuts the door and calls his wife, leaving me to my bedroom, which is really the living room with a smelly couch patterned like a bad Hawaiian shirt.

"This isn't how my life was supposed to turn out," I think. I can't conceptualize my fear yet, but deep down, I realize that I'd been working overtime to accumulate all the cultural symbols of success—things I didn't necessarily want, but feared I needed in order to be loved—and it had all backfired. "Where did I go wrong? As long as I can remember, I've been looking for a solution to life," I think. "But I haven't found any answers in a thousand books—mostly contradictions. Nor have I met anyone with satisfying answers or proof—mostly dogma and theory."

As I sink deeper into the must of my hand-me-down couch, I realize that I only have one life, one chance, that I don't want to be the guy lying on his deathbed full of regrets and what-ifs, I wonder, "If I could do anything, what would I do?"

I roll this thought around inside my head, listing all the things I enjoy and don't enjoy, and imagine possible and impossible.

After an hour, when the answer to the meaning of my life still eludes me, I growl obscenities and sink deeper down into the couch, resigned to a life of mediocrity, when during a moment of peacefulness the "impossible" answer pops into my head:

"Why not ride a bicycle around the world?"

Surprised, I sit up and think, "Yes. Why not just experience life for myself? Why not find the answers? Why not go find happiness or die trying, because if I can't find happiness, life ain't worth living?"

Eventually I would discover a dog-eared copy of *Walden* by Thoreau, one of many synchronicities that would propel my trip. It summarized and reinforced my motivation: "I went to the woods because I wished to live deliberately, to front only the essential facts of life, and see if I could not learn what it had to teach, and not, when I came to die, discover that I had not lived."

The idea grows out of control, like a virus with its own mind, and the following year I test myself by riding across the USA from border to border and coast to coast. The year after my 6200-mile warm-up, my friend Dennis, whose bicycle path I crossed in the Grand Tetons, asks, "Scott, were you serious when you said you wanted to bicycle around the world?"

"Of course, I'm serious," I reply with bravado.

"I've decided—I'm going to do it, and I invite you to join me." Dennis has always been good at following his heart without analyzing the logistics and taking the path "less traveled" without regrets; whereas, my nature is more like the first stanza of Robert Frost's poem:

Two roads diverged in a yellow wood,
And sorry I could not travel both
And be one traveler, long I stood
And looked down one as far as I could
To where it bent in the undergrowth.

Dennis concludes with an ultimatum, "If you don't want to come, I'll find someone else."

Our friend, Vilmar, witnesses the exchange and makes a comment that would echo throughout the trip, "Why don't you guys just go sit on a beach in Mexico and have the cabana girls bring you umbrella drinks everyday for four years?"

I'd already made the decision, but if it weren't for Dennis I may never have had the courage to begin. After three years of preparation (including knee and eye surgery) and just five days before the destruction of the Twin Towers in New York City, I leave behind everything that I think I am—or so I thought—and make the first pedal stroke of a four-year quest that would cover 41,444 kilometers (the equatorial circumference of the Earth is only 40,075 kilometers) through 50 countries and 6 continents (not including boats, planes, trains and automobiles).

2 ◯ How do you ride a bicycle around the world?

If the first question a person asks me is, "Why?" I know they're a person who makes their decisions based upon emotions; whereas, if the first question they ask is "How?" I know I'm talking to someone who's very rational, and like myself, much more likely to get bogged down in details before, if ever, doing anything.

Since the world is mostly water, Dennis and I had to be creative with our definition of cycling around the world. I considered cycling every continent and every country, but the definition between continent, continental plate and island aren't clearly defined; and Dennis said it was silly to zigzag between the invisible and often disputed political borders. So, we defined bicycling around the world as cycling the equivalent distance of the circumference of the Earth without treading the same ground twice, while visiting as many cultures and world wonders as practical. Dennis discovered that by crisscrossing the equator (the seasons are in opposition), we could follow a perpetual summer around the world. As far as planning specifically when and where to go, including visas, guidebooks and maps, Dennis made the prophetic remark, "One wrong turn and everything will change. I don't see the point of planning." The challenge was saving money. Dennis estimated an average expense of 20 United States dollars (USD) per day (including supplies, food, airfare and entertainment) about the same cost as an average car. (To Dennis' equation, I added 10% for ignorance, and 10% for stupidity, which proved to be a very accurate budget.) By "depriving" myself of fancy food, fashionable clothes, beer, coffee, music and movies, I was able to reach my goal in three years. (In retrospect, compared to the average world citizen, I was still living a life of luxury with hot and clean water, a warm and dry bed, three meals a day, a car and bicycle. I even had a cushy job making art on the computer.) So, we each bought a steel mountain bike (steel can be welded back together if you happen to snap it in half), filled our panniers with a repair kit, spare parts, maps, guidebooks, shortwave radio, medicine, tent, sleeping bag, stove, water filter, clothes and food; and, late summer in San Francisco we aimed south and began pedaling.

Six weeks later, after a false start in Tijuana, where we discovered our credit cards didn't work in the cash machines, and had to return to America, we reach the heart of the baking furnace of Baja, Mexico, where even the cacti must suffer heat exhaustion. A Mexican asks Dennis where we're going. Dennis replies, "We're going to Argentina." Telling people we're cycling to Argentina is much simpler than telling them we're cycling around the world, which results in a lot of blank stares and non sequitur comments as if people are deleting it from their memory as soon as they hear it. Conversely, rather than denying the idea, other people become confrontational, essentially accusing us of being fools for taking such a huge risk with no obvious payoff or guarantee of success. Dennis and I both have the impression these people find a simple idea threatening.

Americans often respond by asking, "Argentina? On a bike? Is that possible? Do they allow that?" (Presumably, "they" means the government.) However, the Mexican isn't surprised but does exclaim, *"¿Por aqui?"* (Through here?) and looks around, as if for the first time, at the barren landscape shimmering in the heat. In the future, anytime our situation would look grim, Dennis would echo, *"¿Por aqui?"*

Explaining how to ride a bicycle around the world is a lot more challenging than I imagined. Once, I explained circumnavigating the globe to two Egyptian men with the aid of my map. "Is this America?" they asked.

"No, that is Australia." I turned the map right-side up. "Here is America."

"What is this?" They then asked.

"That is New Zealand."

"What comes after New Zealand?"

On my map, New Zealand happened to be in the corner. I rolled my map into a cylinder to demonstrate the world is round, but their expressions were as stone-faced as Ramses' granite statue until they switched topics, "And where is Egypt?"

I was surprised; was it possible these two men, fluent in several languages, wise in the culture of Egypt and the religion of Islam, have never seen a map? "It is here."

"Ah! You see. Egypt is in the center of the world," they proudly exclaimed. "That is the problem with Americans. They think they are the center of the world, but they are not. They should remember this before the Arab nations teach them."

One Egyptian pointed to my bike and asked, "How do you cross the oceans?"

"I put extra air in my tires," I laughed at my old joke, but they weren't amused.

After Baja, Dennis and I take an overnight ferry to the Mexican mainland. (In the beginning, dolphins surf our wake; and, in the end, the septic system overflows and sewage runs throughout the ship.) We cycle past the heat and annoying American tourists into the cool mountains, through rainbow-colored pueblos, up cobblestone streets with mountain streams flowing on both sides, through the smells of roasting meat and corn, past young machismo men wolf whistling at our spandex tights and young women in tight jeans slung low on the hip, past old women bent into peculiar shapes after a lifetime of scrubbing clothes or making tortillas and asymmetric men with every sinewy muscle formed to wield a machete. We attempt to cycle the old Mex 15 highway, but the traffic is like a forest of leaves flowing down a narrow, twisty creek, and a rock tossed by an adolescent riding in the back of a sugarcane truck leaves a nifty scar in my helmet. Nearby, two policemen appear to be guarding the carcass of a recently deceased cow. I stop to ask if this road is safe for cyclists. They give me the dumbfounded look—*¿Por aqui?*—and gesture to the cow. Its heart has been ripped out and is lying on its ribcage. "*¡No, no es seguro!*" We've heard many rumors of corrupt Mexican police, but rather than blackmail or bribery, they suggest we reroute ourselves down the new Mex 15 *Autopista* prohibited to cyclists. "Perhaps, it's more paperwork to guard dead cyclists," Dennis remarks.

We have a general idea of where we're going—following a coin toss or a pretty line on a grossly outdated and inaccurate map—but at any one moment, we're essentially lost. Often I ask myself, "*¿Por aqui?*" That is one of the main differences between Dennis and myself. He's happy wherever he is and cycles because cycling itself is a reason; I cycle because I'm going somewhere looking for something, some absolute answer to the meaning of life, specifically mine... or, at least, a pleasant distraction.

Where three mountain ranges collide and the roads average twice as steep as considered legally safe in America, and I'm too tired to make any profound observations other than I wished I'd paid someone to suck the fat off me, we visit the Monarch Butterfly Sanctuary. We climb 11 kilometers (KM) to an elevation over 3200 meters. My lungs nearly implode. My muscles burn. And I feel as if I might fall asleep while cycling—my first experience of altitude sickness.

We park the bikes and hike further and dizzier up the mountain to view a colony of millions of monarchs clinging to the pine trees, hundreds weigh down each bough like a heavy snow. I'm expecting the trees to be on fire and skies alit with flaming flakes of monarchs, but it's a cold and cloudy day. The butterflies huddle close for warmth, the backsides of their closed wings appear like rusty-brown autumn leaves. Some, frozen helpless, tumble end over end to the ground.

Once, while cycling through Bolivia, we followed the Rio Negro where it gutted the Bolivian Andes, dumping them into Argentina. Everything was mud. Dozens of waterfalls flowed down the cliffs and under or over the road. We rolled through them or portaged our bikes over them. Hundreds of butterflies fluttered by the puddles in the road, soaking up the moisture. They appeared like gems scattered in the mud. Species I've never seen, like a black butterfly with wingtips colored the bluest of blue oceans, another was striped like a desert sunset, and my favorite, a tiny, rust-colored butterfly whose wings tapered to teardrop shapes. I wondered where nature finds the energy and innovation to produce such precious colors and delicate shapes? And to what purpose? Even the word "butterfly" delicately flips and flaps over my tongue and teeth. The Greek word *psyche* may be translated as *soul* or *butterfly*. Some ancient European cultures thought dreams were the soul-butterfly wandering through other worlds.

I was dismayed to see construction workers knocking the Bolivian mountains into the river valley. In a year, that road will be paved. Then the cars, trucks and buses will come and their radiators will filter the butterflies out of the thick atmosphere. Likewise, chainsaws fell the monarch's homes in Mexico to be reshaped into the homes for people in the nearby, ever-hungry megalopolis of Mexico City. The butterflies never return to the exact grove of trees and the lumberjack's roar seemed an ill omen. (The following year a freak storm and lack of trees would kill several-hundred million monarchs, nearly the entire population in Mexico.)

The monarch is the only insect that migrates, the only animal to migrate over several generations; and, there-fore, the only migratory animal that dies before returning home. They begin around the Great Lakes, near my childhood home. It takes them four generations to reach the mountains of Mexico and return to the cool forests of the Midwest and Canada. As I investigate the monarch moun-

tain, I shuffle my feet through the piles of butterflies trying not to crush the frozen grandchildren of the butterflies that had tickled the flowers in my parent's garden and ponder: Do caterpillars dream of the Great Lakes or Mexican mountains? Do butterflies wake from their metamorphosis and think, "Where am I?" or, "Where am I going?" Do they ask, "¿*Por aqui?*" or, "Why?" or, "How?"

Am I, like the monarch, born with an instinct to migrate? Is my trip like a chrysalis? Will I return home metamorphosed? Or, will my great grandchildren complete my journey?

I don't know what I'm looking for, but I presume I'll know it when I flutter by it.

Meanwhile, it's relatively easy to cycle around the world as long as I keep those wheels spinning, especially considering I have lots of stubbornness and angst to fuel my legs. Or in Nietzsche's words, "He who has a *why* to live for can bear with almost any *how*."

Monarchs clinging to a branch.
Opposite: Washing the mud off my bike during a river crossing. In Bolivia, the riverbeds were used as impromptu roads.
Photo courtesy of Dennis Snader

Part I:
Survival

He who cannot change the very fabric of his thought will never be able to change reality, and will never, therefore, make any progress.

~ Muhammad Anwar El Sadat

3

How are you?

He had arrived in Alexandria aboard the first transatlantic steamer whose primary cargo was "picnickers and sightseers"—tourists. It was shortly after the Civil War when African Americans were freed yet the Native Americans were still being hunted in the Indian War. During his "pleasure excursion" Mark Twain reported:

> *A howling swarm of beggars followed us—surrounded us—almost headed us off. A sheikh, in flowing white burnoose and gaudy headgear, was with them. He wanted more baksheesh [a tip or bribe depending on your point of view]. But we had adopted a new code—it was millions for defense, but not a cent for baksheesh. I asked him if he could persuade the others to depart if we paid him. He said yes—for ten francs. We accepted the contract, and said: "Now persuade your vassals to fall back."*
>
> *He swung his long staff round his head and three Arabs bit the dust. He capered among the mob like a very maniac. His blows fell like hail, and wherever one fell a subject went down. We had to hurry to the rescue and tell him it was only necessary to damage them a little—he need not kill them. In two minutes we were alone with the sheikh, and remained so. The persuasive powers of this illiterate savage were remarkable.*

During my pleasure excursion around the world on a bicycle 135 years later, I visit the Great Pyramids of Egypt. Now America's "War on Terrorism" occupies the globe and the cultural gap between the West and the Middle East—including the Egyptian Arabs—seems to be widening into a chasm. The howling swarms of beggars still exist almost unchanged except they've evolved their trade into an art form as if Twain had inspired them with tales of Tom Sawyer and Huckleberry Finn.

Simply arriving at the Pyramids of Giza is a challenge: On my first attempt, I'm befriended by one of the New Age con artists, an *amigo falso* as the Latin Americans call them. "How are you?" he begins, the most popular question in the world; a question that in the States has become rhetorical, but in other cultures is of utmost sincerity. I believe the frequency and simplicity of this question emphasizes how important it is for people to feel connected; and, because this question plucks the heartstrings is why it also begins most scams, intending to befriend and disarm the mark. My false friend shepherds me to the "government stables" promising a cheap tour of the pyramids on camelback. I suspect he and the tour guides were in cahoots and their sales pitch includes every low and high ball in the book. I promptly feign a migraine and leave. On my second attempt, I succumb to a relapse of Egyptian Giardia while waiting hours for the bus, which, being labeled in Arabic numerals, I'd probably missed several times. Finally, I rely on my steel horse and risk Cairo's lawless roads. I arrive shortly after sunrise just as the gauntlet of hucksters, panhandlers, touts and merchants begin formation. Acting uninterested so as not to invite solicitation, I ride past the piles of plastic pyramids, armies of Anubis, masks of Tutankhamen, litters of sphinxes and the other paraphernalia of ancient Egypt resurrected by its children; and past the modern usurpers of culture: Coca-Cola, Cadbury Chocolate, Nescafé, Marlboro cigarettes, potato chips, bottled water, toilet paper and their various generic incarnations. I hitch my bike to a post near the armed guards and enter the side gate.

To my amazement, I've circumvented the hordes of tourists—I'm alone. I wander through the desert paths and climb atop the wall before the Sphinx, like a tiny mouse just about to be pounced upon, and ponder the riddles of life. In the distance, the jagged form of the Great Pyramid of Cheops emerges as the Saharan sun evaporates the spirit of the Nile. Mesmerized by the new mystery, I leave the contemplative sphinx, cross the road and tread through the rose-colored desert. I expected to be swimming in sand; however, my feet crunch through gravel and rocks, occasionally wading through small pools of sand. I spiral around the Great Pyramid—the only surviving Ancient Wonder of the World—until I can see the grain of the rock like the whorls on a giant's toe. As the sun rises behind the apex of the pyramid shrouding it in a sparkling halo, I wonder about the motivation of a civilization that devoted so many resources to building a mountain of rock in the desert. Then the sun passes the peak and my retinas explode like a fireworks display. At any moment, I half expect, half hope the pyramids to funnel magical, cosmic energy into my spirit.... Except, a policeman beckons me, disturbing my anticipated catharsis. Apparently, I've crossed an invisible line or broken an unwritten law, but after consultation, "How are you?" he only offers his image to my camera in exchange for baksheesh. "Or—" he rubs his fingers together "—you climb." He gestures to the top.

The spell—whether it was spiritual energy or just wishful thinking—is broken. I expend most of my efforts for the rest of the day keeping the money in my pockets. For instance, even circumnavigating the Great Pyramid I can't escape being harangued by Mohammed and his camel, Charlie Brown. Not until I hide among some guards is Mohammed forced to leave when they flog Charlie into a trot. Several hours later, Mohammed, along with his nephew, Ali, corner me in the Western Cemetery, out of sight of the guards. Finally, I concede, "For the experience, as you say," and hire one con artist to keep the rest at bay, negotiating an average sum for a one-hour tour through the desert atop Charlie Brown. I'm sure Ali contrives to make it as hot, boring and bone jolting as possible, stopping every few minutes with pleas for baksheesh—"How are you, sir? You like? Gimmemoney."—until I'm happy to jump off the flatulent camel (Egyptian music according to Ali) after only 30 minutes and begin limping bow-legged back through the desert to Cheops; however, Ali has seen my money belt and approaches me aggressively, "Gimmemoney now!" I've learned—or is it instinctual?—that when threatened by a bear to become the lion. I cross my arms, veins and muscles popping, and put on my best make-my-day expression. Ali's steps stutter and stop; he glares angrily, hops on Charlie Brown and trots away.

Later, I'm separated from more Egyptian Pounds when an American woman purchases the last 19 tickets to enter the tomb of the Great Pyramid. "Please, I just need one ticket. I've come a long way and I must leave tomorrow," I say.

"I've got a tour waiting, and don't have enough tickets myself. They paid a lot of money and came all the way here on a bus." She points to a first-class, air-conditioned tour bus with a television and toilet.

"I came all the way here on a bicycle," I plead, but she simply walks away counting her tickets; however, the guard at the ticket booth winks at me. Some magic must still be left in the air because a little baksheesh materializes another ticket.

Only once do I gratefully pay baksheesh to a guard, when for a moment we're alone in the Great Pyramid, he photographs me lying in the red-granite sarcophagus with my wrists crossed over my heart just like King Cheops had over 5000 years ago. I nearly fill the length and width of the sarcophagus. The sarcophagus used to contain the coffin and the mummy of King Cheops (unless you subscribe to the popular theory that the sarcophagus was actually a battery casing and the pyramid was an Atlantian power plant). I always thought the pharaohs to be gigantic because weren't they, in fact, gods? However, it seems they were mere mortals dwarfed by a plebian, corn-fed American.

I avoid 23 schemes to lighten my wallet. However, in the end, when heat and thirst have dulled my mind, I'm trapped. As I enter the Eastern Cemetery, an official-looking Egyptian guides me towards the Queen's Tomb. I stand in the queue and when it's my turn he says, "How are you? May I see your ticket? Thank you. Please, hurry!" He motions for me to enter. "We are closing soon." I descend a small shaft that angles steeply into the earth for about 25 meters and opens into the square tomb. The room along with its cubicles and shelves is carved out of one huge stone. It's an unremarkable experience until the power fails and I'm temporarily trapped in the tomb with the imaginary ghosts of ancient Egypt. I bumble up the shaft towards the light, fearing I've been forgotten. I barely emerge before the Egyptian holding my ticket is walking briskly away. "Hurry. We are closing. The Tomb of the Engineer is this way." I dash after him mainly to recover my ticket so that I may exit the park without hassle.

"Do you work here?" I ask suspiciously.

"Yes. We must hurry. We close in twenty minutes." He's trying to distract me and I know his guided tour will cost me money, but my eyes are weary of inanimate monuments and my spirit craves excitement. We stop at two square shafts ten meters deep that lead to some tunnels. "Secret passages," my guide says. "This one leads to the Great Pyramid and this one to the Sphinx. Offerings of money, beads, scarabs and food were thrown into the pits so the souls of the Kings may survive in the afterlife." He leads me around some more block structures. "The tombs of the slaves who built the pyramids. There were more than three-hundred-thousand slaves, working for thirty years." A few more twists and turns. "This is it." He disappears into a small hole. Like the other tombs I visited, tomb robbers had ripped the hole through the stone walls. I crawl through the hole, dragging my backpack behind me, mindlessly following my guide. We jump down a meter into a small chamber behind an iron gate. Mohammed Ali (not to be confused with the camel drivers Mohammed and Ali) puts his index finger over his lips and whispers, "This area is closed. Prohibited. But for you I make special trip."

I pause to assess my predicament: though I think of people like Mohammed Ali as hucksters, they think of themselves as businessmen because both parties always agree upon the prices. I've heard few stories of thievery (which is punishable by having your fingers cut off) and no stories of violence (which presumably has more heinous consequences). However, within the constraints of the law, it's an Egyptian-eat-Egyptian world. Survival is generally governed by power and money. For instance, power rules the apparently lawless roads. The largest, most powerful vehicle has the right of way. Smaller vehicles must move or be crushed. As for money, it governs the people. There are legions of Egyptians proposing, "Anything you want—papyrus, perfume—I can get. Very cheap. I have friend. Very nice."

My guide waits patiently, his face is creased in a pleasant manner, his tummy bulges slightly, his arms show no veins or muscles, which suggests that he's not a strong or mischievous man. I judge that I'm the one with the advantage in size, strength and money. Besides, the ground is covered in footprints. I'm not the first fool. "Come. It is not safe to stand by the gate," my guide prompts.

Full of pride and overconfident of my abilities, I follow him around the corner and down a few meters. On our right, a tunnel hewn through the stone leads to the bottom of the shafts that I'd peered down moments ago. "The engineer built this secret tunnel so that he could steal the sacrifices," says Mohammed Ali; however, there's nothing left to steal except, perhaps, a Coca-Cola bottle floating in the sand. The super-secret tunnels illuminate our path and the clouds of dust we kick into the air. We follow a tunnel to the left and enter a small chamber containing five blocks of white granite with mummy shapes carved into them. They appear to be lidless coffins that used to fit into the rectangular holes in the floor. I'm taller and wider than any of the blocks. The ceiling is low, so we duckwalk through the coffins, hop down another shaft, walk hunchbacked through a short tunnel, and emerge in another small chamber. Coffins, including tiny ones for children, lay helter-skelter on the floor. I imagine they were heedlessly shoved around in a frantic search for treasure. The sarcophagus of the engineer is a large granite box recessed in the opposite wall. It's still covered with the granite lid ajar. I crawl through the coffins and peer inside the engineer's last accomplishment. "The mummy," my guide whispers over my shoulder. It appears to be a box full of dust and cow bones—I've seen thousands of cows in various stages of decomposition alongside the road that had failed to yield the right of way, and I happen to know the mummy of the engineer is in the Cairo Museum. Still, it's a tantalizing thought. My eyes and nose burn from the dust; if anything remains of the engineer, I must've inhaled some.

There are still more catacombs beneath us. My guide permits me to go a little farther. "Just look. It is not safe," he cautions. Shafts of light from mysterious sources crisscross the lower levels. The passages are flooded in dust—it seems as if over the millennium the tombs have filtered all the dust out of the Sahara. Slabs of stone have collapsed blocking some passages.

When I return, my guide is sitting in a coffin and gestures for me to sit opposite him. I expect he'll expound the history and mystery of the pyramids, but he merely begins the haggle, "How much is this worth to you?"

"You work for the pyramids. Why should I pay you anything?" I begin to stand: a bluff intended to lower the price.

He moves to block my exit and his pleasant wrinkles invert as he sternly commands me to sit. "I do not work for the pyramids."

With my bottom nestled in the rounded mummy shape of one coffin and my feet in another, I suddenly feel as if I've desecrated the tomb. I've been cursed and the ancient spirits of Egypt have trapped me in the Tombs of the Slaves with a sacrilegious, greedy man—an ancient tourist trap. I imagine he has a friend hidden in one of the tunnels and that I'll be clobbered and robbed of my money belt and camera. Or, what if he refuses to lead me back to the surface so that he may run off before I alert the guards? I'm reminded of my mother's driving lessons in the cemetery: "If you kill us, we won't have far to go." I think, "I could end up buried among the slaves. I'll probably be found in another 5000 years and displayed in the Cairo Museum as,

"The Gullible Tourist. Circa 2002. Giza."

After several minutes of negotiation, where my survival tactic, rather than become a lion, is to become the benign sheep, mimicking his lead, and slipping his grasp, I convince him that I'll reward him for his favors once I safely reach the surface. Of course, I'm saving the option of running. He scurries out of the tomb and I must race to keep him in sight. I'm tired and panicking; twice I bang my spine into the ceiling, once drawing blood. For the final few meters, I drag myself through the dust and pop out of the tomb like a prairie dog. I'm covered in Giza-colored powder indistinguishable from the rocks. Or so I'd hoped. In front of me, astride a camel, is a guard dressed in a ragged uniform, a rifle propped upon his shoulder and grinning like a Nile crocodile, haphazard teeth whittled sharp by decay. I grin back with canary-yellow, coffee-stained teeth, "How are you?"

"How are you, sir?" He asks, but his expression reads, "How much is a trip to an Egyptian jail worth?"

With a smile, I pay baksheesh to my self-appointed guide and protector and run into the desert and secret myself among the ruins. When the path is clear, I dash for the gates, unhitch my bicycle, run Cairo's chaotic gauntlet in reverse—yielding to all vehicles larger than myself and forcing aside the pedestrians—and collapse in the sanctuary of my hotel.

In retrospect, my bicycle trip has generally been rather uneventful and full of kind people and pleasant experiences. My trip to the pyramids was a melodramatic adventure and, though I knew better, I still voluntarily walked into trouble; however, isn't stepping from the known into the unknown bound to be full of mistakes, isn't that how one learns to walk, by falling down a thousand times? With a full tummy, hot shower and soft bed, I ask myself, "How am I?" and realize, "I'm very naïve and lucky, yet quite pleased with my misadventure."

Legend says that a traveler must answer a riddle to be granted safe passage or be devoured by the sphinx. Is this a metaphor for the perils of a spiritual journey if one does not answer their own riddle?

4 ⊙ Where are you going?

I'm standing outside McDonald's near a smog-choked, double-decker intersection lined with mega and mini malls. It looks like Anywhere, Planet Earth, but is actually Bangkok, Thailand. My life came to a halt here 45 minutes ago, when my love of Thailand collided with my irrational need to prove I can achieve the seemingly impossible. But if I go, where would I go? Should I risk Cambodia? There are many rebels and the monsoons have just started. I could get stuck in the mud again, and there are too many landmines to risk bush camping. However, Angkor Wat is one of the most renowned temples in the world. Or I could go north through Laos to Hanoi and escape the monsoon, or south to Singapore and take a boat to Indonesia. Or I could marry a Thai woman and live a simple and beautiful life as a coconut farmer. I fish a hefty, ten-baht coin out of my pocket and prepare a toss. When I was an indecisive child, my father gave me an ultimatum, "If you can't decide, I'll decide for you." I realized that sometimes there aren't any right answers—that it's more important to choose a course of action and follow through. In lieu of my father, I will let the coin direct my fate. I've done this a dozen times, and it hasn't failed yet. As I toss the coin, the whistling and clapping from a man distracts me. "Tuk-tuk?" He's asking if I want to hire his motorcycle rickshaw.

"No, thanks."

"Where you go?"

Everywhere in the world children play peek-a-boo, and everywhere in the world people ask: "Where are you going?" Essentially, I think they're asking, "What the heck are you doing on that bicycle?" In the beginning, when I answered Westerners, I felt proud to have a monumental goal; now I feel uneasy, people, especially villagers in Buddhist countries like Thailand, seem to be wondering where I'm running to (or away from) and what's the hurry.

"Nowhere," I respond and glumly mumble to myself, "I'm not going anywhere."

"Okay, two-hundred baht. I take you Nowhere." The tuk-tuk driver says.

"What?" I laugh and think the coin toss works in mysterious ways. "You're going to take me Nowhere for two-hundred baht!"

"Okay," he concedes, mistaking my laugh for doubt. "Half price. One-hundred baht. We go Nowhere."

"Isn't this Nowhere?"

"No, this MBK." ,

"How long does it take to go Nowhere?"

"One hour."

"Do you know where it is?"

"Yes." He shows me a licentious picture of two Thai women in the Patpong district, Thailand's infamous Sex Capitol of the World. He points to one girl, "No—" and then points to the other girl— "and Where. No. Where. Nowhere," he smiles. The long, dark whiskers on his mole flap in the wind.

"That's very funny."

"You no like?" He furrows his brow. "What you want?"

"I want to go Nowhere."

"Please write." I write it down for him in block letters and he recites, "N. O. W. H. E. R. E. Nowhere." He consults some other tuk-tuk drivers, then says to me, "Yes. Nowhere is on Petchaburi Road."

"Really," I say, amused. "Okay, Let's go. I want to see this."

We board the tuk-tuk, an ornate birdcage on three wheels, and roar off in a puff of blue exhaust. We both grimace as we pass a gruesome accident where a motorcyclist slammed into the side of a car. My driver is not deterred. We speed down the wrong side of the road, across sidewalks and through parking garages. Bangkok has 2000 unclaimed corpses per year from road accidents. "Two thousand people going Nowhere, and I may be one of them," I think.

My driver looks at me in the rearview mirror, smiling the famous, all-purpose Thai smile and asks, "Why you go Nowhere?"

On a deeper level, perhaps he's asking: "What's the meaning of your life?" To me, this is the most important question, but one that most people never ask directly. I've noticed that when people question me they seem to be taking inventory of their own lives, asking themselves the same questions they ask me. I wonder if the reason this question isn't popular is because people are afraid to ask themselves what their life is really meant to be, and why they're not living their dream. Perhaps this is why some people overreact to me—they feel as if they're being forced to confront the possibility that they're wasting their lives. Maybe they're like me: subconsciously thinking it's safer and more comfortable to sit on the therapeutic couch daydreaming "maybe someday" than it is to overcome the innate fear of failure, take a step of action and risk "proving" oneself "inadequate".

If these people could read my thoughts, they'd realize that I'm nobody special—I fooled myself into taking the trip by denying it was actually happening and am as scared and clueless as anyone would be.

"I've heard a lot about this place. I want to see where it is."

"Just looking?"

"Yes, just looking," I say, and think, "Just enjoying the moment."

"Where you from?" For some reason this question consistently comes after "Where're you going?" In other words, my cabbie is more interested in my motivation than who I am.

"America."

"Ah. U. S. A." This is the part of the conversation that often goes sour when people either beg for money and visas, criticize the government for its meddling in the Middle East or accuse the citizens of being ignorant, bloated pigs. Instead he asks, "You like Thailand?" Like most people I've met along my journey, he's proud of his country and wants to make a good impression on his guest. Some countries challenge my optimism, but Thailand meets all my requirements: friendly people, liberal attitudes, breath-taking scenery, inspiring art and architecture, delicious food, affordable prices and beautiful women. Thailand's weather, however, is troublesome. It's monsoon season. Around mid-afternoon, the storms start. First, the winds blow all the dust and leaves off the ground, then big globs of rain slap them back down. So far, the monsoons have been predictable and not nearly as fearsome as a Midwest thunderstorm, which can pick you up and drop you off in the next county. Thailand's heat and humidity is my greatest challenge. The humidity has caused groin rash and glued my thighs to the tuk-tuk. It also causes splitting headaches from heat exhaustion and salt depletion, which is generally cured by a plate of chicken fried rice with an extra helping of salty fish sauce and a pitcher of ice water. In Thailand, all the water and ice is filtered and shipped to the restaurants. It's a relief not to have to filter tepid tap water, which turns into steamy, moldy soup in my water bottles. I eat about five times a day, not counting snacks of fried bananas or mangosteen. Thailand is on top of my list of places to tell people not to go for fear of them ruining it.

We've arrived somewhere. Photos of glamorous and childish women frame the entrance. "Is this Nowhere?"

"Yes. Nowhere. You go look."

I enter a tacky parlor, encircled in mirrors, with a long bar brightly lit in neon signs. The exotic women promised by the advertisement are positioned strategically and posed like mannequins in a department store. "Hello," they chime. A man wearing a tatty silk suit approaches. There's no flicker of the all-purpose Thai smile.

Holding back my laughter, I ask, "Is this Nowhere?"

"Please, come this way." He leads me to a stool in front of a large window. Seated behind the glass are approximately 50 thickly-painted women, each wearing a number. They come to life as if my host has pushed a button under the table. Smiling, waving, blowing kisses, winking, cooing—all the women have a trademark move and sound bite.

"Where are we?"

"Pick one." He appears perpetually blasé, with a hint of irritation.

"I'm not interested."

"You no like girls? What you want." Thailand offers a wide range of options, and judging by the mind-boggling and eye-bulging pictures on the street, he could probably market me anything I can imagine.

"Really, I can't. Is this Nowhere?"

"No, this is Cupid's Massage." He points to a neon sign on the wall decorated with hearts and cherubs.

"A massage parlor, of course," I laugh. "How much is a beer?" I'm thinking of buying my driver a beer so we can sit with the ladies.

"One-thousand baht."

"Wow, are you serious? That's twenty-five dollars."

"Yes," his expression conveys little emotion, but his deeply furrowed brow suggests he used to be a passionate man.

"What's the real price?"

"That is the real price."

"Does that include a *massage*?"

"No."

"Well, I should go, anyway."

"Where are you going?"

"I'm going Nowhere. Do you know where it is?"

"Nowhere?"

"That's right."

"Why?"

"I can't see the world and not go Nowhere, can I?" I giggle, warming to my joke.

"Just looking?"

"Yes, just to look."

Presumably, he gives my tuk-tuk driver directions in Thai to Nowhere, and soon we're speeding down the wrong side of the road again. The driver turns to me and asks, "You want go Manhattan?"

"Is that on the way to Nowhere?"

"Yes. Just looking."

I agree, and moments later we pull into the Manhattan House of Silk, and I'm being coaxed into silk shirts. They're tempting, and only cost as much as one beer at Cupid's Massage, but I'm no judge of silk. I decline his further offers of more massage parlors and jewelry stores, and the tour comes to an abrupt end where we started. We've arrived 16 minutes ahead of schedule. I'm disappointed. Obviously, we've gone nowhere, but I don't feel as if I've actually been anywhere.

Then I realize I've lost my polarized sunglasses, which are essential for cycling and potentially irreplaceable. "This figures. To get Nowhere, you drive in a big circle, end where you started, with less than you had to begin with. Dammit, I've been doing this for two years. I knew I was going nowhere all along.... Okay. Okay. Relax. Think. Where are your sunglasses?" I tell the driver to turn around. "My sunglasses. I left them in Manhattan."

"What?"

"Manhattan. Hurry."

The driver turns his tuk-tuk into a maze of one-way roads and jams us into traffic. "Damn! Now I've somewhere to go and I'm going nowhere fast. Is he doing this on purpose to raise the meter?" I grumble and stomp my foot while the driver revs his engine, enveloping us in a blue cloud of acrid exhaust. I can hardly breathe and my eyes are watering. I keep rocking the tuk-tuk by leaning out one side and then the other analyzing the traffic. Finally, the driver tells me to get out and walk. I peel my legs off the seat too fast, causing my groin rash to flare, and run through the middle of the belching traffic, following the driver's directions. I make a couple of turns and stop. There's nothing but moldy shambles in every direction, like cardboard boxes melting in the rain. Manhattan is nowhere to be seen. "Damn! He left me in the middle of nowhere! Now what—" Then I realize what I'm saying and where I am. I laugh a 10,000-baht laugh.

Eventually, I find Manhattan and my driver waiting with my glasses. He deposits me back where I started. I walk past the queue of tuk-tuk drivers towards my hotel. Each one, as if the others are nonexistent, asks, "Where you go?"

"How much to go Crazy?"

5 ⊙ Give money?

As I squat behind a rock, I admire the scenery. The sun pierces the thin atmosphere, bursting through brilliant white clouds and shattering into sparkles on the rocks. Shadows pan across the ground and up the mountains like disco lights. It looks as if I've entered a floorshow, "And here we have the deluxe, super-size Himalayan Model."

The prevailing winds push streams of rose, orange and yellow sand up and over the mountains. I wish it were so easy for me. Eight other bicyclists and I are riding on a gravel road up the World's Longest Hill. We joined forces in Kathmandu to buy the visas, permits, truck, driver and guide that the Chinese require for travel down the Friendship Highway in the "liberated" and "autonomous region" of Tibet.

After my potty break, I coast alongside the New Zealander, Edwin. Although Edwin is the strongest rider in the group, he always waits for the weakest member, in this case, me, as I'm sick. My intestines feel as if I swallowed a boa constrictor, and my back end makes noises like a squeeze bottle. During my absence, a Tibetan shepherd has found Edwin. Nearby, the shepherd's large flock of sheep graze the small plants hiding among the rocks of the high-altitude desert.

Edwin says, "I'm teaching this guy that pens don't grow on trees."

The Tibetan turns to me, holding out his hand, "Hello. Pen?" a variation of the ever-popular question: "Can you give me some money?"

Somewhere in Africa tourists began giving children pens, which the children were required to have in order to attend school. This tradition of giving away pens soon spread through Africa, sailed across the Indian Ocean, sped over the plains of India, through the jungles of Nepal, up the switchbacks of the Himalayas and swept into Tibet like the People's Liberation Army of China.

Long before it reached Tibet, this tradition, initially a humanitarian gesture, began teaching millions of people to panhandle. I remember riding through the Great Thar Desert in Rajasthan, India, where an adolescent spied my foreign-white skin glinting in the sun. He ran a kilometer barefoot through the thorny desert to the road, and then padded alongside me for another kilometer as I struggled against a hill and wind. "Hellomoneyschoolpen," he said in increasing decibels. He was a muscular lad wearing colorful clothes and large, dangling, gold earrings. Clearly he wasn't in desperate straits, and pens were never required for school enrollment in India. He ran with one hand on my panniers as if to threaten to overturn or drag me to a halt. When I escaped his grasp as the hill declined, he hurled insults and rocks after me. He was like the dirty, mangy, wild monkeys of India that people have cajoled out of the jungles with sweets. When the monkeys don't get what they want—what they feel the world owes them—they sneak into your room, set banana peel booby traps, steal a kilogram of peanut brittle, then sit on your bicycle, snarling and threatening to give you a thrashing.

Give a man a fish and feed him for a day; teach a man to fish and feed him for life— this ancient Chinese proverb is both my philosophy and Edwin's, and soon to be the Tibetan Shepherd's.

The Tibetan is approximately our age, in his early thirties, though wizened by the sun and tooth decay. Still he's a handsome fellow with a broad face, strong cheekbones and golden skin. He has long hair, braided with colored string and wrapped around his head framing his face—the traditional style for men and women. "Hello. Pen?" he parrots.

"Hello. Sheep?" says Edwin.

"Hello. Coca-Cola?" I say, thinking he'll know this word and realize his absurd demand.

The shepherd points to Edwin's pen and then to himself.

Edwin points to a sheep and then himself. "You want a pen. I want a sheep. We all want something, but you have to work for it, mate." Although neither Edwin nor the shepherd speak the same language, Edwin's voice is soothing and fills the gaps. "Baa. Baa," he bleats to clarify his intent.

The shepherd looks confused, so I point from the sheep to Edwin, then from the pen to the shepherd. Grasping the idea, he imitates me and we all nod in agreement. The shepherd walks to his flock and deftly scoops a lamb from her mother.

"What are you going to do with a lamb?" I ask.

"Don't worry. He'll never trade a lamb for a pen. I just want to teach him a lesson."

"How much is a lamb worth?"

"I don't know, but a lot more than a pen."

What the Tibetan knows is that all the shepherds are selling their spring lambs. Lambs are a common source of food for the locals and, I believe, the desert can't support all the newborns. Of course, the shepherd knows the value of both lambs and pens in Tibet.

When the shepherd returns, Edwin tries to swap but the shepherd refuses and reopens the negotiations. Now he wants the pen and money. Edwin looks dismayed and jockeys his bicycle around the shepherd pretending to leave. The shepherd holds the lamb in front of Edwin, turning her from side to side. Then he shoves the lamb in my face and turns her from side to side. Her blue eyes sparkle, and her thick white fleece, adapted to the Himalayan winters, smells like dung. Again Edwin offers his pen for exchange.

This time it's the shepherd's turn to act his part in the bartering drama. He gets angry and pantomimes, "This is a tasty lamb. You're stealing the food from my children's mouths." (In my opinion, over-population is the main problem in the world. If anything, people should give away condoms. "Hello. Condom?") The shepherd backpedals toward his flock. He's using the basic argument I've heard all over the world, "You have everything. I have nothing."

Edwin holds up his pen and flicks the button several times, scribbles on his hand then tucks it into his shirt pocket by the clip. The Tibetan is entranced and, suddenly, he agrees to the exchange, sealing the bargain. So far, the bartering has followed the usual custom and Edwin has to follow through, or risk insulting and angering the shepherd.

The shepherd reaches for the pen, but Edwin, still intent on proving the value of a pen, indicates he wants the lamb first. After a couple bungled attempts, they swap simultaneously and I photograph the moment for posterity. The shepherd quickly stuffs the pen behind the silver buckle on his belt and Edwin is left cuddling the lamb. For a moment, Edwin's brown eyes are as big and bewildered as the lambs. "I never thought he'd go for it," he says, wincing at the loss of his pen.

"What are you going to do with her?"

"Don't worry," he brightens, "It's a bluff. He'll never let me ride away with his lamb."

"What if he does?"

"Then we'll have a mascot."

"We can eat it," I suggest.

We mount our bicycles, and as we pedal away, I think, "Lamb noodle soup. Lamb steamed dumplings. Fried lamb chops." Meanwhile Edwin is wondering what to name her, "The Dalai Lamb-a or Bo Peep, the bicycling sheep." He struggles to hold the lamb in one arm and navigate his bicycle over the dirt road. The lamb bleats pathetically and 100 meters down the road, near the edge of the flock, she wins Edwin's heart and we stop.

The shepherd stares at us with a twinge of curiosity but shows little concern for his lamb. Perhaps, the shepherd has called Edwin's bluff.

"Dang," Edwin pouts, "That was my last customized pen."

"We can still eat it. Jabu and Dongteng [our Tibetan guide and driver] will know how to cook it."

"Maybe we could just keep her in the truck," he moves her from one arm to the other, away from me. Edwin is a vegetarian and I don't think he can bear to be responsible for anyone eating his lamb.

"Someone has to eat it."

Edwin puts the lamb down and begins herding her towards her mother. She bolts underneath the legs of the nearest sheep. Edwin chases the lamb. The lamb scrambles from sheep to sheep and Edwin scrambles after the lamb, zigzagging through the flock until, suddenly, he's face to face with the shepherd. "Just give me my pen. You see—there's your lamb."

While Edwin was causing a stampede, the shepherd has gotten his sling out and loaded it

with a rock. He swings it around several times and sends the stone soaring over his flock. Edwin doesn't seem to notice. With a soothing voice, he keeps talking to the shepherd. The shepherd reloads and releases a second stone with a crack and it buzzes through the air, causing me to cringe, and shatters against a boulder. Undeterred, Edwin advances, "Just give me the pen." He points to the hidden pen and then himself. "Hello. Pen?"

"They've both gone crazy," I think, laying my bicycle down and preparing to rescue Edwin. The Shepherd sees me approach and grabs his dagger out of the ground and begins waggling it at Edwin, then me, then Edwin, while yelling, "Stay back or your friend gets it," or so I imagine.

I freeze, but Edwin encroaches on the shepherd's territory holding out his hand, "Hello. Pen? Give Pen!"

The shepherd is behaving like a madman now. He shouts, lunges and feints a stab towards Edwin's belly. Finally, Edwin holds his arms above his head. "All right, keep the pen," he says. "Keep the pen."

When Edwin retreats, I'm laughing so hard that my gut twists painfully. "Buddy! What were you thinking?"

"I just wanted my pen back," bemoans Edwin. "Just wait until everyone finds out that I—a New Zealander—traded a pen for a sheep."

By now our Australian friend Matt has arrived and we laugh. The competitive and mischievous Australians have given New Zealanders a notorious reputation with their sheep jokes.

"But you don't have either."

"That's the worst part." He closes his eyes and sighs, as if imagining the embarrassment of confessing to his Kiwi mates.

"Aw. You made a cute couple."

Some Tibetan women tilling the rocky fields invite me to share lunch.
Previous: Some "average everyday" roadside scenery in Tibet.

6 ⊙ What do you want?

Lake Malawi is about eight kilometers below the starboard bow of my airplane. Malawi and Mozambique seem to inch past my window even though one hour in an airplane is two weeks on a bike. The brown land is flat and scrubby. I can't see any paved roads, but sandy-dirt roads spread hundreds of meters wide through and around mud pits. As we enter Tanzania, the snow-capped volcanic cone of Mt. Kilimanjaro looms in the distance, peeping through a halo of clouds.

I've been traveling for 45 hours, including 21 hours in the Johannesburg airport. I slept on a bench, using my handlebar bag as a pillow. Hundreds of Africans were sprawled across the floors and benches: all the Europeans went to the hotels. Compared to a wet sleeping bag in freezing temperatures or a hostel with the noise of drunken brawls echoing off concrete walls, I had luxurious accommodations. I've been reading my "Crowded Planet" book to pass the time and pinpoint a bed in Nairobi. "'Nairobbery' is now regarded as the most dangerous city in Africa.... The largest slum in Africa...." (I would witness a man steal a suitcase, and then be chased down and beaten by every able-bodied vigilante within earshot. I've had a perpetual fear of my bicycle being stolen. Once I told Dennis that I didn't know what I would do. He replied, "I'd say, 'Now don't forget to oil the chain and the back tire needs a little air.") My guidebook also says that anti-Americanism is on the rise. In 1998, the terrorist group Al-Qaeda bombed the US Embassy in Nairobi, Kenya, killing 224 and seriously wounding over 4500. (Later, I'd meet a man whose brother died in the explosion.) My Adam's apple catches in my throat with the familiar thought, "What was I thinking?"

I knew Africa was going to be challenging. A week ago, I went to get my booster shots. The travel doctor said she was surprised that I didn't already have malaria, then she gave a long lecture about the dangers of Africa, repeatedly trying to sell me a rabies vaccination for 270 USD. She was flabbergasted when, after making excuses, I finally gave her the bottom-line, "A vaccination is only going to buy me twelve to thirty-six hours, if I'm in the middle of the African bush and get bit by a rabid animal, I think I'm probably going to die with or without a vaccination, so I'd prefer to save the money."

The plane swoops past Kilimanjaro's neighbor, Mt. Meru, and begins descending. My passport is scrutinized and stamped with a frown. My bike is waived through customs with contempt, never mind the New Zealand microbes and plant matter (I had to wash and sterilize my bike entering Australia and New Zealand). The ATM accepts my card and I find a charming, over-priced cab driver. In record time, I pitch camp and am sitting by a fire amongst nappy travelers: a couple who drove a truck across Russia in the winter; a medical student who brags about giving birth to two mango fly larva from his own stomach; a woman doing her thesis on the consequences of education on traditional pastoralists; and three Germans who have bicycled down the Saharan sandy tracks, past mobs of stone-throwing Ethiopians. I'm relieved to be rid of the lustful, drunken and drugged backpackers that plague South East Asia, Australia and New Zealand.

I spend the first day assembling, cleaning, fixing and painting my bicycle. On the second day, I feel ready to risk venturing into Nairobi. I invite myself to the market with Dan, an American, figuring he'll run interference with the vendors and cab drivers, leaving me free to admire the sights. We venture down congested roads. "Might is right" reigns again. Only a critical mass of pedestrians can interrupt the traffic or, more likely, pedestrians must wait for the cars to jam before crossing. I walk down a tightrope of concrete, mud on one side, bustling traffic on the other. A bus blows a contrail of black exhaust, flapping my clothes. The smoke silhouettes Dan, just a meter ahead, and makes my vision swim, lungs gag, and sinuses blacken.

The buildings are classic Third-World concrete block with a bit of flair and occasionally flanked by a mirrored skyscraper bringing squares of sky down to earth. The dilapidated bottoms are held together by the glue of posters and the paint of gauche adverts. It reminds me of an American ghetto: my stomach knots from the Pavlovian fear resulting from having the wind knocked out of me numerous times in the schoolyards of Milwaukee by a gang of African Americans. (I find it interesting that African African's refer to themselves as being from a certain tribe, or as "Black people," but seldom from their particular country, such as Kenyans.) Kenyans not only look differ-ent—skin a vibrant purple-blue-black, lanky bodies ending in bulbous hands and feet, topped by shapely heads with features so plump and round the African sunlight cas-cades off them like water—they act differently—their body language is relaxed, open, their smiles flashy and eyes cheery. The most voluptuous women in the world bat their eyes (white men are *en vogue*) and men with bodies sculpted even more perfectly than statues of Adonis shake my hand, "Welcome, friend." The poor are clothed in the usual tattered T-shirts and sandals, and dusted in gray, while rich men wear suits, and rich women wear modern clothes or *kitenges*, an African sari.

Ironically, I feel more at ease among my African brothers, where I am a minority, than I do in my own country. Everywhere I've ever been has proved more frighten-ing in my own mind than in reality, making me my own worst enemy; nonetheless, I'm shocked that people are so friendly, proving that the racism in America is just a state of mind, and that the backlash of racism is fueling the problem simply by telling people there's a problem they must fight against, which further polarizes the races. Then again if there were no backlash, there would be no reason to change.

We enter the market and are swarmed by a hundred vendors—or is it one vendor with a hundred arms like Shiva?—pulling me in every direction, asking, "What do you want?" ad nauseam. This question assumes that everyone must be lacking, and if one can determine what that need is, they can separate you from as many dollars as you'll foolishly agree to; so, if you aren't lacking to begin with, you'll certainly be lacking to end with.

After years of being harassed by touts, I lose my patience and snap, "What I want is to find the meaning of life, enlightenment, immortality, peace, love, happiness—do you have happiness?"

"Yes, sir. I am very happy."

"How much does that cost?"

"No cost."

I admire some sandals made from old tires and seatbelts. The vendor wants 35 USD. I furrow my brow and he flips over the sandal, "Michelin Tires," he justifies.

"No, thanks."

"How much you want to pay?"

"Nothing. Just looking."

Another vendor jumps on this opening, "Looking is free. Come, I want to show you my art. I am African Picasso." (I'll meet three more African Picassos that day.)

"I don't want anything." Any response gives them a weak link to chink. Meanwhile, Dan is being swept downstream by the crowds.

"Why not?"

"I don't have much money."

"Don't worry; you will go to America and get more."

"I need my money now."

"What do you need your money for?"

"Food."

A hand shoves some rainbow-colored Maasai jewelry through the mob. "You like? Almost free."

"Can I eat that?" My response baffles them and they produce a variety of objects: necklaces with bone carvings of lions and elephants, gazelle bookmarks, ebony or rosewood statues, ceremonial masks, ceramic plates decorated in tribal motif. I keep repeating, "Can I eat that?"

"What do you eat?" the ringleader asks.

"Same as you."

"Tell me."

"Bananas."

Everyone echoes, "Bananas."

"Bananas only cost three shillings."

"I eat many bananas."

"How many?" He's searching for a weakness.

"Three per day."

"That is only ten shillings, maximum."

"I'll be here for seven months."

He scribbles arithmetic on his hand, then nods, "Twenty-one hundred. This is a lot." He confers to the group in Swahili. Someone produces a golden picture of a rhinoceros, a collage of plant leaves.

"Can I eat this?"

A school of ivory smiles appear in a sea of ebony. "Yes, you can eat this."

The mob is motionless as they wait for the hook to sink. "What is it?" I ask.

"A banana painting—made from banana." They crowd echoes gleefully, "Bananas."

The African market is unique because it's a co-op. The prices are fixed and self-employed salesman—usually drunks with bloodshot eyes and stale breath—follow us from stall to stall claiming to be the artist or the brother, son or grandson of the artist. They earn an additional commission above the fixed rate. It's most economical for the buyer and most profitable for the artisan to buy directly from the source. Dan suggests we go in search of the artists. We hail a *matatu* (a minivan) and the driver, like a magician passing one deck of cards through another, transports us to the next market.

I show interest in an ebony statue of an elephant, and vendors appear out of the nooks, each with a statue in hand. I feel surrounded by a herd of elephants and a pack of lions.

"Do you know how much this is?"

"No."

"Do you want to know?"

"No."

"Two-hundred."

I should be quiet but I can't help commenting, "This is *mzungu* [foreigner] price. I'm *mwafrika* [African people]." I show them the freckles on my arm. "You see? Little bit African."

"I can see you have spent much time in African sun. I will give you local price."

"I don't want anything." Diverting them, I point to Dan, "He wants something. I already have something. Look—" I show them my banana painting of a rhinoceros.

They're undeterred. "One-fifty."

I use reverse psychology to make my point that no means no. "I'll give you three-hundred," I tell a beautiful woman with hair woven into a glistening hat-shape, and holding an ebony elephant.

She smiles, thinking she's met a charitable foreigner. "Okay. Three."

"On second thought, I think it might be worth more. Will you take five-hundred?" She's bewildered and hesitates. I'm feeling like an ass trying to teach them a lesson like Edwin, but one of my pet peeves is shortsighted, do-good missionaries and naïve tourists that spoil the locals and the economy. An Australian miner once told me how his company hired the aborigines in a small outback village for a "fair market wage". Within a matter of weeks, with their relatively extravagant wages, only a miner could afford a chicken dinner, and within a matter of months, they had purchased and consumed every chicken in the village. Not only were there no chickens, there were no eggs to make either breakfast or more chickens.

Another man accepts the offer, "Five."

"Do I hear six? I have six from the man in the back. Do I hear seven?"

"Seven."

"Eight."

"One-thousand."

All are laughing when one enterprising youth says, "Just give me everything you have."

When the crowd disperses, the beautiful woman with hat-shaped hair, skin the color of violets in a full moon and hyper-feminine curves, makes a final offer, "200 shillings and..." she says with a silky voice and coy eyes, "If you come to my home I will make you a chicken dinner."

Dan buys a pink, soapstone chess set with a Maasai tribal motif from an artist (most are poor craftsmen), while I sit with a family that shows me how to mass-produce identical sculptures of stick figures with jellybean heads embracing, or, if one desires, more erotic poses, such as the "African Kama Sutra." I'm surprised to see mundane materials, such as markers, shoe polish and food dye, used in the construction. I was expecting traditional materials, like crushed berries and goat's blood.

We begin our return trip during rush hour as the office workers are knocking their heads together fighting to board the *matatus*. Night is falling, and thieves are rising, so Dan hails a cab. When we reach downtown Nairobi, University students are blocking the main roads, in protest of a student who was critically injured in a hit and run accident. We're stuck in traffic for 20 minutes, when desperadoes, possibly university students run amok, seem to materialize out of the vapors of the sewers and head towards our cab. "What do they want?" I ask.

"They are very bad men," the cabbie says as he frantically rolls up his window and reaches back to lock the doors. Seconds later, they're pounding on the windows and rattling the door handles. Discouraged, one pulls out a shim and pries the trim off Dan's window and runs away. We're stuck there for eons. The building alcoves are hidden in shadows. There are no people and nowhere to run. "Surely," I think, "They'll bring their friends, break the windows and put knives to our throats—the rich foreigners. Do I have enough money to pacify them? What if the cabdriver tosses us onto the street to protect himself?"

The university students have caused a chaotic chain reaction. Nairobi seems to breed chaos; for example, the electric company switches the power on and off, threatening to strike, possibly causing streetlights to stop working and students to be run over. The recent rains have drowned 15 people in Nairobi. (New Zealand is the second wettest place on Earth and I never saw flooding or heard of anybody drowning due to the rain.) The rains drove a nest of ants into my shoe one day and underneath my tent the next, gnawing several holes in the bottom. Rats regularly stampede through the kitchen of the restaurant at my lodge. The cook told me, "I killed—" he mimes clubbing rats— "two yesterday."

"They must like the food," I said as I imagined rat guts splattering into my *ugali* and spinach.

"It is a good restaurant," he said proudly.

I can't say I know what I want, but I definitely know I don't want to be clubbed like a rat by an angry mob. With a belch of smog, the traffic begins moving. We surge past Uhuru Highway and my knowledge of the city. "You were supposed to turn left," I say. Is our cabby driving us into the ghetto so he and his buddies can rob us themselves?

"How much you want to live?" I imagine him asking. Instead, he insists, "No, it is this way."

We become lost in the suburbs and even our cab driver appears scared. Finally, Dan insists, "I have the map. Just go where I tell you." Dan directs us down a dark road. The driver swerves around potholes and through a puddle that nearly swamps us and sloshes to a halt. We're stuck, perched between puddles that stretch from the wall to the ominous hedge, rumored den of thieves. Eternity ticks past several times as the driver mumbles in Swahili and contemplates—I'm sure—throwing us out of the cab. I squirm in my seat. Suddenly, he guns the car and we plow through a foot of muddy water. I cry, *"Pole, pole. Hakuna matata."* (Slowly, slowly. No worries.)

As a friend told me, my guardian spirits are well trained. Our cab surfaces near our campsite with all I really wanted—I survive my urban safari to die another day.

There are more wooden giraffes in Africa than real giraffes.

7 ◉ Where are you from?

"Where are you? Are you okay?" My mom was frantic.

"I'm fine, mom. It's only been five days. I haven't even left the country; I'm in Yosemite."

"You haven't heard what has happened, have you? You know I always watch the news while getting ready for work... and they showed an airplane crashing into the World Trade Center. I thought it was a commercial for a movie. Then, as I'm watching they showed the second airplane crash into the tower. I called your father—he's an engineer, you know—and he said, 'Those buildings might collapse; they'd better get the people out.' And, I watched... I was late for work; I didn't even know if I should go... all those people jumping out the windows... I couldn't believe they were showing this—on live television—and then one building collapsed and then the other. All those people... Scott, I think you should come home."

After the phone call, Dennis and I gathered in the lodge with several hundred people. We watched the buildings crumble into dust over and over. "I think our trip just ended," I said. "There's gonna be a war. Look how much some people must hate our country. I don't want any backlash because I'm labeled an American."

The remains of the World Trade Center smoldered for a month as we slowly cycled towards Mexico. A plethora of plots to blow up bridges, poison water supplies and release deadly, genetically-engineered viruses surfaced in the dark waters of the media, as if the media were co-conspirators profiteers waging psychological terror-games and polarizing the West and Middle East.

"If we quit our trip, the terrorists win," Dennis echoed the cliché sentiment of the day, and we agreed we might be safer in Mexico. So we continued, declaring ourselves bicycling ambassadors to the States. Unfortunately, terrorism became one of the themes of our world travels.

In Northern Ireland, terrorism had become a tourist attraction: Dennis and I took a black cab tour of the battle-scarred Belfast while our cabbie showed us the site of the previous day's riot where the mob lobbed Molotov cocktails at the police. He explained Northern Ireland's "war on terrorism" or "war for freedom"—the label depends on which side you favor—the Catholics (Republicans) or Protestants (Loyalists). Abraham Lincoln said, "The shepherd drives the wolf from the sheep's throat, for which the sheep thanks the shepherd as his liberator, while the wolf denounces him for the same act as the destroyer of liberty. Plainly, the sheep and the wolf are not agreed upon a definition of liberty." Upon leaving Ireland for Scotland, the border guard patted down our bicycles and said, "No bomb here. It would've gone off by now."

In Amsterdam: I entered a Chess café, people were scattered among a checkerboard arrangement of square coffee tables. I asked a balding Dutchman with a Dutch-boy haircut and spectacles if I could play the next game of blitz chess.

"Where are you from?" Essentially, he's asking: "Who are you?" and "What is your attitude or cultural beliefs?"

"America."

"Ah-mere-ee-caw," he said in seesaw mockery, and then in a derisive tone meant to correct my geography, "The United States."

"Of America," I asserted.

"A Yankee." The Dutch aren't shy and so he began his diatribe, "I hate America. The people are okay—I hate the government."

If I were more eloquent I would've quoted a timeless passage from a famous freedom fighter—or, is that rebel terrorist?—to the British crown, Thomas Jefferson in the Declaration of Independence: "Governments are instituted among Men, deriving their just powers from the consent of the governed. That whenever any Form of Government becomes destructive of these ends, it is the Right of the People to alter or to abolish it, and to institute new Government, laying its foundation on such principles and organizing its powers in such form, as to them shall seem most likely to effect their Safety and Happiness."

Instead I simply repeat the theory I was taught in school, "In America, the people are the government."

"Then I also hate Americans. I will not play you. You are fascist pigs. And you are fools if you think you have a democracy. You are—" he picks up a chess piece "—just pawns of your corrupt government."

So many people have said this I wonder, "Maybe he's right. Wouldn't an American citizen be the last to know and the first to deny it—even to themselves?" I ask, "Have you ever been to America?"

"No, why should I want—"

"Then how do you know these things?"

"Anyone who reads a newspaper or watches television knows these things."

"Do you believe everything you see on television?"

"It can't all be wrong."

"Half wrong—there are two sides to every story. Newspapers' business is to make money—not to report news—"

"Then how do you explain Iraq?" He's backed by a crowd of fellow anti-Americans.

"Let's go to McDonald's; I'll buy you a Coca-Cola—"

"Bwah! Americans. Bush is an oil-hungry megalomaniac—"

"—and we'll talk about how many people the Dutch enslaved and murdered in Indonesia or apartheid in South Africa? Do you think the Netherlands is innocent?"

"Your days are numbered. America won't be able to compete with the European Union or China."

In Egypt: I was zigzagging between pedestrians and cars in a Cairo intersection. Two men had collided and were shouting. A policeman was asleep in a chair on the corner. An Egyptian dressed in expensive linen introduced himself with a smile of cracked teeth. "How long have you been in Egypt?"

"Too long," I said, deflecting potential scams.

"Where are you staying?"

"The Papyrus Hotel," I say, which was the hotel across the street from mine.

"Bin Laden or Bush?" He had detected my American accent.

"Who do you support?" I asked as we weave through the ramshackle crowds and vendors of pita and pomegranate juice.

"Bush is a tyrant. Bin Laden is the friend of the people."

"How is a Muslim who kills children a friend of the people?"

"It is not about the holy religion of Islam. It is about America shitting on the Arab nation."

"So, you're going to shit all over me, and everyone is going to shit in everyone else's backyard until the whole world is shit?" I unknowingly and not so eloquently paraphrase Gandhi, "An eye for eye will make the whole world blind."

"I fought in Iraq with the Americans. We are happy to take your money to fight. Your soldiers are very bad. They are soft like children. Without machines, you are nothing." As I ducked into a watch repair shop to evade being followed to my hotel by my fluent antagonist, he shouted, "You will lose this war. All Arab nations are against you. This is our home. Every man, woman and child is against you."

Inside, two elderly men greeted me reticently, "America?"

"Canada," I tested.

They expose more craggy smiles and slap me on the back, "Friend. Canada."

I fled Cairo's turbulence for the tranquil waters of the Red Sea. En route, at the numerous military checkpoints, I was singled out of the bus and interrogated: "American! Where you go? Why you here? How long you stay?"

Unable to obtain a visa to Iran, war blossoming in Iraq and fading in Afghanistan, I skipped to Mumbai, India: 24 hours after visiting McDonald's, an American icon, in Central Station, it was destroyed by a terrorist bomb.

In a small city in Nepal: Debbie, my current cycling companion, and I cowered in a shop, peering through a grimy window at a mob of protestors burning effigies of the American flag and President Bush. "C'mon, I want to see this. If anyone asks, I'll say I'm Canadian."

Debbie held my arm back, "They might not stop to ask."

In Vietnam, during their Memorial Day celebrations: Posters and murals depicted American soldiers dying and B-52 bombers plummeting in flames.

In some countries: I haven't been able to see the stars and stripes flying in the United States Embassy because it has been removed or hidden by makeshift barricades.

More or less, I understand foreigner's reactions, but what I despise are the American tourists who wear Canadian flags and say: "You must be stupid to be telling people you're American—I never admit it. I'm getting out of America as soon as possible. I hate our government."

I always reply, "Why don't you change it?"

Unfortunately, it seems many people take Jefferson's unalienable rights to life, liberty and the pursuit of happiness by alienating their neighbor's rights to life, liberty and the pursuit of happiness. Benjamin Franklin made a comment that seems prophetic, "The man who trades freedom for security does not deserve nor will he ever receive either." In other words, people, rather than be the warrior for their beliefs, would rather sell themselves into slavery, hoping for an easy life, which may explain the self-induced mass ignorance all over the world, including my own.

Revolution is a common theme all over the world.
Right: Chinese truck in East Africa advertising America's War on Terrorism in the Middle East.
Previous: London graffiti. And, Vietnamese Memorial Day poster.
Page 38: El Che, the world famous counterculture symbol, advertised on the back of a road sign in Argentina.

8 ⊙ What are you doing?

Perchance security didn't like my reason for visiting Israel: "To eat falafel sandwiches." However, maybe the problem started while I was waiting at the squeaky-new airport terminal in Tel Aviv for 40 minutes to answer "some questions for security purposes." Israel is the most policed state in the world and I, feeling impatient and impudent, whispered to a fellow American, "Hypothetically, if I were a terrorist, I'd blow myself up right here and now just out of spite," which ranks as one of the stupidest things I've ever said; however, I meant to show that for all of Israel's security measures, it's still riddled with terrorism, if not causing the terrorism due to their use of extreme force and seeming lack of compassion.

The pudgy custom officer appears harmless in his blue collared shirt and khaki pants. After a perfunctory and ironic, "*Shalom,*" (meaning *hello, goodbye, peace, friendship, welfare, safety, salvation,* et cetera) he begins with the usual questions: "What was the purpose of your visit to Israel? Did you enjoy your stay? Was this your first time in Israel?" Intending to trick me, he rephrases: "Have you ever been to Israel in the past? How long was your visit? Do you have any friends? What is her name? Where does she live? Where did you meet her? How long have you known her? Do you plan to return to Israel?" And, of course: "What are you doing?" and "Why?"

When people ask, "What are you doing?" or "What do you do?" they're essentially asking, "How do you survive?" And in this case, my *doing* seems to be threatening

Israel's surviving.

I say, "I ask myself that everyday." I've become defensive of this question, as if what I'm doing defines who I am; I don't know who I am or where I'm going or what I'll find. Does anyone? Am I trying to find myself? Or lose myself? The reason changes moment by moment, and now falafel sandwiches isn't sounding like a very good reason.

"I'm sorry. Maybe I didn't hear you," he doesn't like sarcasm.

"To do something never done before. To see the world. A spiritual journey. A coming-of-age quest. Because I can't stand being a rat in a cubicle maze, and I had nothing better to do. That sort of thing."

"Where is your bicycle?"

A surprising amount of people—surprising to me anyway—think that I'm lying about cycling around the world. On top of that he probably thinks, like so many "civilized" people that I'm just another asshole American. "I shipped it ahead," I say, thinking that doesn't sound very convincing.

"Where did you go in Jerusalem?"

I'm relieved the questions are more specific and I can give concrete answers. "To the Church of the Holy Sepulcher and the Western Wall," I say confidently.

"And what did you see in the church?"

I replay my visit to Jerusalem in my mind, searching for an answer he'll find satisfactory. The church was a nondescript building constructed out of Jerusalem stone, sandwiched wall-to-wall between other buildings. It had two small windows and two doors, one bricked over. Outside on a staircase, a young woman in military uniform— M-16 slung over her shoulder—was preoccupied with wrapping her plump, glossy, lipstick red lips around a lollipop. I followed the blue-haired tourists inside the church. It took some time for my eyes to adjust to the candlelight. It was the dingiest, bleakest cathedral I've ever seen—no stained-glass windows or paintings. The walls and massive

columns were covered in soot. In the center of the apse, under the dome, stood a small stone building. Tourists were fanned around the building. "What is the Church of the Holy Sepulcher?" I asked my friend, Nati.

"Don't you know? It is the holiest site in the world for Christians."

"Why is it so holy?"

"I don't know. I'm Jewish. You're the Christian."

"I was baptized Lutheran, but I never understood it." I consulted my brochure: the Hill of Golgotha, where Christ was crucified and buried, was razed to accommodate the church.

"What is a sepulcher?" Nati asks.

"I forgot."

We followed the tourists towards a small cube structure of rose-swirled stone. A Greek Orthodox priest with black robes and long grizzly beard—appearing to be the Holy Ghost himself—shepherded pairs of tourists inside the small building. Solemn priests of all denominations scurried in and out, murmuring prayers in ancient languages and wafting incense and candelabras to and fro. I watched this for sometime thinking this must be the sepulcher. The woman beside me reminded me of my Aunt but with a loud, grating American accent. I felt some kinship and risked the embarrassment of asking, "What's in there?"

She looked at me in a mock-friendly way unique to Americans, that doesn't quite disguise her flicker of disdain, "That's the tomb of Christ."

I said, "I thought Christ was buried in a cave."

"He was," she said in a haughty voice. "They carved the tomb from the rock of the cave and the candle altar is what's left of the boulder they used to seal the entrance."

I laughed at my ignorance and out of embarrassment jested, "No wonder, I didn't recognize it."

I queued and was admitted inside to view some paintings, sculptures, candles and flowers. Afterwards, still feeling jovial, I increase my foolishness by jesting with the line of tourists, "Don't bother. The body of Christ isn't even in there. It's all a big scam."

When the veil of reverence dropped again, my shame is sparked by images of the crucifixion. "Why do Christians love to worship suffering," I wonder. "My suffering was almost beyond my capability to endure, and what did I gain?" My mind flashed through the dozens of times I was knocked off my bike, like when I hit a patch of loose gravel and went tumbling into a barbwire fence, and flashed past a dozen other tribulations, like having to repair my bicycle rack with a door hinge and riding a half-broken bike thousands of kilometers.... "All that for what many people label as selfish, or a vacation, or some he-man feat—I just wanted to be happy... and I nearly died a thousand times searching for happiness." I recalled the miraculous, overwhelming urge to exit England's A2 highway, seconds before two cars collided and one flipped over just where my bicycle would've been.... Suddenly, I realized, "It is a *miracle* that I survived thus far. Not only survived, but my body and mind are stronger than ever." I heard prayers murmured around me and thought, "Jesus voluntarily suffered a thousand times more to teach humanity how to love." Caught in the energy of millenniums of faith, my eyes flooded with tears. "If I can cycle around the world, imagine what I could do if I weren't so self-absorbed? Imagine what I could do if I were a humanitarian?"

After reviewing my memories, I feel proud to tell the airport security guard what's inside the Church of the Holy Sepulchre, "The Tomb of Christ."

"Did you go inside the tomb?"

"Yes."

"And how did you go inside?"

I raise my eyebrows and say, as if it isn't obvious, "I walked in."

"For example, did you go up the stairs or down the stairs?"

He's being tricky. "There are no stairs."

"Oh, sorry. I didn't know that. Can you describe the entrance to me?"

"I walked through one entrance into the antechamber and then stooped low to enter the tomb."

"What did you see in the tombs?"

"That's the point—there's nothing in the tomb."

Undeterred he continues, "Where else did you visit in Jerusalem? You mentioned the Western Wall. Can you describe it?"

The Western Wall is another nondescript religious monument, except that it is a beautiful timeworn mosaic of bricks (as if nature has magnified the history of the wall, including the architect's omission to orient all the bricks with the grain) separated by tufts of green plants and a paper mortar of prayers. The wall supports the Temple Mount, the focal point of creation where Adam was born upon the Foundation Stone, the holiest spot in Judaism. The Divine Presence is said to never move from the wall, but tell that to the armed guards.

"I was most impressed by the metal detector and x-ray machine at the entrance, and the two-hundred soldiers with machine guns inside."

He's unabashed. "Can you be more specific? What is the significance of the Western Wall?"

"Something about the temple being the Jewish spiritual center of the world. I don't know—Look, I took a photograph of the sign so I wouldn't have to memorize it. Do you want to see it?"

"No, thank you. Which side was for the men?"

"The men go on the left, the women on the right."

He nods his head like a solemn game show host. "And what do the men do at the wall?"

"They pray like chickens bobbing their heads up and down." I'm losing my patience and insult the Orthodox Jews who punctuate every word of their prayers with a bow.

"Did you do anything special at the wall?"

"I placed a prayer." It's tradition to stuff a prayer to God in the cracks of the wall. (I had an unusual moment of peace at the Western Wall: I was just grateful to be alive and the world seemed perfect, even in the sense that God gave people the freedom to fight amongst themselves, so I just wrote down, "Thank you.")

"What else did you see in Jerusalem?"

"The Dome of the Rock [where Mohammed ascended to heaven and Moses revealed the Islamic prayers]. From a distance. The soldiers wouldn't let me in the Muslim section," I say contemptuously.

My interrogator whispers in Hebrew to his partner, pauses, and asks me, "You don't speak Hebrew, do you?"

"Four or five words."

"I just need to consult my colleague. There's nothing wrong. It's just faster and easier to speak in Hebrew." He's lying. I wonder if they're putting me through the wringer because they suspect I'm a terrorist or because they're on high-security alert. The Palestinian Leader Yasser Arafat officially died a few days ago. Rumors say he's been dead a week while the Palestinians tried to arrange a new government. It was strange to see the news reports of Palestinians shooting guns in the air, stoning the Israeli army and burning tires. "We want the skies to turn black as a sign of respect," they claimed, but from my balcony in Tel Aviv, I saw nothing.

"Do you have any other tickets from your previous travels?"

"No, I told you I'm traveling overland by bicycle. Obviously, I wouldn't have plane tickets." The interrogation was an amusing game to play, but now I feel that my character is being attacked.

"Have you ever been to any other countries in the area?"

"You saw the stamps yourself in my passport."

"What was your purpose for visiting Israel?" He asks again, trying to trip me.

"I felt I was missing the Middle East in my world travels."

"But you went to China?"

"China is in Asia."

"Sorry. We think of Israel as part of Asia," he says with a smarmy smile, but my Israeli friend told me they consider themselves as part of Europe.

"Just a few more questions." They've been questioning me over two hours. "Did you go anywhere else in Israel?"

"Only Tel Aviv and Jerusalem."

"You didn't visit the Dead Sea?"

"I'm bored of being a tourist."

"You came all the way here and didn't want to see anything?"

"I wanted to see my friend. Besides, Jerusalem was bad enough."

"Why is that? It's the most Holy place in the world."

"Only if you are a Jew, Christian or Muslim. Besides I found all the fighting—the stone throwing, the mobs, the children burning barrels of garbage, the armed guards—very hypocritical." I'm very discouraged with Israel. After traveling the world and discovering that people are essentially good, and that we all share the same physical needs to survive and emotional desires for joy, yet are driven mad by the fear of dying hungry, lonely and unfulfilled, that in the "holiest place in the world" neighbors are tearing themselves apart—it's the antithesis to everything I've discovered. I realize I'm causing trouble and change tactics, "Look, I just want to leave. I'm going home. I'm just passing through."

"Then why are you stopping in England for three weeks?" He has my tickets. "Do you have a friend in England?"

"Yes, I already told you—my girlfriend." I mean the woman I love and the woman I intend to make my girlfriend.

"Sorry." He consults his partner and begins a new strategy. "Why did you visit Egypt?"

"You already asked me that."

"Sorry, I forgot. Can you please tell me again?"

"Tourism. What does this have to do with anything?"

"Do you have any friends there?"

After being thrown in prison in Zimbabwe, I should've learned to keep my mouth shut, but stupidity infuriates me—I feel I must make a point. Also, the thought of being imprisoned again, and never seeing my girlfriend, who this minute is waiting for me in London, starts a nervous rumble in my stomach. I defend myself by offending. "I don't have any Egyptian friends—" Actually, I do, but information about my dubious past clearly won't help. "I didn't even like Egypt. Look what's the relevance of all these questions? How am I a threat to the airplane?"

"We don't think you're a threat to the airplane."

"Then what am I doing here—if I'm not a threat?"

"Please, sir. Don't be angry. We're here to help you."

When people feel threatened in Israel, they blow themselves up. He's literally attempting to defuse the situation. "Help me what? Miss my plane? Do you think I'm a terrorist?" They step back, shake their heads, mouths aghast and plead for me to remain calm. "I am calm. Now it's my turn to ask some questions. Have you ever seen an American blow himself up? Do you think I'm a Muslim extremist? If I were a terrorist, would I be so stupid?"

"Sir, if you will just be patient. This is standard procedure. Just look around."

"I've been looking around. I've been standing here longer than anyone else. I don't find this amusing anymore."

"If it wasn't you, it would be someone else."

"What do you expect me to do—walk out of Israel? I didn't bring my bike. Why don't you x-ray my luggage, search me, make a mark in your book in case I ever return and let me get on the plane?"

He agrees, buying time and consults his superior. After some more questions from his boss, they tag my luggage with a red sticker, which cues the inspectors to unpack, unwrap and x-ray everything, giving an extra dose to some suspicious items, like my stone sculpture of a Zimbabwe working woman. They use an electronic wand to sniff everything for drugs and explosives, and even peer inside my toothpaste and ostrich egg. Afterwards, I'm escorted to a dressing room, stripped down to my skivvies (a woman disappears with my shoes, which reminds me of a Zimbabwe prison—now I can't run away) and given the same treatment as my luggage.

I grumble, complain and my self-righteousness schemes ways to prove their manipulations useless. During the ordeal, the Israelis have treated me with the utmost respect; nonetheless, I wonder, "Is this how Palestinians feel?"

A pleasant woman escorts me to the gates, presumably so I can't get any thermonuclear devices minutes before my plane leaves. "Will you ever visit Israel again?"

"No."

"I don't blame you."

When the plane is airborne and I'm assured of safe passage, my temper and arrogance subsides, my brain chemistry achieves a semblance of balance, releasing a few brain cells for rational thought, and I ask myself, "What were you doing, Scott?" I've been told egotism is a cultural disease—and I've surely been infected.

Via Dolorosa (Latin meaning *Way of Suffering*). The path that Jesus walked to his crucifixion. **Page 43:** The Western Wall. **Page 44:** the Church of the Holy Sepulcher

9 ⊙ Are you afraid of people?

I've traveled for several days through a desert worn flat as my flip-flops. It's Zimbabwe's dry season and the dehydrated trees are turning color; if I climb a slight hill, the distant forest looks like a Technicolor Afro. The past few nights, I've found antelope tracks and elephant dung near my bush camps. One question Africans ask frequently is: "Aren't you afraid of wild animals?" I've discovered that most animals, unless they're hungry, obey a law of nature: if you don't bother me, I won't bother you. However, there's one animal that doesn't follow this law—the most dangerous animal on the planet—homo sapiens, which is Latin for *clever apes*. Based on how frequently I'm asked if I'm afraid of people, this must be the number one fear that keeps most wannabe travelers at home in front of the television, including myself most of the time. My world trek has proved to myself that almost everyone is kind, helpful and generous, because whenever I've been in need there's been someone who expended a great deal of time, money and energy to help me back on my bicycle; nonetheless, through the trial and error of my naivety, I've learned it's foolish to be unprepared for the person's who has modified their scruples to their own shortsighted benefit.

I stop at a veterinary roadblock by a policeman searching vehicles "for matters of police interest." Ostensibly he's motivated by the welfare of his country seeking poached or diseased meat, a stowaway tsetse fly, or perhaps stolen goods, but I speculate he's motivated by a thirst for power or greed. So far, in over three years and dozens of countries, only the Italians made a cursory search for contraband cigarettes when Dennis jumped the queue.

"My bicycle is too heavy, and my knees are too weak to carry matters of police interest," I protest and grudgingly open my panniers one by one, though his sighs indicate he'd rather I just dump them on the ground.

The Zimbabwe officer searches my rear panniers (wardrobe and closet), my backpack (kitchen), my front panniers (garage and bathroom), my handlebar bag (office) and my tent (bedroom). "There are no elephants in there, if that's what you're looking for." Humor is my best defense. He appears zombified, as if the burdens of officiating Zimbabwe have dulled his nerves, deafened his ears—as if he's heard everything— even his eyes roll in their sockets with fatigue.

When he finishes, he looks me in the eyes for the first time and says, "How are you?"

"I could use some water," I croak. I've cycled forty kilometers on one liter of water.

"What is your name?"

"Scott. And, you?"

"You did not show me any identification."

"You did not ask."

"I am asking now. Passport please." I remove my passport from its secret hideaway. I know he's a legitimate officer; however, like a conman impersonating an official he holds my passport ransom (a common scam) and writes my name in his book. "American!" he exclaims distastefully.

"Is there a problem?" I begin to speculate how much money is appropriate for a bribe. Perhaps, I should've slipped ten dollars into my passport.

"No. I see you are riding a bicycle and I just want to ask about your journey. Is this not okay?" He smiles and exposes the palms of his hands in a gesture of friendship, but I know he's lying. A dangerous official is seemingly benign, like a leopard stirring the grass like a gentle breeze as he stalks his prey.

Generally, I like to think of myself as a fox, but I'm capable of being the tiger, the bigger predator to scare away the smaller jackals. (Some would argue I'm just a jackass.) Once in India, a man tried to run me over to prove something to his friends and himself. On the fourth attempt, when he successfully bumped into me, I was feeling so righteous and infuriated that I reached into the car at an intersection, and pulled him halfway out of his seat, until his sweater started to rip and he looked like a frightened rabbit; however, I had insulted his honor, so he got of the car and began raging to reclaim his pride. Our battle of neurotic and narcissistic egos was infectious; within minutes, we were surrounded by 200 Indians, if not 1000, and if it weren't for a wise and gentle Sikh with a red turban and handlebar mustache, I might've been stoned to death, because nobody could understand my half of the drama. It would've been wiser to just growl a few times, or wiser yet just to have let the incident blow past like a hot wind.

I have my faults and make mistakes, but I learn, albeit perhaps too slow to ever reach enlightenment in this lifetime; so, now I use a more diplomatic approach. "Of course, you can ask me questions about America, and I'll ask you questions about Zimbabwe—this is why I travel."

The conversation may seem slow and lacking plot and climax; however, our comments disguise our enmity, and between sentences, my mind is racing to analyze statements for hidden meanings and motives: Is he bored? Or, corrupt? Is he honest, upholding his version of Zimbabwe's law and civic duty, or have I violated some unknown custom? I wish I had an omnipotent point of view; how interesting his thoughts must be.

"What are you doing in Zimbabwe?" he asks.

"Many things: learning about the culture, writing a book, eating. Is there a restaurant near here?"

"Tell me about this book you are writing." I suspect he's inconveniencing me, so that I'll bribe him to stop frustrating me. I've developed the patience of an African. I can answer questions for hours, or daydream all day—this is my normal occupation while cycling. Maybe he's going to frame me. In Mumbai, India, I was befriended by a Malaysian man who had just been acquitted after 3.5 years in a Goan prison, because some police officers framed him with a kilogram of marijuana hoping a conviction would lead to a job promotion.

"It's a book about my journey."

"What type of things do you write about Zimbabwe?" I realize what's happening. He suspects I'm a spy or a journalist. The Americans having been putting pressure on the Zimbabwe government to reform. The president of Zimbabwe eliminated the freedom of the press and, therefore, freedom of speech to prevent the Western media from continuing to exploit

Zimbabwe or, depending on point of view, uncovering the evidence of President Mugabe's corruption. I'm sure my journals would be interpreted as subversive propaganda, and if caught I'd be imprisoned—again.

For example, I have the beginnings of a subversive story about a Tanzanian man that made a prosperous career by hiring natives to find and harvest old-growth hardwood deep in the bush. He spoke very fluent English with a broad understanding of politics due to his university education and having lived under three systems: the English regime, the socialist Tanzania and now the free-market. He personally knew the President of Zimbabwe, Mugabe, from when he was a "freedom fighter" for Rhodesia (Zimbabwe) hiding in Tanzania. From the press' perspective, President Mugabe has been driving away or murdering the white farmers and stealing their land, one of the most fertile regions in Africa, plunging the whole country into a depression. However, according to my friend, the problem started around 1898 when England, in the guise of the East African Company, began murdering the blacks and stealing their land and resources. After a civil war and their independence, a treaty in 1985 guaranteed that in ten years England would buy the unused farmland from the whites and give it back to the blacks. This never happened; consequently, in 1998 Mugabe began giving the unused land back to the blacks without compensating the whites. The whites fought back. Many people were killed. The white farmers ceased production. The blacks don't have experience in mass agriculture techniques, and have forgotten traditional methods of farming, relying too much on the modern era. And so the people are starving, as I would if I had to go from graphic designer to hunter-gather overnight.

There are long lines to buy bread as soon as it comes out of the oven (if there happens to be enough ingredients that day). The first people in line buy a whole cart full and then resell it on the street for double price. It's the same for produce.

When people are well nourished they're free to become scientists, artists, or humanitarians; however, when people are starving they become desperadoes, eroding the social structure. Due to hunger, I've had many encounters with corruption and desperation. In Kenya, a giant soldier aimed his AK-47 at me, "Why do you defy my orders," he said as I attempted riding away fearing he was a bandit. He nearly stole my sunglasses, but when I told him I was cycling to Cape Town, he said, "Here—" with a roaring laugh and hearty backslap— "You will need them, more than I."

Not all hunger is literal, Mother Teresa said, "Being unwanted, unloved, uncared for, forgotten by everybody, I think that is a much greater hunger, a much greater poverty than the person who has nothing to eat." In my opinion, hunger can also be the illusion that life is better somewhere else.

Is this policeman a desperado? Is he threatening me? Does he think my life is really better than his? I become suspicious of giving him any information, so I counter, "Nothing special. I write about the culture of different countries, how I experience life on a bicycle."

"Where do you write these stories?"

I avoid revealing my journals and say, "On the Internet." His face goes blank as he processes this, and I realize he doesn't understand. "A computer." I mime a keyboard.

He asks again what I'm writing about; and I expound using simpler sentences.

I believe the policeman is—or at least regards himself as—a good man; however, he's making one simple error—he thinks his need is greater than mine, and, therefore, he's entitled to balance the debt, even through force and manipulation. "So, you lied to me," he says.

I gasp, "Lie?"

"You said..." but his accent swallows the words, or he swallows them to cause confusion, to flush the buck out of the bush.

"I—"

"Ah! So, you didn't say that!" He scoffs, throwing his head back, feigning emotion, as if he has caught my espionage red-handed. Luckily, his amiable counterpart corrects his misunderstanding. "I see," he says. "Tell me—what do you know about Zimbabwe culture? What do you tell your *friends*?"

My liberty depends on a game of Zimbabwe trivia. "I tell them what it's like to drink *chibuku*." *Chibuku Shake Shake* is a sorghum and maize beer, and is recommended to be consumed within a few days after brewing or you may get ill. It looks and tastes like vomit, and, like its namesake, you shake shake afterwards. "I tell them what it's like to eat mealy maize." Also known as *ugali, nsima, sadza*, corn meal, or grits, eating mealy maize, the staple food of Africa, is like eating mashed potatoes with aluminum sprinkles. "I tell them about Victoria Falls and Hwange National Park." Seeing Victoria Falls, one of the Seven Wonders of the World, must be like an ant watching a row of elephants urinate. Visiting a national park is like visiting a zoo except that you're in the cage and the animals are outside. "I tell them how difficult life is now because of— Uh— The economic situation and how friendly and peaceful the Ndebele and Shona tribes are in spite of their troubles, unlike the warlike Zulus in South Africa who have everything." Zimbabweans are remarkably stalwart and peaceful, and I'm customizing my words to appeal to his pride and avoiding any mention of politics.

He's appeased momentarily then asks, "Where will you make your next report?"

"Maybe in Bulawayo. Mostly I don't write anything." I'm beginning to feel like a desperado myself.

"How will you find the *Internet*?"

"There are many Internet cafés." He frowns and I volunteer, against my general principal of never volunteering any information to a police officer, "I can show you on my map." I fumble out my map. It shakes like a leaf in the wind. I contemplate running; I could survive in the bush long enough to cross into Botswana. The problem is he won't give me enough reason to run. He'll lead me step by step—"It's just procedure, you understand, nothing to worry about, but I need to ask you a few more questions in the police station."—until I'm locked in prison watching the animals on the outside.

"Would you like a cookie?" I ask. He takes one without comment. "This is Bulawayo city center." He's as fascinated as a schoolboy seeing my map of the world for the first time. "I'm looking... I don't see one.... Maybe they don't have one. There isn't always Internet access—Wait—" I flip through the pages with a desperation generated by my belief that if I find an Internet café I'll be proved innocent; however, it must be my incompetence more than any other factor that gains my liberty.

He laughs, "You may—"

"Wait—"

"—go." He returns my passport.

"I found—"

"GO!" he commands, but not before he confiscates my cookies.

Tanzanian entrepreneur sharpening my machete on a homemade grinding wheel in the rain.
Previous: Some boys that learned to act tough.

10 ⊙ Are you afraid of animals?

For the record: If a wild elephant charges you, run zigzagging through the forest. If a rhino attacks, climb or hide behind a tree, or remove your shirt and at the last second step aside like a matador. If a tiger is stalking you, stare it in the eyes to intimidate it. Never run away like prey.

As Debbie and I cycle through India's Corbett Tiger Reserve, a nearly pristine wilderness just out of sight and hearing of the helter-skelter dustbowl of everyday India; however, locals still illegally shepherd their buffalo through the park or cut down the foliage and carry it home. Within moments we glimpse a jackal bounding through the bush, and an old pile of wild elephant dung big enough to fill a pannier. A few kilometers down the road, Debbie finds a fresh pile.

"An elephant must be nearby," I say excitedly.

The stone and dust road, makes my legs and nose burn, and shakes the bolts out of my bicycle. The valleys and riverbeds are dusty sand, and my strength is useless to pedal my weight (75 kilograms for me, 45 KG for the bike and gear, plus food and water) through the dry quicksand. Occasionally, the ground is damp, smooth and pungent, giving my legs and nose a few hundred meters of rest.

As we penetrate deeper, freed of hungry Indians, India blossoms into a jungle. The road meanders through a tunnel of foliage, numerous species of trees and bushes that I don't recognize from the surrounding farmlands. Thick, thorny bramble barricades the road. I can't fathom how a tiger could prowl through this undergrowth or an elephant could stroll through the dense trees. The most intriguing aspect of the jungle isn't the flora or fauna but, simply, the light. This canopy is sparse compared to a Costa Rican rainforest where several layers of foliage and mist blocked the sunrays, or the dense pine forests of Germany that consumed every photon, making a flashlight necessary even at midday. The Tiger Reserve's sunlit canopy—leaves burnt yellow or transparent as if overwhelmed by the sun—gives the sal jungle the appearance of being illuminated from the inside, a yellow-orange light reminiscent of a perpetual sunset and a tiger's stripes. The wind shimmers the leaves and grass as if the jungle itself is stalking us. Several times my heart skips when the forest shakes, but either it's a troop of common langur monkeys tumbling through the trees or a herd of spotted deer fleeing with tails waving an alarm.

We exit the park 70 KM later and the surroundings turn back into a dustbowl, and we're not allowed into the second half of Corbett Tiger Reserve because the rangers tell us that we need to ride around the park 90 KM—rather than 40 KM through the park—to the opposite gate, buy permits and then come back. Besides, the ranger says, "It is not safe for riding bicycle."

I contest, "But we already rode halfway through the park."

"You were lucky," he says.

"Tiger no problem," I say extending a fistful of rupees as a bribe.

But he doesn't take the bait. "Tiger no problem for you. You problem for tiger." His logic is irrefutable. There are only about 4000 wild tigers left in the world, and they aren't expected to last another decade. I'm sad not to see the endangered Royal Bengal Tiger. Instead, all I encounter is a plague of paper tiger's amidst India's urban jungles. After losing a day to the infamous bureaucracy, ejected and dejected, we decide to abandon India.

Weeks later, still in quest of wildlife, the military guarding Nepal's Royal Bardia National Park from poachers let us enter on bicycles without any trouble. I'm surprised because cars are timed to prevent them from either speeding or stopping. The highway burrows a wide track through the dense jungle with a bed of flowers like purple mist. It's an old-growth sal forest that makes Corbett Tiger Reserve's jungle seem like scrub brush. It's difficult to see through the sun and haze west of the road, so I focus my attention on the east side where the sun penetrates underneath the trees. I'm searching for wild elephants or rhinoceroses. There are numerous tracks and piles of dung where the grass was trampled and trees snapped by passing animals. My guidebook says, "Nothing infuriates a rhino more than a bicycle." I imagine a rhino walking through the forest, "Dammit! Who left this bicycle here?"

I observe a large gray shape among the trees. I circle the road peering into the east forest only to determine it's a fallen tree. I wait for Debbie thinking, "No self-respecting animal would traipse around the road." When, my ears are relieved of the whirring of my wheels and the rhythmic clanging of pans in my panniers, I hear the rustling of leaves and snapping of tree branches from the west side of the jungle. The trees are swaying back and forth. I'm about to go inside and see if people are illegally harvesting fodder for their cattle when I glimpse an elephant's rump like a great boulder amidst the trees.

Debbie arrives looking panicked. "I think I just saw an elephant," I say excited.

"That's what I've been trying to tell you," she whispers hoarsely.

We've been jumpy lately because we've been camping amongst the densest population of tigers in the world, and we've been kept awake at night listening, presumably, to the drums of shepherds keeping the tigers at bay. Last night something was prowling around our camp, perhaps a laughing jackal or Maoist rebels patrolling the woods, perhaps even a 275-kilogram tiger—we've been warned against camping for these reasons. Often the locals ask me, "Aren't you afraid of the tiger?" a peculiar phrase, which makes it seem like every village has its own tiger. Last night, it seemed even a leaf hitting the ground echoed through the forest like a gunshot. After I realized we'd never hear a tiger coming, and while I watched over Debbie, I read my guidebook: "...nocturnal creatures [tigers] that have grown old or been maimed have been known to prefer human flesh. Humans are easy prey, and once the taste is acquired, eaters of human flesh lose interest in their natural prey."

As I stare breathlessly at the swaying trees, I think I'm imagining things, so I creep backwards peering into the jungle. I spot the backbone of an elephant glinting in the sun. I fumble my camera into position. Even with the zoom it appears little more than a gray patch among green leaves. Meanwhile, Debbie is pantomiming hysterically—she's so frightened she's lost her voice. Finally, she squeaks, "Behind you. There's an elephant behind you." Where I initially stopped, about 100 meters away, an elephant lumbers through the tall grass onto the road with her baby waddling close behind, its trunk tucked in a curlicue.

The endearing qualities of mother and child, the cute proportions of a miniature elephant, the miracle of life and the thrill to see endangered animals thriving: these sentimental thoughts are trivial compared to the fear of being trampled. Elephants won't hesitate to protect their young.

"What's our strategy if the mother charges?" Debbie asks. "Should we run into the bushes or ride away? I'm going to try riding away."

Bull elephants can briefly run faster than the world's fastest human. I'm reminded of the old joke: I don't need to outrun the elephant, I only need to outrun Debbie. "Don't move. Don't make any aggressive gestures." I turn. Debbie is already riding away. "Stop! Don't move," I hoarsely cry as three more elephants cross the road.

Debbie is shaking. "My legs are jelly. I don't think I can run."

"Stay calm. They won't attack us for no reason."

In no way is my experience like watching a nature show narrated by a calm, husky voice. I'm spinning in circles. First, I'm watching the elephants, then scanning the shaking trees, then looking behind me for more elephants. Can I hide in the grass? Crouch among the saplings? Run into the forest? Climb a tree? Five more elephants emerge and I snap several photos. I'm both exhilarated and frightened: my instincts for survival barely overrule my panicking emotions. Two more elephants emerge— bull males—the most gigantic creatures I've ever seen, dwarfing the rest of the herd. One male notices us. He takes one step towards us. Two steps. I prepare to drop my bike as a decoy and run. Our eyes lock. Time stretches toward the infinite until the 5000-kilogram animal turns back and rejoins his comrades.

For a long time, the elephants block our path, crashing through the forest on both sides. The elephants from the east side encircle us as a bus and motorcycle pass. The drivers don't notice the elephants. (They are probably preoccupied with even more exotic animals—Western cyclists.) So, I surmise it's safe to pass. "C'mon," I say, "We should go. They are coming this way."

As we ride forward, I scan the west for the remaining elephants hoping they won't unexpectedly emerge. Suddenly, on the east, the 5-meter tall grasses shake, rustle and part like a wave on a rock, as five to six elephants spook because they couldn't see or hear our bicycles. They stumble and bump against each other, their eyes wide with fright. The females trumpet alarm. Debbie and I zoom away. I rein my speed to pace Debbie, my head craning backward, watching the tall grasses sway with hurricane forces and expecting a mad bull elephant to emerge, thinking if he charges, I'll veer into the jungle, dump my bike and run zigzagging through the trees, leading it away from Debbie like a rodeo clown with my flaming orange shirt. Fortunately for us, they quit the chase, maybe the dirt ditch slowed them down; however, within my imagination I remember, as if it really happened, a bull elephant chasing me down the road, with thundering steps, trumpeting a battle cry, breathing on my neck.

Later, Sitaram, our Nepalese guide, says we were twice lucky. First, seeing an elephant brings good luck; in seven years, he has never seen so many elephants at once.

(There are only 60 wild elephants left in Nepal, and since most also forage through India, they're counted twice.) Second, we were lucky to save our lives. I reckon we were 22 times lucky since there were at least 11 elephants.

A few days later, Sitaram takes us for an elephant ride on one of the wild elephants captured in Nepal, broken (trained) in India and returned to Nepal to entertain the tourists. The elephant's bulk and thick hide easily parts the brush and saplings of the thickest jungle. I realize I wouldn't have had a chance hiding from an elephant. Our friendly but sad elephant walks right up to a spotted deer transfixed by his benign magnificence. Effectively we're invisible atop the elephant, even a tiger wouldn't run away from us. When we return the mist has still not settled, and I'm the first to discover a tiger kill: a deer surrounded by paw prints, with a broken neck and a large chunk missing out of its rump. It's only a few hundred meters from our lodge, just inside the park fence. In the afternoon, Sitaram guides us to his secret spot, and we wait several hours for the heat to inspire a tiger's thirst, when from my perch in a tree, 500 meters down the river, I spot a great bulk part the grasses and take some sips of water—a royal Bengal tiger. This time there's no fence between us. My skin prickles. He lies down on the riverbank. I can barely discern the shape of his pointy ears through my binoculars, but somehow hearing our excitement, he stands, looks right at me with his binocular-like eyes, transfixing me with his magnificence, then in a flash, disappears into the tall grass.

Butterfly with tiger eyes. **Previous:** Captive elephant with weeping eyes.

11 ⊙ Were you ever robbed?

I'm in the Zimbabwe courthouse in Victoria Falls. It looks like a bad film from the seventies with faded, off-key colors and old-fashioned decor. A man dressed in a brown suit with a wide collar and fat tie, presumably the head attorney, whispers to another lawyer, "Have you informed the *mzungu* of the charges against him?" *Mzungu* is the Swahili word for the dirty foam on the seashore.

"No one has told me anything. What charges?" I ask.

"We are charging you with a crime."

"What crime?"

"Changing money on the streets."

"But... I told the police that I didn't know it was illegal."

"In Zimbabwe, ignorance of the law is no excuse, same as America."

"The police said they weren't going to file charges."

"It is no longer a police matter."

My heart flip-flops as I suddenly become mired in the bureaucracy that has become world famous for its Land Reform Policy—"Africa for Africans"—that has murdered hundreds of white land owners, especially farmers, ruined food production, crashed the economy and started a small war. Am I about to become a statistic of Zimbabwe's genocide? "What is the penalty?" I ask.

After consulting the law books and each other, they say, "We don't know."

"What do you mean you don't know? Aren't you the lawyers?"

"It is for the magistrate to decide."

"Can he send me to prison?"

"Yes."

"Prison! I've just been robbed of a hundred dollars, and you think I'm the criminal. The police asked me to find the thieves to help make Zimbabwe safe. The reputation of your country is very bad. There are no more tourists. What happens when I leave Zimbabwe, and I tell everyone that I was robbed and you put me in prison?"

A beautiful, stylish and seemingly sympathetic young woman asks me to describe the crime. Halfway through my story, I become suspicious, and ask, "What is your job?"

"I'm a prosecutor," she says demurely.

"A prosecutor! I've been charged with a crime, may be imprisoned, and I'm being interrogated by the prosecuting attorney. Where's my defense attorney—where's my advisor? Even in Zim I'm entitled to a defense. I read the sign."

An officer steps forward, "Please remain calm, sir," he whispers. "You are not helping yourself."

I think, "Keep your mouth shut, Scott, before you get in more trouble." But I can't help exasperating, "I'm the only honest man here," which in retrospect is a lie even to myself. It's an odd glimpse into my mind's ability to jump around seeking a set of self-justifying events to focus on, effectively rewriting history to absolve itself of guilt, rather than just accepting responsibility that perhaps I'm not such a nice or wise person, and moving forward towards that goal instead of denial.

The officer escorts me out the backdoor of the court office into a holding cell where I slump into a chair and succumb to melancholy. "You're afraid?" he asks me.

"I've done nothing wrong. I don't want to go to prison."

"Where do you think prison is?" He sweeps his hand over his head in a circle.

I'm inside an aluminum fence topped in spooled razor wire, surrounded by a sandy yard and concrete wall. In the center is a mat with cabbage, a bag of mealy maize, a jug of oil and worn plastic dishes. Under a tin roof in the corner, two men, dressed in identical dirty white T-shirts and shorts, cook lunch in blackened pots over a wood fire for the guards. Two of the men that robbed me, Ivan and Vanilla, sit in the dirt in the opposite corner. Vanilla ignores me, and Ivan glares at me with hatred. Handcuffs are cuffed to the fence. Outside, there's a guard with a shotgun. "Oh no! I *am* in prison." I bemoan and the guard laughs.

My chattering mind is shocked into silence. I feel my consciousness shoot down a tunnel, and my surroundings become hyper-real as if illuminated by a bolt of lightening in the middle of the night. Then I laugh, thinking, "That's just like me not to see the bars for the prison. How many more prisons have I created for myself?"

I've been jailed for three thirsty, hungry hours. The courts will break for lunch soon and may not have time to finish my case. I'll be reprimanded for the weekend because I "have a passport and may flee the country." I would too. Zambia is only two miles away. An officer is typing my statement. There are no copies of the forms so he must retype everything one letter at a time, pausing every sentence to poke the keys loose or wind the ribbon manually. The clickety-clack, like a dripping faucet, is driving me mad. Outside the fence, a guard, who's been pacing back and forth, grins, pumps his shotgun, chambering a shell. "You see, *mzungu*, I don't need a typewriter or pen or paper."

After five hours, the inmates are lined up against the wall. It's time to go to court. Vanilla, Ivan, and Scott: accused numbers one, two and three. We're escorted into the "box," facing the courtroom. I gaze across the crowded room, fearing repercussions from Ivan and Vanilla's friends and family; but the crowd is only curious to see the *mzungu* be prosecuted, as if I'm a substitute for a television show.

The beautiful but devious prosecuting attorney, reads us our rights first in Shona then in English. I barely understand her, but the gist is clear: "Whatever you say or do will be used against you."

The well-fed, well-groomed magistrate droops over his chair and desk, is either narcoleptic or eternally bored, but as soon as Ivan slumps against the box the judge, without looking, says, "Do you have problems standing, gentlemen?"

All three of us snap to attention. "No, sir," I say, but I do have a problem: I can't see the judge without leaning forward over the box, and I can't understand him unless I can read his lips.

"Do you see me wearing a hat?"

Vanilla removes his knit cap revealing patchy hair and lesions covering his scalp. His bony features and pallid skin are symptomatic of AIDS.

The magistrate begins his interrogation. There's a pause, until a lawyer tells me to answer him. "Excuse me. I couldn't hear you."

This gets his attention. He looks at me for the first time, as if I'm being contemptuous, and enunciates, "Did you give these men money?"

Against the advice of the police I tell the truth. "No. I gave the money to their leader. There were about ten men involved maybe more. Ivan and Vanilla were the only two I was able to identify."

"How do you know these are the men?"

It seemed everyone in Victoria Falls knew Ivan and Vanilla but were too afraid to confess their names. Playing snitch on behalf of the police and determined to turn from victim to victor, I had finally convinced one man with a simple statement, "You are an honest moneychanger. These men, who robbed me, are also robbing your business.

If you tell me their names, I will make sure they stop." Then I confirmed the names with several people, and by pretending to want to exchange more money, discovered their habits and whereabouts and delivered the information to the police. Shortly thereafter, the police captured the men and requested that I come down to the police station to identify them. The station was a generic, yellow cinderblock building with the clacking of typewriters, shuffle of boots and ringing bells of rotary phones echoing throughout the halls. I noticed a sign on the wall: "Do not change money on the street, it is a crime.... Enjoy your stay." Next to this was a poster of Mugabe (the visionary president or racist dictator of Zimbabwe depending on which news source credited) and a service charter: "Together we will fight crime."

The police put six of the moneychangers in the lineup instead of mixing in a few innocent civilians. "Please identify the men that robbed you." This was my second lineup during my trip. The first time I was paid by the Scottish police to sit beside a man accused of molesting some girls. I was identified as Mr. Teddy Bear. ("Mr. Teddy Bear, please stand. Face right. Face left. Thank you.") After the girls identified Mr. Tree, their own father, I went to the pub with Mr. House, a gigantic Irishman, and he confessed, "If I ever see Mr. Tree again, I'll beat him to within an inch of his life, cut his bullocks off and make him eat them."

I thought of the disheveled, unshaven, rheumy-eyed, sour-smelling Mr. Tree, and his sprightly, towheaded daughters and said, "I wouldn't blame you."

I tell the Zimbabwe police, "They all look familiar."

"You must pick out Ivan and Vanilla. These are the names you gave us. They are here now."

"Look, you wanted the names. I don't know which name goes with what face. There were over ten men."

"Just tell me who you think it is."

"They are all guilty."

The officer leaned close and whispered, "The dreadlocks and the box cut. Don't worry. We know they are guilty. We will take care of the rest."

"Okay," I said too loud and conspicuous, "Um— The man in the dreadlocks and— Ah— That man—with the box cut and football jersey."

The officer thanked me and said, "Please come back tomorrow to sign some papers. We will try to recover your money."

And so here I am—one small step from signing some papers to being charged with a crime. I'm afraid I don't have enough evidence to convict Ivan and Vanilla. I'm the only one clearly guilty, since I'm the only who admitted it. The magistrate asks me the obvious question, "Then how did these men participate?"

Ironically, I had began the day buying supplies in Zambia, assuming that Zimbabwe wouldn't have any modern products left on the shelves and reducing my Zambian kwacha and chances of being swindled by the moneychangers. On the streets of the Zambian border, I changed my kwacha beside several police officers ensuring a legitimate transaction. I entered Zimbabwe with no formalities but a stamp and pedaled to the banks intending to withdraw some local currency using my debit card. However, I began to think I was carrying a dangerous amount of cash (640 USD hidden in various places), and perhaps I shouldn't withdraw anymore for the thieves to steal. The moneychangers saw me pause and swarmed me. "Change money. Change money," they chanted and rubbed their fingers and thumbs together.

Even changing money in a bank isn't reliable. I remember in Guatemala when the teller asked, "Do you want quetzals or dollars?"

"Both."

"You can only have one."

"Okay, dollars."

"We sell quetzals only."

"Okay, quetzals."

"You must come back tomorrow. There is no electricity now."

Sometimes moneychangers are the only option, and they always have the best rates, but.... "Isn't it illegal in Zim?" I asked.

"Oh, no. It is perfectly legal. The banks just put that sign there because they want more business." Of course, he's lying, but there's also a grain of truth to what he's saying. Why should the banking corporations profit and not the people? Why should I support Zimbabwe's failing economy, effectively propping up their failing government? In retrospect, this is what psychologists refer to as rationalization.

I tell the judge, "They asked me if I wanted to change money. They contributed their Zimbabwe dollars to the leader. And they contributed to the general chaos to exhaust and confuse me." I show the courtroom the roll of worthless money, called "a bomb." The worthless 10-dollar Zim bills wrapped in a 10,000-dollar bill—the ancient bait and switch.

"There," he addresses Ivan and Vanilla, "You heard it from the horse's mouth. That is how you work—as a team."

They deny everything, shaking their heads vehemently.

"Ivan, you don't have to say another word. We all know what game you are playing," the judge refers to his second offence. "And, Vanilla, you are a moneychanger. I'm not asking you—I'm telling you—you are a moneychanger. You forget we all are on the streets. I am on the streets. I'm not blind. Am I blind? No, good, I didn't think so. I see you and I think, 'Ah! Someday you will be in my court and I will remember you.'" He turns to Ivan, "The only reason you are pleading innocent is because you didn't make the exchange, isn't that true? And now it's all gone. You and your friends spent it all in one night on alcohol, didn't you? That is the worst part. You didn't even think of your family."

I wonder if he's speaking English for my benefit. Ivan continues to deny everything, and Vanilla quakes with fear.

"What is your recommendation?" he asks the attorney.

The attorney stands and glances at me with her doe-eyes. "We recommend the full penalty, your honor."

"Mr. Stoll, how much money do you have?" This is never a good question.

This time against the advice of the police, I lie to the magistrate, "About eighty-thousand Zim dollars."

"Do you have more money in your lodge?"

"Yes."

The judge pronounces the verdict, "I find you all guilty. Defendant number one: six months and five-hundred-forty-thousand dollars [100 USD]. Defendant number two: six months and five-hundred-forty-thousand dollars. Defendant number three," I brace myself. "Two months and one-hundred-thousand dollars." (About 18 USD.)

I swoon in the courtroom, and lightheaded and bewildered, before I gain enough strength to hop the box and run back to Zambia, the policeman escorts me back into the prison. I think, "Two months in prison. There has to be a mistake. How will I survive?"

Luckily the police officer tells me that I am mistaken. The magistrate said, "Two months or one-hundred-thousand Zim dollars." I wasn't given a mandatory prison sentence; however, no one can leave prison without paying his fine. The judge knew that I'd be left in prison without food, at least for the weekend, or much longer if my friend from the lodge, Gaëlle, didn't come to rescue me as promised. However, I anticipated this and have extra money in my pockets and 100 USD hidden in my shoe. While I'm fumbling for money, Ivan and Vanilla are forced to change into their prison garb: dirty white shorts and shirt, and their shoes are removed so they can't run away. I hurry to pay my fine and leave before the magistrate discovers my white lie. I'm issued a receipt as a "souvenir," and the man with the shotgun slides open the gate and slaps me on the back, "Thank you for your business. Have a nice day."

Ivan rattles the fence, "Why, Scott? Why?"

"You know why. Tell the police who the other men are and they'll reduce your sentence, otherwise they say they will not feed you until you confess."

"Help us. Give us some money," Ivan pleads.

"You want more money from me?" I force a laugh, which must sound like an evil cackle. I take the evidence out of my pocket. "You want this?"

They recognize *the bomb*. Vanilla stops sobbing and gets off the ground to plead, "Yes, help us. Even ten-thousand. Buy us some days, Scott."

"Let bygones be bygones, brother," says Ivan. "Mugabe gives land to his generals and ministers. Where's my farm, brother, you know what I'm saying? Brother, we are not from different corners of the world—there are no corners—now we both have nothing. Yeah, man, that is the will of Jah [the Rastafarian God]. From bad things come good. You will see. Jah isn't stupid; he doesn't smoke ganja like us."

"Give me one reason, Ivan. Did any of my money feed your baby? Or did you spend everything on *chibuku?* Where's your money Vanilla?" They're speechless. At least, they've stopped claiming innocence, but in the back of my mind I think, "It's easy to be a critic."

I throw the bundle of money over the fence. The bomb hits a tree branch—Boom!—the bills sprinkle down into the enclosure. The officer guarding the prison with a shotgun laughs as Ivan and Vanilla scramble to find the red 10,000-dollar bill, but they succumb to their own scam. I had removed the 10,000-dollar bill behind my back.

Overall, I'm impressed with the fair and practical judge, and same-day service. But it's not poetic justice. I could've titled this story: "What was the most arrogant thing I've ever done?" But nobody has asked that question. Vanilla has a bad cough, possibly pneumonia in addition to AIDS. He may not survive the poor nutrition and mental stress of prison. And Ivan has a wife and baby that need him. She's already waiting outside with his dinner and his baby. Prisoners aren't fed anything except mealy maize and cabbage to save money and, more importantly, to starve their strength and will-power, making their own bodies a prison. As for me, I'm guilty of pride: "How could I be so foolish? How could these drunks have tricked me? I'll make them pay." These were my secret motivations. Of course, the police manipulated me for their own gains in money or promotions or pride; nonetheless, I was naïve to think I wanted justice or that justice would be served. My real penalty is shame.

The next morning as I'm preparing to cycle out of town, hoping Ivan and Vanilla's moneychanging friends aren't going to ambush me, Gaëlle, who's been witnessing my soap opera, comes to wish me farewell. One benefit of my experience is that I realize more deeply the value of friends and family.

During my travels I've made many true lifelong friends, whereas in America my life just seems to plod along monotonously. What has been lost in my own country that friends have become more like accoutrements? In San Francisco, my ex-girlfriend, who ironically had a doctorate in relationship counseling, once said, "You didn't know that? If you're smart, that's how you do things here. You get one friend that's a lawyer, one friend that's a financial advisor...." And sure enough, when I observed more closely, her "friends" were like interchangeable parts in the mechanized plan of her life, which made me feel like a spare cog, check on the list and toy poodle. Perhaps her attitude is a variation of what caused the dramatic dance in Victoria Falls—an attitude of enslaving people with saccharin words in an attempt to appease one's ego-importance and ensure survival, in other words, a variation of entitlement—a corruption of the rags-to-riches American Dream.

Gaëlle says, "What is this feeling between us? I don't know.... You prepared me the worst coffee of my life and it was the best one!" (I made her cowboy coffee, where you boil coffee, sugar and dehydrated milk in a pot and must sift the grounds through your teeth when you drink it.) "Maybe *if* I buy a bike and follow you it would change my life. But with *if* you can rebuild the world. The only thing I know is I would be very happy to see you again one day.... Not too far I hope! *Bonne journée.*"

Statues left to rot. One could argue the Zimbabweans were robbed of their businesses by their government.

12 ◉ Did you get run over?

Months of planning to cycle through Vietnam are coming to fruition: my border crossing went smoothly; the food is excellent; I find the French colonial-style architecture charming; and, I've left the monsoons behind a ridge of mountains. A beautiful woman with a ponytail down to her seat cycles beside me, holding an umbrella to shield herself from the sun. She practices her English, "I love you. Will you be my boyfriend?"

Soon after my newfound girlfriend leaves, a man on a scooter sees me and begins swerving side to side, each arc bringing him closer. I stretch out my arm and splay my fingertips to keep him away. He aims straight for me. My gut constricts and adrenaline enflames my skin. At the last second he swerves aside, ruffling my fingertips. Minutes later, another scooter crests the small hill I'm climbing. The driver sees me and leans his scooter at an extreme angle. The scooter seems to pause before it slings towards me. I stick out my arm. It's going to be very close. I balance my bike on the edge of the road, unsure if I should play the chicken in his game.

I've replayed the following scene in my head dozens of times. I tell myself that it happened too fast, that I was looking at the road not my antagonist, or that I would've crashed had I swerved suddenly, or that if I rode into the muddy berm, my wheels may have dug into the soft gravel, catapulting me into the ditch, or that I really didn't think anything would happen, or.... But those answers aren't very satisfying, and I wonder if our self-conceit—or is that self-deprecation?—magnetized us together. At the least, my stubbornness and outstretched arm caused me to lean into danger.

Colors flash in my peripheral vision. His bike rips through my front pannier, crushes my fuel bottle, breaks my pump, resets the combination on my lock, wraps my rack around my front axle like a wet noodle, rips my shoe and snaps my pedal. "Is this a nightmare?" I wonder. The driver's face and his two companions smash into my outstretched arm just below the elbow. I pinwheel off my bike. My thighs catch the seat and the titanium strut snaps with a sound like breaking glass; simultaneously, I land on my tailbone. Agony whitewashes my vision, and I crumple on the ground believing I've broken my back. "It was only a matter of time...."

I've learned a lot from roadkill. Every animal has a quirk that drives it to its doom: rabbits can't decide which way to run; deer become mesmerized by headlights; snakes and lizards are basking in the sun when a passing motorist flattens their middle; porcupines and echidnas curl into a ball to defend oncoming disaster with their quills; turtles hide in their shell to be crushed like eggs, (I rescue the living turtles, but sometimes I find dead turtles with no apparent damage; I suspect they died of fright waiting to cross the road); kangaroos, which can't walk backwards, bounce straight into danger; cattle are bred to ignore impending slaughter; the butterfly's wings suck them into the draft of passing vehicles; crows, vultures and dogs often join their road-kill dinner; the herd instinct can drive a whole flock to their doom; I've even seen fish washed out of a river by a flash flood and run over. Most animals are either too small to comprehend their danger, or too big to feel vulnerable. As for humans—specifically me—I'm still puzzling whether I'm too smart for my own good or too stupid to know any better.

My body is vibrating and numb with shock. I can't feel my legs. "Just get up," I think. My legs move, but don't cooperate fully. I stagger to my feet. My left arm muscles are knotted and the veins gorged with blood, and my legs are bleeding and imbedded with gravel. Slowly my surroundings come into focus. My panniers have been torn from their hinges and lie in the ditch alongside my bike. Hordes of people are running to see the pandemonium. I regain my senses and become enraged. I turn about, intending to break the nose of my aggressor. The three teenage men, the scooter and their luggage are scattered on the ground. The driver is face down, spread eagle and motionless. Drops of blood coat the ground like rain. A broken fan slowly spins. The two passengers grab the unconscious driver and drag him to his feet. He topples like a puppet whose strings have been cut. They try again and this time he falls atop the hot muffler—sizzle. On the third try, he wobbles and lolls between the two men as if they're passing him back and forth. The crowd is gawking. "Don't stare at me. Did you see what he did?" I shout and turn to the driver, "I hope you're hap—"

He turns towards me, appearing as if he has been dunked in a bucket of blood. There's a long gash over one eye, black blood gushes over his brow like a waterfall. His nose is already broken and dark streams of blood run out of his nostrils. My anger deflates into shock and pity.

The other two men, also bleeding, prop the driver between them on the scooter and drive away. The mob turns towards me. They laugh and chatter and point at me. They seem to be saying "Vietnam" over and over.

"Hello. Help. Police. Water. Ice." I gesture at my limp arm. I know the words for water and ice in Vietnamese, to no avail. Nor does anyone help me drag my broken bike and panniers to a nearby shack selling junk food. "Hello. Help." I call. The proprietor happens to be the old woman with rotten red and black teeth who's following me. I ask for water and ice again. She shakes her head no. I see a bus and run into the road and wave with my good arm refusing to move myself until it stops. The driver speaks some English and agrees to take me to the hospital in Hanoi. He throws my broken bike and gear on top of the bus, charges me three times the price, doesn't give me a ticket and pockets the money.

An hour later, as all the damaged tissue begins to swell and crush my nerves, I stare dumbfounded out the window, an ambulance passes with sirens and lights blazing. Inside the driver of the scooter is lying unconscious with a bandaged head.

If I were smart, I'd have gone back to Laos immediately. Instead, I spend a week in Hanoi. An Englishman confirms, "You're lucky they didn't call the police. If you get in an accident here, it's automatically your fault. Some of the Vietnamese don't like foreigners, and they think you have too much money. They will sweat you. You're expected to pay for all the damages, and then the problem will disappear."

I confess my worries, "I must've been the only cyclist to cross the border that day. How hard would it be to find my name and alert the border guards?"

"In that case, you better hope he isn't dead. You'll really be in trouble. They'll try to take everything your family has." I begin considering buying a boat and paddling across the Mekong to Laos.

After a clever mechanic using a hammer and wood blocks bangs my bike back into shape, I brave the countryside with a bruised tailbone and gimp arm, hoping to forget my woes. Vietnam has been invaded at least 11 times (most recently by China which saw an opportunity after America withdrew), which has created a macho and xenophobic society. Many men ride war-era Russian Minsk motorcycles, wearing cheap, durable army fatigues and pith helmets. The Vietnamese appear mobilized to repel the latest invasion—tourism. Daily, the young machismos play chicken, jousting with their vehicles, or dancing in the street like matadors, jostling my bicycle or whipping me, shepherding me forward. I intend to lose every game of chicken, but sometimes

I can't get off the road fast enough. Twice, truck drivers have pulled over, gotten out and grabbed the back of my bike, and shoved me into the ditch, bending my rear rack. What can I do? The last time I defended myself, I made matters worse: anger, confusion, alienation, and four injured men.

Another variation of playing chicken involves eating, drinking and smoking noxious things in mass quantities until one party quits or passes out. One day, I accept an invitation to a drink. It's mid-afternoon and there's nothing open but the beer gardens. In Vietnam villages, signs advertising *Bia Hoi* (draft beer) are every 50 meters. This can be a keg of Beer Hanoi or, more likely, an old 2-liter plastic soda bottle filled with beer by an enterprising local and distributed to the keg-less poor. They only cost 8000 dong (about 50 cents). We drain three liters by the time my bowl of eggs arrives with a side dish of spiced salt, chilies, ginger and mint leaves. I crack open an egg and am revolted by the sight of a chicken fetus. I ordered the wrong type of egg, the white one instead of the brown one. The men laugh, and for a horrified second I think they expect me to eat it. Inspired, I slide the fetus over to my neighbor, "For you. Gift." Nobody is salivating over this Vietnamese delicacy. But, they have another treat in mind. They fetch a bag from their scooter. Inside is a cobra squirming and puffing its chest. I'm offered the honor to drink a cup of rice wine with the cobra's heart floating inside, still alive and beating the wine red; after which—the pantomiming becomes especially elaborate—we will go to the brothel to celebrate. I'm thankful that it isn't the end of the lunar month, when the male-bonding ritual involves eating *thit cho*, roasted dog meat, which smells good, but I've seen where these dogs come from—diseased, mangy strays yanked out of the Laos rice paddies.

After Vietnam draws second, third and fourth blood from minor accidents, twice more being run off the road, I return to Hanoi. Occasionally, I venture to the restaurant for a pate baguette, or to the beer garden for some draft beer and giant snails. I visit the tomb of Ho Chi Min and marvel at his resemblance to Colonel Sanders. I spend a few hours teaching English to an enterprising midget. His family bought him a store the size of a small closet. He sleeps on the top shelf in a space so small not even he can stretch his legs; and on the bottom he sells soda and cigarettes. I am going to buy a soda but he wants 10,000 dong, three times the price. "You can afford it," he says. I admire the fact that he survives by selling one Coca-Cola to one tourist per day, profiting about 60 cents.

Generally, I hide in my hotel room. I even hide from Spring (that's her Anglicized name, her real name, which is equally beautiful, is pronounced "Swan"), the hotel manager, who's as sweet and colorful as dragon fruit and delicate as the flower in her hair. Spring, who calls me "Mr. Sky" because she can't pronounce my name, discovered my broken body and broken bicycle at a Hanoi bus station, and escorted me to her hotel in a taxi.

I've discovered that I have a marketable talent of drawing pictures and trading them for food, beer and lodging. (It's amazing how much free time I have since I can't watch television, surf the internet, drink, smoke, gossip or have sex, which only leaves eating—I eat about five times as much as the average Vietnamese.) One day while practicing in the restaurant, I soon have a line of guests and employees waiting to be drawn. Among them is Spring. My drawings are flowing onto pieces of paper, into happy hands and out onto the streets of Hanoi. Three times I draw Spring, but I can't capture her essence. My heart pangs at her disappointment that her picture, maybe even she herself, isn't as beautiful as the other women. "Don't worry," I say sincerely, "You're too beautiful. I am not a good enough artist," and I whisper, "Everyone else is easy to draw, because they are not as beautiful."

Some days later, she says, "Mr. Sky, I know you love me."

"How do you know?"

"I can see it in your eyes," she smirks and struts away, intending—I think—for me to admire her figure. Maybe I'm getting clucky. I've been on the road a long time. But, the Vietnamese women play their own brand of chicken: they head straight for you with all their sex and charm. Most want money or a visa to America. I've had five marriage proposals already. On my first day of cycling a foreign country, I was given two pieces of advice (or gossip depending on your opinion) by a matronly woman named Maria that have held true in almost every country: "Remember the *federalis* and *policia* can shoot you dead, no problem." And, "In Mexico, you don't just marry the woman—you marry the whole family."

After a fretful month in Vietnam, I'm ready to leave. Spring, with her mischievous smirk, asks, "Sky is there anything you'd like to tell me?"

"I'll miss you." I volunteer, hoping not to betray that I've grown fond of her, nor to give her any hope.

"Sky—how can I say?—if you come back to Vietnam, I will be here. You don't forget me."

I don't have the heart to tell her I'm never coming back... but there's a chance I may never leave. She gives me her phone number. "I may need this," I think as I board my cab. Beside learning that it would've been better to lay down my pride and get out of the line of fire, better yet, not to even arrive for the war, I learned that when I needed help the most, it manifested in one of the kindest people of my trip—Spring.

If the Law of Attraction did magnetize me to my foe, like matter and antimatter, I should be glad that our collision vaporized some of my conceit. It also serves as a warning that someday, if I were to become even more angry, fearful and egotistical, that I may meet someone who cancels me out entirely.

I check my bicycle and baggage into Singapore Airlines and think, "The police must know I'm here now. They're probably waiting for me. It's not my fault, but if those teenagers are dishonest, or their parents are desperate, or the police corrupt— I'm in big trouble." When the immigration official gives me trouble because the guard at the Laos border didn't give me the proper paperwork, my body becomes tense and flushed, despite telling myself, "Don't be so bloody obvious." After a delay, in which I'm sure the police are being summoned, he allows me to pass.

I wait at the gate and wonder, "How'd I get myself into this? I knew cycling around the world sounded like a bad idea. I just had life too easy and too much time to accuse myself of being unhappy." If I were born in a Vietnamese rice paddy in 1970, I'd be too busy surviving to wonder if I were happy.

Some police walk past, wearing the same drab olive uniforms trimmed in red and yellow from the Vietnam War (they call it the American War). Have my uncle's war stories and too many movies instilled me with dread? Am I paranoid? They turn in my direction and look at me. My guts, in a fight-or-flight response, are intent on jettisoning any unnecessary cargo, fouling the atmosphere with my flatulence despite repeated trips to the toilet. Finally, it's time to board the plane. Four police march to the gate, two on either side. "This is it! They've come for me. Do I play ignorant?

Do I run?" I have a seemingly simple and obvious thought, which to me is a minor epiphany, "Happiness is just getting on that plane." The boarding pass is trembling in my hand. I give it to the stewardess. She runs it through the machine. My name comes up. Nothing happens. As I march down the ramp, the four police hardly notice me, except maybe for the smell of fear.

Children are often in charge of the family water buffalo.

13 ⊙ What was the worst thing that happened?

I find it discouraging that this question is so common. It seems the average person would rather be horrified than inspired. Does it give them a sense of superiority to think they would've made better decisions? Does it justify that theirs is a wonderful life, and it'd be foolish to risk it on something as obviously silly as being a stranger on a bicycle in strange lands? On a positive note, do people like cheering for the underdog? Or, are they adding up the pros and cons of making their own adventure?

My relationship with the "woman of my dreams" is going up and down—mostly down—despite my best efforts. We had met in Christchurch, New Zealand from a chain of coincidences that glued me to a bench with tendonitis, and while I was feeling sorry for myself and contemplating the feasibility of cycling Africa on one leg (as I did sections of Tibet), across the park I saw the most beautiful women in the world so far. A voice inside my head, not quite my own, said, "You could be happy with her." Then, as if my thoughts were magic, she sat down beside me as if she knew me. After the usual perfunctory comments, our conversation grew until we were speaking like old friends. "Of course, I care about your eternal soul," she said. I was flattered and entranced by her strange choice of words and mesmerized by her beauty. Her teeth were like a string of pearls set between glistening lips that swept up in a perpetual smile. And her eyes were half blue and half hazel, like the ocean washing over a sandy beach. However, it wasn't her lips that I loved, but her smile. It wasn't her eyes either, but the twinkle. Nor was it her graceful, lithe form, but being hugged tight and the tingle when our skin touched. Since then, I've chased her halfway around the world.

I remember the moment I fell in love with her: I cycled past a man in Tanzania, and we both rang our bicycle bells simultaneously in greeting. Normally mine tolls, "duh-ting," but for a moment our bells sang in harmony, "Ting-Ing-Ing-Ing-Ing," and I realized that being beside Jasmine made my spirit sing. I can't speak for her experience except to say that she told me a hundred times she loved me. However, as time passed, she grew more conflicted and often said, "I feel as if God is testing my faith." Her problem—or is that my problem?—is that she's a born-again Baptist, a fundamentalist, and I'm not anything, or as I tried to explain in the following letter:

> When I became a more experienced traveler I would carry two or more maps, because the mileage, spelling, roads and villages would never be the same on any two, and I preferred to have one road map and one relief map showing the mountains and rivers. I also realized that the only true maps existed in the memory of the locals, so I would ask for their guidance dozens of times a day. As time progressed, I learned to read the terrain, weather and people and guide myself. I believe religions are like maps. Even if I had all the best maps in the world, they couldn't describe something infinite and ever-changing—they aren't the same thing as actually traveling the road. That's partly why I left: to throw away my maps, trust my inner compass, feel the grass between my toes, get lost in the woods and discover panoramas never seen by any cartographer.

My philosophy not only made her more conflicted, but drove her further away.

In Guatemala I receive disheartening news from her father: "Try not to end up in jail again, as Jasmine says she will not be a visitin'. She's hanging out with a guy from church, so it's all grist to the mill. Women are strange creatures, often saying things like, 'I could never end up with a man like him, no way in a million years.' Then next time you see them they're married." (Unbeknownst to me he's lying, presumably to protect his daughter from me, the pagan.) Not only does it seem inappropriate to receive this news secondhand, but Jasmine's fickle emotions and new boyfriend seem to nullify the love we once had.

I jog into the midday's burning sun, a few kilometers outside Antigua, down a major road closed for construction, free of dust and exhaust. I run until the pain burns so much my heartache is forgotten—for a moment. I collapse in the shade of a peaceful wood overlooking Antigua's cathedrals.

I cry to the sky, to Jasmine's God, the God that preordained everything including my suffering, the God her father said would damn me to eternal hell if I didn't do something so simple as believe, the God her pastor said Jasmine would always love more than me. "Why did you bring her into my life only to take her away? Am I supposed to suffer some lesson? Are you sacrificing my soul to save hers? Or maybe you tricked me into loving her, so that I'd come crawling and crying to you. What kind of fucked up world is this? You might as well strike me down now and burn me in hell, because I'm not going to be your puppet. I don't want to be part of that kind of world." I scream and grovel and, even, threaten to kill myself to get straight to the answers. When my fury fizzles, and there are no thunderbolts in sight, I mourn, "Scott, she's gone. You have to honor her decision."

As I jog back down the empty road, two burly men that I've seen before are waiting for me. I switch sides, but they intercept me. The lead man reveals a silver revolver from beneath his shirt. *";Que es esto?"* (What is that?) I laugh thinking they're playing a joke.

"Un pistol. Darme su telefono." (A gun. Give me your phone.)

My gaze never falters from the gun. It appears real. And there are bullets in the chamber. *"No es un telefono...."* My Spanish falters.

";Desea morir?"

My mind churns the phrase into English: "Do you want to die?"

The man turns to his friend to give instructions. His pistol swings aside. Now is my moment to grab the gun. But I can tell from his thick forearms that he's much stronger than I am. His friend raises a sawed-off shotgun from underneath his jacket, and points the gaping black muzzle at me. I have no money, no credit cards, no phone. When I was in East Africa, rumors abounded about robbers beating their victims senseless to make sure they had no valuables and then writing "NO MONEY" in their back with a razor blade as a warning to other potential victims. In South Africa, robbers don't stop to negotiate; they kill you first and then search for valuables. I have only one second to act before they coordinate their weapons and intentions. I always wondered what I'd do if someone pointed a gun at me. Option A: I could give them everything I have and pray, not that praying has been working. Option B: I could call for help with my whistle, but there is no one near. Option C: I could fight, simply jabbing my keys into his larynx, but even if I disable one, the other would have plenty of time to fire. I choose option D: I run, though I'm trapped on a road lined with concrete ditches approximately 1.5 meters wide and barbwire fences, I sprint for the opening 500 meters away.

"Alto o te mato." (Stop. Or I'll kill you.) The man with the revolver shouts. They are both carrying big sticks, and his friend, who's a few paces ahead, gets a full swing and thumps me in the chest. I hear something crack. The man behind me swings, aiming

for my neck. I block with my arm and keep running. I'm faster, but they break my stride by bashing my legs. I pull ahead, but while watching out of the corner of my eye, I see the man with the revolver take aim. In desperation, I shriek, *"No. Por favor. No."* I realize—and I nearly laugh—that I don't really want to die after all. I slow, so that I'm between them and they can't fire. One man cracks me in the back aiming for my spinal column. They know all the soft spots. The other takes a grand-slam swing. I'm afraid that if I duck or block or become too canny, they'll use their firearms, so I allow him to hit me. He bashes me just above the temple. The world goes black. My hand spasms and my tape recorder falls to the ground with a crunch. My feet keep moving despite running in blackness. Their footfalls diminish. Twice before, men have shot at me, once on accident and the other time either as an impudent joke or warning. The bullets buzzed past like an angry bumblebee. I bragged about this to my grandpa, who was a decorated World War II veteran. He wasn't impressed, "It's not the bullet that you hear that you have to worry about; it's the bullet that you don't hear that gets you."

I hear nothing.

Still nothing. I'm in too much shock to feel pain. Have I been hit already?

My vision is streaked with stars. I slow and risk turning around. The men have stopped to retrieve my tape recorder. They got what they wanted, even though it's not a phone, and even if it survived the fall, they might not realize the batteries are

Another lost and wandering soul following me through the marketplace.

dead, wound down by my grief.

Ironically, two hours after Jasmine's father warned me to stay clear of prison, I end up in the police station wishing for Jasmine and despising her father. The police record my report, give me one copy and stuff the other in a cornflakes box used as a filing cabinet. "Now what?" I ask.

"We are finished."

"What are you going to do?"

"Nothing." But as a consolation they offer, *"Tienes mucho mucho suerte.* [You're very, very lucky.] You should never run. Normally, they would kill you. It is very popular in Guatemala. We recommend you visit the hospital."

Later the doctor says, *"Tienes mucho mucho suerte.* A couple centimeters lower—" he gestures to my temple which is so sore I can barely swallow— "it would have been very serious. You could have been killed." My Spanish is weak, so he emphasizes, *"Muerto."*

"Dead," I echo.

"Do you want some medicine for the pain?"

"No, it's nothing compared to a broken heart."

The next morning, I have breakfast in Antigua's market. I want to ask for a cup of strong coffee, and it comes out, "Can I have a wife?" The women laugh, and the gossip ripples like a wave through the marketplace. They work twelve-hour days every day, but they're full of smiles and dreams. Annabelle brings a jar of *pico de gallo* that she made just for me, and my favorite breakfast, scrambled eggs and tomatoes without salt, and double-strong coffee. I can barely chew and swallow my breakfast past my aching temple and the lump in my throat.

I've been plagued by nightmares. My mind is clouded and my thoughts spin, "Is Jasmine the same woman that I loved?" and, "I gave her everything and it wasn't good enough," and, "I rode my bicycle around the world and I'm still not good enough," and, "Did she really love me," and, "If not, did I really love her?" and, "What did I do wrong?"

But as Dennis advised me, "You'll never figure out the solution, because half the problem is gone." And, Samuel advised, "Stop eating for a week and you'll forget all about her."

My hands shake. My eggs have no flavor. My coffee is bitter even with a tablespoon of sugar. My *pico de gallo* has no *pico.*

After a restless day, I spend a restless night on the rooftop of my hotel, where poisoning myself with alcohol and nicotine seems like a soothing pastime. I'm comforted to be in the Northern Hemisphere again and to see my eternal travel companion, Orion, back on his feet. (In the southern hemisphere, Orion seemed very undignified standing on his head.) Suddenly, atop El Volcan De Fuego where there's just an innocuous puff of smoke during the day, a plume of lava erupts, like a gigantic Roman candle, obscuring Orion. Moments later the lava and rocks run and tumble down the side, girdling the cone in glowing orange, and life seems beautiful.

The question that hardly anyone asks and that I admire most is: "What was the best thing that ever happened to you?" Ironically, the best and worst things that happened to me are the same thing—maybe it isn't ironic at all; maybe following a dream is like dancing on the edge of the unknown and one step could mean gaining or losing everything or both.

It's also ironic that after cycling past the great cultures and wonders of the world, and being robbed and beaten, the most joyful experience is being in love and the most sorrowful experience is being out of love. On one level, it seems childish, but on another, she provided the greatest lesson in life: that it doesn't matter what you do, if you feel nothing.

I also learned that love isn't just a helpless feeling, it's also a thoughtful action—accepting and giving love, valuing everyone every moment for who they are and what they could be, combining your energies to plant a seed that grows into a tree that bears joyful fruit.

It's also cliché but true to say, I have my health and I have my memories: once, in a crowded London corner shop, Jasmine sang to me, "I had the time of my life... and I owe it all to you." I'm certain of one thing: Jasmine was the woman of my dreams... for a time.

(Postscript: Why is it many years later, looking backwards, it's so easy to see the forks in the road of our lives, and realize that sometimes no matter whether we went left or right we'd still end up going forward, and that perhaps everything worked out just as it should have because if it could have been different it would have been different, but we still wonder: "What if?")

The literal and figurative fork in the road, one of many places where I nearly quit.

14 ⊙ What was the hardest part?

Number 35 struts towards me in a manner seemingly calculated to jiggle her wares, like a flashing neon sign in a shop window. Her chest is polished and sparkling with glitter. I imagine I could coast my bicycle from the tip of one breast, swoop down into the valley of her cleavage and soar gracefully up the other side. The women in the Czech Republic are possibly the most beautiful in the world. She pauses before me for a moment to admire her reflection in the café window. She sucks in her gut and sticks out her chest then struts past my bike laden like a beast of burden, my sweaty body and lame greeting without a flicker of acknowledgement. This is common in the "civilized" world, and my heart pangs. I miss countries like Argentina, where the women would call across the crowded street, "I love you. Will you marry me?" or romantic Italy where women called from their flowery balconies, *"Ciao, bello."*

My Turkish coffee tastes like a Bolivian mud road splattering off my wheels; however, my chicken breast atop a pile of fries and smothered in gravy is just what the bicycle ordered. This is my first hot meal in three weeks. I'm breaking my fast on the terrace of a Czech café to alleviate my ennui before it mutates into depression, I'm watching beautiful women walk past—*girlspotting*. Most people think that the most difficult aspect of my trip would be something physical like climbing the Andes Mountains with food poisoning and intestinitis; however, the hardest part for me is the boredom and loneliness, and it's ironic that the most difficult section of my trip is the pinnacle of Western civilization where it's easy to survive and thrive, perhaps because life is too easy and I have too much free time to indulge my egotism, meaning the aspect of myself that feels inadequate and likes to prove itself worthwhile.

Not long ago, I was lost, circling the canals of Belgium, and suddenly was attacked by grief and loneliness and crumpled to the ground, tangled in my bike. I'd fallen many times from accidents due to physical exhaustion, but that was the first and only time I've ever collapsed from emotional exhaustion. "My heartbreak has provided me with a frightening glimpse of the hole in my self-esteem," reads my latest journal entry. "I suspect I've been filling this hole with a woman's love and my bicycle trip. But, I have no love, and I've decided to quit my trip. I'm limping as far as possible, but it's only a matter of time before my hole swallows me and my bicycle."

There's no end to the stream of gorgeous women passing the café. It's a shame I can't see their personalities so easily. Why is it so hard for me to meet a woman? One that I love, anyway, and one that loves me. I feel cheated by love. Why is this the strongest urge in my life? Is it a Freudian desire to return to a state of atonement a child has with his mother? Being in love feels like the closest I've ever come to experiencing enlightenment. Possibly it's lack of love for myself that compels me to seek an outside source. Maybe my faith is weak; I believe in God—or should I say a creative power?—but I don't feel any love pouring down from the heavens. My expectations of God and love must be immature and flawed. Dennis said more than once, "I don't think you know the difference between love and lust." All I know is that I pine for women more than I dream of finishing my trip, which I find pathetic, why can't I find life in general as beautiful and thrilling as women?

My lust and loneliness are making me weak. My Canadian friend Wade, who hosted me for several weeks in Lueven, Belgium, told me I'm a Calvinistic prude, and that Europeans have a much healthier view of sexuality. "Why don't you just go to Amsterdam and get it out of your system?" he said. "Why do you criticize something you've never tried? Two consenting adults can do whatever they want. You're so typically American, you'd rather stay home and watch blood and gore on the television." Since sneezing is the closest thing to an orgasm I've had in ages, I plan to go to a brothel tonight to celebrate my birthday and cure my loneliness, or, at least, satiate my lust and free my mind to worry about bigger problems, like what to do with my life.

A week ago, I tried the opposite, jumping into my loneliness. I found an old logging trail in the woods of Germany. I portaged my gear over the fallen evergreen blocking the trail, cycled deep into the woods and pitched my tent on the edge of a clearing. In accordance with my new motto, "I have nowhere to go and all the time in the world to get there," I stayed for a few days, sustained by some rice, one can of tuna, wild apples and blackberries. At night, I medicated myself with some contraband that I imported from

Holland in my seat post, read *Crime and Punishment*, watched the embers of my camp-fire glow like a mini-universe and contemplated my sadness. It made no sense to me. On a bicycle, I've endured far worse physical pain, which never lingers in my psyche.

As I suspected, there are some brothels on the Austrian border. I skip the first in favor of a well-kept building, inconspicuous aside from the neon sign "Nightclub" with a flashing heart. The interior is decorated in a cave motif. I have the original Budweiser from Pilsen, which they claim the Americans stole. Though I don't smoke, I buy a pack of cigarettes and smoke like a Guatemalan chicken bus to ease my nerves. I've never slept with a prostitute. Many of the women appear beautiful at a glance, but after closer inspection, seem like worn mannequins, mechanical and artificial like sex robots. I begin to think that I can't even get laid in a brothel.

On my third beer, mid-afternoon, more women emerge from their bedrooms to begin work. Claudia, the most beautiful, gravitates towards me immediately. She has Scandinavian ice-blue eyes and hair swept back like a raven with his feathers puffed. The angular lines of her aristocratic nose and cleft chin accentuate the streamlined curves of her body. She doesn't speak English, no one does, but she speaks Spanish and says, "You're very handsome. Why do you come here?"

"I need to spend my koruna before I go to Austria," I joke.

She giggles and, despite myself, her calculated charms win my affection. "Do you want a girl?"

"I don't know. My heart is infirm."

"No arriba?"

"Si, no arriba."

"No problemo. I am like doctor of love."

I change the subject, "Do you like your job?"

"Why not?"

"There are many ugly men."

"No, not many. I choose who I like."

"Wouldn't you prefer another job?"

"Yes, but the money is good." She leans against me, enveloping me in her enticing fragrance. "Will you come with me later?"

I hesitate; if I don't agree, she'll leave, and I'll have no one. "If you're nice—if you like me—I'll go with you," I say reticently, feeling as if I've just jumped overboard and must figure out how to swim. She brightens and asks to see my bicycle. She models for me until she tries to swing her leg over my bicycle and her plump alabaster breasts nearly pop out of her faux leopard bikini and I begin laughing.

Suddenly she's impatient, grabs my hand, and leads me directly to the cave-like bedroom illuminated by lava lamps. Her clothes fall to the floor as if I were her aged husband. I'm left to disrobe myself. She makes appropriate coos and clucks, then pulls me into the shower, and tries to tease me to life. Normally, the sight of a woman like Claudia fevers my blood, but I'm impotent. Claudia steps forward, grabs my hands and kisses me tenderly. "We aren't supposed to kiss or hold hands," she says.

"Why not?"

"It is too intimate."

"That isn't necessary," I say.

"I don't do anything I don't want. I like you very much. I wish you could be my boyfriend."

"You are a very good actress. I almost believe you."

"Don't worry. I will give you a massage instead."

After an hour, and the knock on the door, I cycle away, feeling as if my loneliness was waiting at the door and is racing to crash into me. Nearby I travel down sandy tracks, deep into a forest and pitch camp near a flooded quarry next to the border. There've been record rains this year in Europe. Only 86 KM away half of Prague is underwater, including the zoo. Two manatees were last seen swimming upriver towards Germany, and the gorilla disappeared after the zookeepers opened the cage so it wouldn't drown.

The quarry waters are like liquid sapphires. I swim among the submerged pine trees, like a bird soaring through a forest, occasionally roosting in the treetops to breath deep. I swim until my bones ache from the cold, and then scrub my skin raw with sand. Afterwards, I sit on the cliffs and watch the sun set amidst colors that only exist in the sky, wondering if someone on the opposite side of the planet is watching the sunrise. First, the mosquitoes discover me. Then, the bats come out and I throw pebbles into the air for them to chase until a whole flock circles above. An owl with a wingspan of a meter glides over me two arm lengths away; and, a wolf bolts into a corner of the quarry and with no place to hide crouches and stares at me.

When night drops its veil, I follow the trail back to my tent. The trail forks numerous times. Already the spiders have spun their webs across my path snaring my face, raising the hair on my nape and giving me goose bumps. The mosquitoes buzz around my head further disorientating me. I can't find my tent. I shrug the spiders off and panic—everything looks the same. I stumble through the woods blind except for the few meters my flashlight illuminates, until it occurs to me to turn off my flashlight and let my eyes adjust to the moonlight. My tent is only 50 meters away, appearing like a fat glowworm in the moonlight.

After dinner, as I chronicle the day's events, something snaps a branch beside my tent. My heart pauses then resumes beating so furiously that I can't hear anything but the blood rushing through my ears. Do wolves step on branches? Maybe it's a bear. There are two recommended courses of action if it's a bear: If it's angry, I shouldn't antagonize it, and if attacked, as a last resort, I should lie down on the ground and cover my head. Most likely, the bear will knock me around a bit before losing interest. However, if it's a hungry bear, I should defend myself: yell, shout, bang pans, throw rocks—the worst thing I can do is play dead.

It's back, circling my tent. How do I know if it's a hungry bear or angry bear? I risk yelling and clapping my hands. It stops. Is it the gorilla? Should I throw my bananas outside? Now, there's two on my left and one on my right. They're chasing each other. I hear strange chirping barks and hoof noises. Pigs. Wild boar! That explains the signs that I saw in Germany that said something like, "*Achtung!* Don't tease the wild boar." Normally, there's no wildlife anywhere near a road. (I looked under every rock in the Baja and never found even one scorpion.) Boars are very aggressive and territorial, possibly more dangerous than a bear.

I'm scared. He's just a few feet away. I assume it's a male. He's pawing the ground and snuffling. I hope it is not mating season, or that they're protecting their young. Maybe I should light a fire? I don't have any gas and I used all but two matches smoking cigarettes. I'm such an idiot. I wish Dennis were here. He'd know what to do.

I grope for my knife, while mesmerized by the side of my tent flapping with his snuffling. Am I going to die on my birthday? Too bad I lost my pepper spray. I don't know what to do: be aggressive or be quiet? Maybe I should empty my bottle of urine on the ground, mark my territory. Is it the flashlight? Turn off the light—

Motionless in the dark, I think, "I'm not bored or lonely now, am I?" I'm reminded of Claudia. She was more pleasant than a one-night stand, but it was too clinical and mechanical, like the irresistible urge to defecate, leaving me with a mixture of pride and disgust with what my body had produced and the desire to dig a hole, bury it and never acknowledge it existed.

Of course, what I want most money can't buy: love is a gift. Rather than fill my spiritual hole, Claudia seemed to pry it open; whereas, I enjoyed swimming among the submerged pine trees as much as anything in my life; and the wildlife, even the boar, are exhilarating.

When my fear dissipates, I drift to sleep, my spirit comforted by the company of the rooting boars and the whispering wings of owls.

For a long time, I puzzled whether to admit my trip to a brothel, but if I bury all my mistakes how will I ever learn, and wouldn't it make me a hypocrite to pretend I'm better than everyone else? Carl Jung said that if you refuse to acknowledge your shadow-self, it controls you and you become a victim. He also said, "The most terrifying thing is to accept oneself completely."

This may explain the dichotomy of my life.

15 ● Where do you go to the toilet?

I'm camped beside the chief's hut in a large village in Malawi. When I awake, the chief already has a pot of clear, warm water ready for my bath. I wash my face and hands, then pack my gear and plan to find the nearest clump of bushes. I haven't seen any latrines, and my coffee has given my bowels a jumpstart. Remembering a very embarrassing moment in a small Thai village where I did a chicken dance and pantomimed laying an egg, I decide against pantomiming Mother Nature's call.

"Where do you go to the toilet?" is another common question that mystifies me. Are people really that curious about my bathroom etiquette? For the record, I'm not picky; in fact, I'm a bit like a dog, I cycle along until I see a favorable tree; I don't require hot water, and I carry soap and toilet paper; nonetheless, this simple act has been one of my greater logistical concerns. I'm rarely lost, seldom can't find food or water, but frequently, desperately, seeking a toilet. Though somewhat predictable, there's a small window of opportunity, especially due to the quantity of food I eat. As Dennis said, "I don't have time to open a newspaper much less read it."

The chief gives the warm water to the kids, and they stop gawking at me and turn a patch of orange dust into mud. I realize that warm water for washing is a luxury, an honorable gift from the chief; the villagers probably can't afford to burn the wood for anything except cooking. I pay my respects to the chief and give him some sweets and cigarettes. The kids escort me to the road running barefoot with synchronized steps, taking shortcuts through the bush, and leaping out of the tall grass to wave goodbye. I don't understand the language here, but I spoke bad kitchen Swahili in Tanzania where the kids would often greet me with, "Uncle," or, *"Shikamo,"* (I place your feet on my head). It's a sign of respect for elders, and I'm supposed to reply in a grumbly voice, *"Mara haba,"* (Please stand).

Malawi is a bountiful country, but Malthus' theory is proving true: Malawi is one of the most densely populated countries in the world, and the people are on the brink of starvation having stripped the land of its resources and ability to replenish itself. It takes me four kilometers to find a secluded spot. I'm still paranoid from years ago in Mexico. I was hiding in the woods, or so I thought, paralyzed with Montezuma's Revenge when a truckload of sugarcane workers drove past. The Mexicans, like prairie dogs, had a lookout in every direction. Immediately, one shouted, "Look! Look! An American without clothes." Suddenly, about 30 Mexicans hanging over the edges of the truck, sitting on the roof and standing on the running boards had a clear view of me with my pants down precariously perched on the edge of a cliff, a typical impromptu garbage dump behind a shrine to the Virgin of Guadalupe. *"Hola,"* I waved meekly.

By now I'm fully dilated, and bushwhack an overgrown trail to perform my daily duty. I dig a hole beside a tree with my machete. The first time I had to commune with nature as a young boy, I didn't know how to squat. I wandered through the woods looking for something to sit on that resembled a toilet. I tried sitting on a stump and hanging my bottom over the edge, but it was like sitting on a bed of nails. I almost solved the problem by leaning against a tree in a sitting position, except that my feet slipped out from underneath me halfway through. Now that I've mastered squatting, I never want to sit on a bacteria infested toilet seat again, or be splashed by a urinal. I love squatting. It stretches the muscles in my aching legs; my bad knee pops soothingly; it applies pressure on my bowels; straightens my intestines; and spreads my cheeks clear of harm, as if saying: "Ready, set, go!"

In lieu of a newspaper, I admire the unique plants, the fragrant breeze, peculiar insects, and songs of unfamiliar birds. I clean myself, stand and begin an unpleasant traveler's necessity, I examine my feces for signs of disease: blood, pus or worms. A healthy bowel movement should be reddish-brown, firm enough to hold its curlicue, and light enough to float on water. I admire my work—picture perfect—if I can say that about feces. To aid decomposition and prevent the spread of any microbes that may be hitchhiking to the next human, I stir it up and bury it, another unpleasant necessity on an overcrowded planet.

Back on the road, I'm being watched by a group of woodcutters, barefoot and dressed in rags. I begin to itch. I was caught in some burrs, there are dozens of varieties in Africa. I remove them and give my boys a good scratch. The itching intensifies until my legs and nether region sting and burn. The pain is unbearable. I hop, slap and scratch. The giggling woodcutters approach. "Problem, sir?"

"My skin. I itch."

"Very bad plant in there, sir." He says with a smile, before translating for his friends. They roll their heads back and laugh, exposing cavernous mouths and ivory teeth. Some begin a jiggy dance imitating me. "Don't scratch," he advises.

"What can I do?" I ask hoping he'll fetch an ancient jungle remedy.

He shrugs. "It will last only some hours."

My skin is twitching with pain, and a ring of fire is spreading across my chest and arms. I cycle up the mountain at a breakneck pace to sweat out the poison. I fear my whole body will be engulfed in the red tide and swell like a balloon. I swat, scratch and slap as if hounded by a swarm of tsetse flies, whose bite is reputed to make a heard of gnu stampede. The men follow me, laughing and shouting up the road to their neighbors, and then the neighbors laugh and shout to their neighbors, and so it follows me, like jungle drums, up and over the mountain and seemingly all the way to Cape Town.

I have a small realization, conceivably why people ask such a mundane question is because we all share a common fear of being humiliated and ostracized from the community. This isn't the life changing experience I'd hoped to gain from my travels—or is it? Embarrassment—the great equalizer.

16 ⊙ Did you get sick?

I'm composing this travelogue while sick in my hotel but temporarily lucid. People often ask about my worst experiences, such as getting sick, now I can reward them with a disgusting and horrifying story that depicts how far humanity has evolved (or not) in the last thousand millenniums.

My Tibetan hotel has no heat, so I huddle beneath four thick blankets quilted in flowery pink and green patterns that the Chinese favor, drink from the bottomless pot of tea and hug bottles of hot water. I wonder if I have the disease of the year, Severe Acute Respiratory Syndrome (SARS). Though there are no confirmed cases in Tibet, the Chinese have closed their borders and rumor says they'll evict all foreigners. Our group composes nine of the remaining 35 foreigners in Tibet.

The high altitude, freezing temperatures, poor hygiene, and the stress and physical exhaustion of cycling 6-10 hours per day have kept me perpetually sick for months, making me suspect I'm masochistic, because I keep going. Currently, I have at least four diseases and one parasite. It started in India when I got boils (skin abscesses), on my legs from thorn scratches that became infected, possibly from dried goat's dung blowing around. Boils are agonizing sores that ooze blood and pus and caused my flesh to swell to near bursting. I've been to three "doctors" and taken three rounds of antibiotics to cure my boils, but they seemed to have migrated from my legs to my throat. My throat is nearly white with ulcers. I can't swallow and during one coughing fit, the pain was so intense that I think I blacked out for a few seconds. It makes dengue, the break-bone fever, which I caught in Mumbai, seem like the sniffles. Currently, I've lost my voice and a drooly gob of snot goes in and out of my nose like a yo-yo, same as every Tibetan kid. I've been so sick that I spent the last three days being shipped to Lhasa in the back of a truck, hiding underneath blankets at the Chinese military checkpoints, because my permit is valid only for cycling Tibet, and apparently not for riding in the truck, especially the cab, though I was suspicious that my guides simply wanted to quarantine me. I felt so ashamed and angered by missing the ride into Lhasa that I sobbed, and vowed again—realizing I couldn't live with this feeling of failure—to cycle around the world or die trying.

Aside from being exposed to foreign germs, my main problem is that I can't stay warm. On my first day in Tibet, it rained. Soaked, frost biting painfully into my fingers, and my stomach battling foreign particles of feces, I succumbed to a cold. After which, I've been too exhausted to recover. Even if it isn't raining, at high altitudes, the temperature drops about five degrees per 1000 meters, yet as the atmosphere thins the sun's radiation becomes more intense. At one moment, I began to burn and sweat and had to pull the brim of my cap around my sunglasses; then a moment later, the sun disappeared behind a cloud and my sweat began to freeze. My body temperature went up and down like the snot in my nose, and my clothes went on and off, which amused many locals. Every night I stuffed two bottles of boiling hot water in my sleeping bag, and if they happened to roll onto the ground, by morning they were frozen solid.

Where do these germs come from? About ten percent of the locals, especially the Chinese wear face masks to prevent respiratory diseases, but this hasn't deterred the majority of people from spitting in the streets or in their shops and restaurants. I went to a pharmacy indicating that I needed some lozenges when the owner coughed up a loogey, spat it on the ground behind the counter and then rubbed it into the floor with his foot, and proceeded to sell me cures to respiratory diseases infected with respiratory diseases—the Chinese are reputed to be excellent businessman.

Nearing Lhasa, one of our hotels had a small courtyard where cars were parked, garbage strewn and firewood stored. The urinal was a trough that drained through a hole in the wall and the toilet was behind a broken truck sunk in the frozen mud and indicated by the pyramids of frozen feces. Of course, there were no sinks so everyone must rinse their hands in water and shake off the excess like a wet dog. In India, the locals wash their hands over their plate of leftover food and then spray their neighbors with flecks of rice coated in a sauce of their personal diseases, which turned my stomach even more then when I was served a plate of *abu gobi* in Southern India with flies stuck to the top and even stirred in, and being forced to eat it because there were no other food sources for miles. Flies swarming around a restaurant aren't flies roaming the desert that coincidentally happened along a bonanza; they're most likely bred just outside the window beside the stove where the leftover food is dumped.

I think my diseases have combined into a toxic potluck party, making me feel like a balloon animal about to pop. During a break near a Tibetan monastery and a cave where an aesthetic monk survived on lichen for two years until he turned green, there was a Tibetan-style latrine. "Ah, a little bit of civilization," I thought, thankful not to have to run off behind some rocks with the peeping kids lurking about. It was a two-story stone structure with the business end exposed to the sky. I walked up the narrow, uneven, stone staircase with no handrails. The wooden door swung open with little effort revealing a dirt-covered, wooden floor with a hole in the middle. This two-story construction, as opposed to a simple hole in the ground, I presumed was necessary because the waste freezes before it can degrade and needs to be shoveled out. Five piles of feces, nowhere near the hole, dotted the floor like landmines. I was reminded of bush camping in Croatia. "Dennis, did you read the guidebook? It says never go off the beaten track or wander in the fields because there are still landmines leftover from the war."

"Remind me to read it beforehand next time," he said in his remarkable regret-free manner.

I squatted and released trillions of Giardia protozoa into the abyss while staring at the weathered piles of feces and feeling nauseous. While waiting for the rumbling in my guts to subside, I heard a sound like running water and looked below, between my legs and beneath my dangly bits, to see a furry Tibetan dog, who had apparently come running as he saw me climb the stairs, as if I had rung a dinner bell, and was enthusiastically lapping up my porridge-like stool. Later, I would learn these pig toilets, supposedly an ancient Goan, ecologically-friendly invention, especially eco-friendly for intestinal parasites, are made to accommodate pigs, dogs and, even, yaks—and,

you can guess who has been eating the yaks: yak butter tea, yak dumplings, yak noodle soup.... Just the thought of it makes me want to yak.

Photo courtesy of Edwin Tucker

17 ⊙ Where do you find water?

Before sunrise racing the Mexican, Baja sun, Dennis and I share a frugal breakfast of coffee and apples and decamp. I carefully pluck my clothes off the cacti thorns where I was irradiating the bacteria, but now they're damp from a thick fog. I've discovered four types of cacti needle firsthand: one plump, purple cactus like a pin cushion that stabbed me; another unidentified cactus left a dozen spears in my foot; an inconspicuous green, leafy shrub that implanted an array of barbs in my shin; and, once I cut open the red bud or fruit of a mission cactus to see the inside. It took half an hour to pick the fine bristles out of my hands with a tweezers.

We push our bikes down a sand track that the garbage trucks bulldozed through the cacti forest, where they randomly dump their load to desiccate and blow away. The tracks are the few places we can penetrate the wilderness without a flat; nonetheless, it appears my bike discovered a thorn. Waiting for the fog to clear, I disassemble my bike. I can't find a leak. Perhaps my tire deflated because of the 16° C (61° F) ambient temperature difference between predawn and mid-afternoon. The surface temperature of the roads is much higher and can cook an egg. I have to use Dennis' pump. Yesterday, the intense heat evaporated the grease in mine and destroyed the o-ring.

Just as I enter the volcanic reserve, 70 KM into the day, I run out of water and Dennis has cycled out of sight. I'm already thirsty as I climb the flank of the dormant Las Tres Virgenes volcano. Below me, an immense forest of giant saguaro cacti fills dozens of square miles. As I desiccate like a piece of garbage, my mouth goes dry and I have a horrible alkaline taste in my mouth. My eyelids are sticking to my burning eyeballs, making me perpetually squint. Every breath dries my throat. It itches. I cough and try to gather enough stringy spit to keep my throat moist. My sweat is diminishing. My heart is laboring to pump thickening blood. And, my joints ache, lacking lubrication.

I find some shade where the road cuts through a hill and sprawl against the relatively cool rocks, and watch ranks of cacti, like green Martians with arms raised in salute, march up the flanks of the candy-striped volcanoes. My thermometer has maxed out at 50° C (120° F). Dennis always says, "It doesn't matter what the temperature is. I can't tell the difference over a hundred-and-five, and what can we do about it anyway?" He also made a gloomy forecast, "If we're having such trouble finding food and water in a developing country, imagine what it will be like an undeveloped country." (The Baja would prove to be one of the most challenging stretches of road.) I shake the last few drops out of my bottles; this effort costs more sweat. My skin is triply pink: sunburnt, flushed with blood, and coated in rosy desert dust. After 15 minutes in the shade, my thermometer still registers 50° C, which means the ambient temperature is over halfway to boiling; and, I'm shivering cold and delirious, telltale symptoms of heat exhaustion.

I'm dehydrating fast. I don't have much time, and there are no buildings, people or cars. Cycling can actually be cooler than sitting in the stagnant hot air; so, despite common sense urging me to wait for help, I enter the baking sun and hope I can make 20 KM to the next town. The road is polka-dotted with flattened scorpions, fat green caterpillars and green goo. Swarms of gnats polka-dot my glasses. And above me, turkey vultures circle. "I'm not dead yet," I taunt them in a gravelly voice, wasting precious moisture. I search the riverbeds for puddles. The rivers flowed once three weeks ago after a hurricane dumped 51 centimeters of rain on the Baja; by the next day, all the water seeped into the desert, as if it never happened except to turn a few patches of the asphalt road into rubble. There isn't even mud to suck. I look at the clouds wistfully as if I could inhale the vapors.

Where are the rich gringos with their refrigerators on wheels? Many times they've passed me honking and scaring me into the berm on my bad wheel. (I've been popping spokes.) Even in Mexico they think they own the whole road. (The Mexicans have been very courteous drivers, perhaps because they're accustomed to dodging cows and donkeys, but I think they're just more sympathetic to the common man.) I scan the ditch for bottles of water tossed out of recreation vehicles, but there's nothing but bottles of urine tossed out by impatient Mexican truck drivers. I can't even contemplate drinking my own urine, because there's none left.

Every muscle, bone and joint aches—the toxins are building in my bloodstream. My speed is diminishing. My temples are throbbing. My veins are engorged with blood—or are my muscles deflated? My skin is dry; all my sweat—if there is any—is being whisked away. Difficulty swallowing. Headache. Tired....

Every thought is engrossed with water: cold showers, mountain streams, glaciers, swimming pools, great lakes of water, my whole life full of faucets perpetually flowing hot and cold water, mostly going down the drain. One swallow, all I want is one swallow to take the fire out of my mouth and one drop for each eye. I realize, when I'm considering drinking a bottle of truck driver's urine, that I will not survive the day without water. I might not even survive another hour. I would trade my bicycle for a glass of water. "Water. Water. My kingdom for a glass of water."

I have no regrets except that it seems there's so much more life to live than I've been living. More importantly, I realize that I didn't truly say goodbye to my loved ones because I thought I would see them again, I thought they'd always be there. I never said that I would miss them. In fact, I don't think I've ever been deeply honest about my feelings with anyone.

I crest a hill and see a dusty, wind blown town housing the Mexican military and fueling the trucks and drivers. Dennis is waiting at the barricade. He has run out of water, too. We head to the nearest shop and both buy a gallon of water. I hand the cashier a wad of pesos with shaking hands. Once, confusing the exchange rate, I nearly paid ten dollars for a gallon of water; now I would gratefully pay a million. My gallon of water is chilled. I cradle its coolness against my bosom like a baby and carry it outside. It sparkles in the sun and glistens with dew. I take a sip. My saliva glands spasm as they return to life.

The first few gulps feel like swallowing lumps of ice, but once my throat is lubricated, I pour half a gallon down my gullet until my brain freezes, and my esophagus and stomach feel lined in ice. Waves of tingles radiate from my belly. My eyes tear. My pores open like 100,000 floodgates. I'm drenched inside and out. The dry, hot wind suddenly feels cool and tickles my skin. I shudder as in the peak of an orgasm. I've never experienced such bliss. Heaven is a cool glass of water in a hot desert.

Finding and filtering an average of 12 liters of water per day could take hours. Eventually I discovered that I could siphon water through my filter, which took even longer but at least I could conserve my energy for cycling.

18 ⊙ Don't your legs get tired?

The Vietnamese summer has melted my malaria pills into a yellow lump. The tape and glue I used to Jerry-rig my bike has also melted. The seals in my pedal bearings have burst. The algae in my water bottles have died. My temples throb, my skin is flushed, my thoughts are like butterflies caught in a monsoon. The sun, even through the clouds, spark pinpricks of pain through my flesh like fireworks: I have heat rash and heat exhaustion.

A thousand meters below me, I can see the road winding through a valley of monumental, conical limestone hills. I should've read my guidebook before deciding on a shortcut (which has turned into a long-cut) down the old road. My guidebook reads: "Highway 6 is a euphemism at this point as atrocious road surfaces, switchbacks and steep climbs make it an arduous stretch to say the least—a four-wheel drive or robust motorbike are the only feasible vehicles. Buses are only for masochists." I wonder: *What are bicycles for?*

The road is so rugged that I've had to cut an innertube into strips and tie everything down. I need to rest and reevaluate my options. I slow, switching gears by kicking the chain over with my foot (a week ago a chain link popped loose and ripped the derailleur off). When I dismount my bicycle slips out of my sweaty grip, splashing down into a pile of water buffalo dung. Not far behind, I flop down beside a road marker shaped like a tombstone. *If Scott passes out does he hear himself hit the ground?* My curiosity of Buddhism has given me many koans to contemplate today. The tombstone radiates heat like an oven, so I roll onto the ground and sprawl in the dusty grass, but the ground is too hot, so I sit up and fan myself with my floppy hat. Even this requires too much effort. Without a puff of wind to cool me, my groin is like a Petri dish, sweat tickles my skin like flies and runs uselessly onto the ground. I feel like the sun is wringing me dry, turning my blood into sludge. I'm fearful that my heart and brain will explode from heat stroke, just like mom warned would happen if I wasn't careful.

A woman with a baby in a basket strapped to her shoulders and a young boy stop to gape. It's so hot many men and women and most of the children are topless. The woman uses a fan that she crafted from a plastic bottle and piece of bamboo. Sweat coats the boy's shorts and runs down his legs like urine, and the baby reminds me of a baked potato.

"*Nuoc.* Water," I keep repeating with different stresses and tonal variations and pantomiming. Finally, they shake their heads no and point up the hill. (Once, I wanted some rice or noodles, and went through all the tonal variations, before the restaurateur motioned me to stay while she went to purchase ingredients. Many restaurants won't actually purchase the food unless they have a customer. She returned, looking very proud, with a box of laundry detergent.)

Fifteen minutes later, the locals still gaping, I stand and push my bicycle up the hill. Walking feels cool with the slight breeze my motion generates, but my feet are blistered and raw from trying to get traction on my bicycle cleats. I wish I had my hiking shoes. I bought them in Kathmandu for the cold trek up Mt. Everest. They were stylish and had sentimental value, but my knees objected to carrying the extra weight up Vietnam's steep and rough roads. A week ago, I traded them with the

owner of a guesthouse-restaurant-gift shop. She whittled down the bargain to dinner and a beer, then she over-charged me for my room, rounded all the numbers up to the nearest thousandth and short-changed me. I had arrived at her guesthouse after a minor crash (dodging a minivan), bleeding, desperate and too dizzy to monitor my pocketbook, which is a never-ending travel chore. When I recovered my senses, I calculated that instead of profiting 40,000 dong, I paid her 5000 dong (about 33 cents) to take the shoes.

After 200 meters of trudging up the mountain, my body is burning. I stop. The villagers stop. Rest. Push 200 meters. Rest. Push. Again and again with diminishing results. I'm still 20 KM from my destination and I've been averaging less than four kilometers per hour (KPH). I have no water and only one-hour of sunlight remaining. No buses, minivans or jeeps have passed. I consider turning around and coasting downhill, but I don't recall any streams or camping sites; Vietnam is over-populated and deforested compared to most places. I'll have to go all the way to the bottom and buy supplies and camp in the schoolyard; but, I realize this is impossible because the heat of braking has been causing my rims to burn through my tires and brake pads. Furthermore, the town is full of pranksters. A group of adolescents saw me coming and dragged a log into the road to block my path. They surrounded the log with arms crossed and grins on their faces. I simply rode in the squishy grass alongside the road. *If riding around the road is easier than riding on the road, is it still a road?* However, I did have one of the highlights of my trip when a young boy, clearly being abused, put his hand on his oafish father, who was probably illiterate and couldn't speak English, and said, "This is my dog."

A motorcyclist stops and for a hefty price offers to tow me to the mountain pass. On our first attempt, the rubber straps snap. On the second, slower attempt, as he motors away, the tension slowly increases until, suddenly, I'm slung into the ditch. The next few running starts tow me a few dozen meters, but since I'm manually holding the straps to prevent being dragged behind his motorcycle, I can't control my steering.

After the motorcyclist leaves, and three more pushes up the mountain, I see a group of small children near a long house atop a hill on the side of a mountain. I climb the hill looking for water, but unlike almost everywhere else, the children shriek and scatter before me. After much shouting, I attract the attention of a man. I go through my pantomiming routine asking permission to pitch my tent anywhere. He giggles. I ask for water. He giggles again. It appears everything's very humorous. I suspect he must be high on opium, a common crop and pastime in the mountain villages. I help myself to the water in a barrel fed by a system of bamboo troughs and hoses and return to the main trail. Four stocky women dressed in black clothes with colorful embroi-dery are leading horses home burdened with fruits and vegetables. I ask if I can sleep on the ground beside the trail, the only flat spot I've seen. The leader refuses to look at me and shakes her head no. Four more women and horses approach, the women don't acknowledge my greetings, and two foals fright and flee down the mountain.

I continue until I find a flat spot where a landslide destroyed the road. The sun has set. A young man finds me waiting for the skies to darken before pitching my tent in the bushes. He slaps his legs and winces, asking if I'm tired. Often people ask if my legs hurt. It's my grinding knees that agonize me. No matter how stubborn I am, my knees have executive power over me; they're mechanically unsound and cease functioning at odd times, and often threaten to quit the trip.

The young man insists I go home with him. I decline repeatedly until a military jeep drives past. Not long ago, foreigners were required to sleep only in special, over-priced, tourist hotels where the guests were registered with the police. I'm certain camping is still forbidden. Darkness is imminent and I wonder why they don't offer assistance or arrest me for loitering.

I accept my newfound friend's hospitality, concluding, perhaps, it's safest and that we'll both benefit from our cultural exchange. It takes both our efforts to push my bike up an even steeper dirt trail, 1.5 KM into the mountains. It's dark and I can barely see the silvery trail in the moonlight as I stumble over rocks and roots into a stream. We arrive in his village of the H'mong tribe. There are no lights. The geometric planes of the long house jut from the sinuous black jungle. We carry my bicycle over the threshold of his house and lean it against a wall. The embers of a fire illuminate bulky shapes. I grope towards the fire pit after the man. I'm offered a child-sized bench. My knees crack when I sit. There are four women and five children who hide behind the pillars and furniture. The women wear fancy embroidered clothes covering T-shirts of defunct dot-coms. The young man wears pants and no shirt, and the children wear shirts and no pants. They're all covered in a coat of grime. My efforts to converse cease when I ask the man his name and he doesn't respond. He appears content to smoke his tobacco pipe. (One puff makes my head swim.) His wife and her sisters gossip while their hands languidly and expertly embroider clothes. His wife says only one word to me, which I interpret as tea, but my drink is like bitter water. The children play with large emerald-colored grasshoppers. The desperate grasshoppers cling to any-

thing and the boys use them as cranes to move matchboxes across the table. There's neither art nor books or music.

I remain here for two hours, exhausted, swooning and mesmerized by the fire. Before my trip, I had trouble climbing a staircase; now, combining all the hills I cycle in one day, I routinely climb about 20% of Everest's elevation every day. Today, even in the heat, I far exceeded that energy output. I hit the wall about a dozen times, each time thinking I could go no further, but that salvation was just around the bend. I'm angry with myself that I didn't quit long ago; however, I'm amazed at my strength and endurance, and wonder what I could do if my life were in jeopardy; I admit that when my life is safe and easy, I seldom have such interesting experiences, because I'm too lazy and too cowardly to get off the couch. It occurs to me that my mind must be as lazy as my body; what could I do if I learned to focus my mind and emotions in one productive direction?

When it becomes clear, I can't sleep or eat anytime soon, I pantomime that I would like to wash my face and fill my water bottles. The husband leads me 500 meters up the hill to a hose attached to rickety bamboo piping on stilts and siphoning water from a small stream. He disconnects the hose, and I wash in a field of weeds that make my legs itch. When we return to the house, my bladder is pulsing. My body is purging itself of lactic acid and reestablishing a balance of electrolytes and water. I communicate that I have to urinate by grabbing my guts and wincing.

He shakes his head in a baffled manner.

I grab my groin and jump up and down.

He shakes his head again.

I use my thumb as a phallic symbol and twist my hips side to side.

Smiling he shakes his head in a baffled manner.

I put my water bottle between my legs and squeeze out a stream of water and act relieved. "Ah."

He stands there bug-eyed.

I duck into the woods, but he follows me. I motion for him to stay, three times, but my gestures mean nothing to his curiosity. Finally, I just turn my back and pee.

He's still laughing when we return to the hut and soon all the women are too. I'll have to endure this story repeatedly as visitors arrive, to gawk at me.

It takes two hours to cook dinner: a pot of sticky rice and a pot of salty spinach. By now, the grasshoppers have lost all their legs and have been thrown into the fire. My hands shake from exhaustion, and I spill all my freshly filtered water in the darkness, coating myself in a layer of grime. With dirty hands, my host and I dine first, followed by the women and children. During the lull when the kid's mouths are occupied, I curl up in my designated spot on a wooden bed frame built into the house. There's no mattress or pillow just a dusty, moldy blanket. I pretend to sleep. The others bumble about until eleven o'clock and then it takes the kids 30 minutes to cry themselves to sleep. I awake in the middle of a monsoon and pee outside between the planks of the wall. My hosts never showed me the bathroom, if they have one.

Everyone awakes at four in the morning and begins their chores: the husband husks longan fruit, two women mill corn with a machine that looks like a museum piece from the Old World, one woman boils corn mush in two big cauldrons, and the last minces a huge pile of greens onto the dirt floor. I'm still exhausted and itching to leave, but I accept their invitation to breakfast. I sit on the stoop and watch the sunrise. When they seem to grow bored of their chores, they take another two hours to cook breakfast: a pot of grits and a pot of noodles with salt.

Breakfast ends—my stomach is full, but I'm still weak from malnourishment— and I'm free to leave. I sacrifice some candy to the kids, which I need to fuel my trek up the mountain, take photos, thank each person with a prayer and a bow, and begin to push my bike outside. I've planned a small gift for the husband hoping he'll buy his kids some pants, but before I can offer, he blocks my exit and writes a number on

the wall with some charcoal. My bill for room and board comes to 100,000 dong (about 7 USD), a week's wages to the average worker, or a night in a hotel with air-conditioning, hot water, satellite television, Internet and breakfast. Never before has anyone charged me for an invitation or act of hospitality. I feel demoralized and robbed and further drained of my vitality. I negotiate a discount and am left to find my way to the road. I climb down cliffs and wade through streams. *If I carry my bicycle and panniers is it still a bicycle or is it a backpack?*

19 ⊙ Do you ever get lost?

Dennis and I cycle through the mountains of Greece, past the monasteries of Meteora (meaning *rocks in the air*) built atop gigantic pillars of sandstone and containing racks of monk skulls; through olive grooves hundreds of kilometers long; past ancient Greek ruins, like Delphi on a spur of Mount Parnassus the site of the ancient oracle (where are the oracles and prophets now?) and into the heart of the "beautiful monster" Athens.

I was told by my cynical Portuguese coworker that I wouldn't have to worry about being robbed in Europe because the social programs keep all the lazy and desperate people swimming in booze and floating on cigarettes. (Since I like to think I'm an optimist, I'm sure I'll be swindled somewhere.) Greece being on the fringes of Europe has some economically depressed areas. We passed several shantytowns constructed of haphazard sheets of plastic, corrugated metal and scrap lumber: a construction technique that is ugly and inefficient, making living conditions far inferior to the simple mud-brick villages of South America. (Some of my favorite structures were the African villages, which are sculpted with handfuls of mud and straw, giving them elegant flowing shapes, each hut perfectly engineered per the inhabitant's sensibilities. The cave-like interiors are cool and soothing, and taking a midday nap made me feel like I was recharging in the womb of Mother Earth.)

The clothing of the gypsies were pieced together like their shanties; and, rather than the friendly greetings of the Greek country folk or the unilateral indifference of big-city folk, the gypsies stopped and stared as we passed, a look I associate with the desperation of poverty, but, perchance, was the curiosity of kindred spirits living on the edges of society. I don't mean being poor is bad; some poor people are the happiest, most generous and proudest people I've met; for example, Dennis and I met Monso in northern Argentina. He showed us his empty wallet and joked, "How many dollars do you want?" Monso didn't have even one extra peso after a day's work, much less the money to buy his children schoolbooks, which is a shame because his eldest daughter seemed to be a budding Shakespeare, "A banana in every language is still a banana."

Nonetheless, Monso invited us to dinner. He had a hunk of beef swarmed by flies hanging from a hook in the shed. He hacked it apart with a machete. *"¿Bueno Carne, Si?"* He beamed.

Dennis and I felt a bit ill, but we beamed back, *"¡Si, bueno carne!"*

I felt obliged to eat everything, even the bits I couldn't cut. The mother brought me three knives and I still couldn't cut the gristle apart. Nor could I chew the meat, but swallowed big chunks, fearing I would insult my host. Monso just laughed and asked if he should get the sword off the wall, then leaned over and cut apart my meat with his razor sharp bowie knife, that I imagined he also used in his handyman work. Monso extended his invitation to camping in his yard with the ducks, turkeys, dogs and a parrot that didn't know how to fly. Monso's wife swept the dirt smooth as asphalt everyday. (I'm not sure how she didn't sweep a hole in the ground.) Colorful plants and a fresh breeze surrounded us. How much of a "sacrifice" would the richest person in the world have to make to equal this gesture? In contrast to Monso's family, whose lifestyle was the norm for centuries, where poverty is surrounded by money there's the perception of the haves and the have-nots. I think this phenomenon is present in Greece and, certainly, in Athens. Perhaps, the lost, desperate and unhappy people migrate to the cities because it seems fast and easy, and perhaps the less scrupulous prey on the rich and ignorant because they feel entitled to the fruits of labor without having to plant the seed.

On our first night in Athens—this always happens in my first few days, as if the swindlers can smell suckers—Dennis and I are approached by an over-friendly Greek who says he worked in the oil business and lived in Houston for eight years. He proclaims, "Americans, they are here—" he pounds his chest— "close to my heart." This begins to make my spider sense tingle—few Europeans like Americans. "Come, I'm on vacation. I have lots of money. I'll take you to a good Greek bar and buy you a beer." He's a clean-cut man with the burly body of a laborer, though he doesn't have the sunken eyes of a career drinker, he stinks of beer.

I'm suspicious and look at Dennis. He shrugs leaving the decision to me. I want to believe our new friend; I've been invited to drinks all over the world, and meeting extravagant people "good" or "bad," experiencing anything other than my Midwestern point of view, fascinates me. "Why not? One beer then we must go," I say planting a seed for our escape. We walk around the corner and down the stairs of a "Nightclub." Of course, it's a brothel and Dennis and I both confirm our suspicion that it's a scam, but I'm curious and, in retrospect, enjoy a haughty game of testing people to see what motivates them. The matronly madam behind the bar opens three mini-beers and hands them to us before we can protest. "How much is this?" I ask, assuming I'll be stuck with the tab.

"Only five Euro. Very Cheap."

"That's not cheap. That's more expensive than London."

"No. Very cheap."

Suddenly, Dennis and I are surrounded by plain women begging for drinks. "Buy yourself a drink," I say.

"Please. Just to say, 'Hello.' If you want me to sit here you must buy me a drink."

"Then go sit somewhere else."

"Okay, I will stay. I like you. Maybe—"

"No thanks." While the women attempt to hook me, and I marvel at how they wear more clothes and are more ordinary than the topless women on the average European beach, I hear Dennis say, "Uh... Scott," and by the time I turn, I only see his heels as he runs upstairs and outside.

"What a goody-goody," I think, annoyed at being abandoned.

Seeing Dennis ditch the tab, the bartender disappears, and a moment later a beefy, surly, mustached man replaces her. "You must pay ten Euro twenty for your beers."

"That's not my beer." I point to Dennis' unfinished drink.

"It is your friend's beer. You must pay now."

"I don't even know that guy."

"You must pay now."

"He's paying," I point to the over-friendly Greek, who's obviously getting kickbacks.

"Pay for your own woman," he says and ignores me by snuggling with a prostitute, who's so disinterested that she appears like a rag doll in his arms.

"You must pay now," the bartender's mustache bristles with anger.

"First I will finish my drink, then I will pay for my drink," I hold up the miniature beer can.

"You must pay for both. Now."

"I didn't order that drink. I'm not drinking that drink. I'm not paying for it."

"It is your friend's drink. Now it is your problem."

At any moment, I expect bigger and meaner bouncers to appear and roll me. I would learn, after relating my story to other savvy travelers, that it's common to be robbed by the bouncers, even being gassed or drugged during the process. I stand, "Now it is your problem." I begin to dash out of the bar. Several women grab me.

"Stop. I'll call the police." The surly man starts to move around the counter towards me.

I shrug off the women easily. It's very foolish for them to try and stop me. My bicycle weighs more than any of the homely waifs, and I carry that over a mountain every-day. Still they chase me up the steps and out the door. I dash down the back streets of Athens, making random turns, losing myself in the Ugly Monster, and losing the bouncers and bouncy ladies, grateful that I'm wearing good running shoes.

Coincidentally, I run in the right direction and stumble upon Dennis at an ice cream shop, and we both laugh at being suckered by the oldest trick in the book— The Friendly Greek Scam.

Quite often I've been lost, both physically and spiritually, and I've noticed three things: I always have an adventure; I always find myself a little wiser; and I always laugh a little.

A view of my kitchen and balcony from the campsite pictured on the right. Notice the small village barely visible in the valley. Three shepherd boys from this village came to visit me.

20 ⊙ Where do you sleep?

The "doctor" calls me, "the husband," into his office and explains, as if Debbie isn't there, annoying her European feminism, she has a severe food allergy. Her symptoms include: diarrhea, vomiting, rash, chest pains, delirium, and she's generally feeling very sorry for herself, as I did when I had dengue fever. The doctor assures me it isn't dengue fever and prescribes a pile of medication and a few days rest. I scoop up the medicine and jest, "Now I'm as good as an Indian doctor." He doesn't laugh, so I amend, "Don't worry. I'll take good care of my wife." Still, I'm the only one laughing.

I met Debbie in Cairo, Egypt and, coincidentally, again in Dahab when she happened to be standing outside my bungalow. When she returned home to England, she discovered that her best friend and ex-lover, in a fit of depression, either jumped or fell off the cliffs of Cornwall into the ocean. I invited Debbie to travel with me to India as a cure to dwelling on her sorrows; and, despite her father's warning not to do something stupid, within four weeks, she took a sabbatical, rented her house, sold her car, bought a bike and flew to India.

I do everything I can for Debbie: zooming in and out of villages to find and filter water, buy and cook food, scout campsites, pitch camp, maintain and repair the bicycles, navigate and negotiate lodging. I do everything short of pedaling her bicycle; still she's still struggling. I had hoped India would give her a new perspective on life, but, as far as she mentions, she finds the struggle to survive depressing and thinks more than ever that her friend wasted a privileged life and regretted it the moment he stepped off the cliff. Most days, I feel she's annoyed with me for getting her into this mess; I, however, find Debbie's deadpan English pragmatism soothing—a perfect balance to India's madness and, perhaps, my own. Once in response to my philosophizing and agonizing, Debbie knocked the butterflies out of my mind by asking, "How do you *unboil* an egg?"

Until Debbie recovers we're stuck in Kalyandurg, a town that reminds me of a phrase in my guidebook that I always seem to violate one way or another, "Whatever you do, don't...." Kalyandurg isn't in my guidebook, or probably any other, but if I ever write a guidebook, I'd say, "Whatever you do, don't go to Kalyandurg."

Almost daily people ask me the mundane question: "Where do you sleep?" Personally, I can think of a lot more interesting questions, like: Would you ever quit if you met the woman of your dreams? (I almost did and would've regretted it.) What do you miss most? (My friends.) What can India teach America? (A sense of community, that people are cooperating together to build something that contributes to everyone's physical, mental and spiritual well-being.) What can America teach India? (Birth control or quality not quantity.) How can I bicycle around the world? (First, you must really want it.) However, people are fascinated with the logistics of my trip. Perhaps, they would travel if they had some guarantee of not being stuck in the Kalyandurgs of the world.

Going from one chaotic town to the next tourist trap would drive me crazy. I prefer to camp. My tent is my portable sweat lodge: zip up the door, shut out the world and meditate to rid myself of accumulated evils. The safest places in urban areas are beside police stations or in a graveyard, but I enjoy the thrill of camping in the starry desert with the coyotes, or nestled deep in the woods with the bears, even amongst dens of thieves with a rope tied around my wrist and to my bicycle. I've camped in places I'd never have imagined, like two garbage dumps. One dump was rather nice, depending which way the wind was blowing; the other with a dead cow and gnats flying up my nose, was missing that "home away from home" feeling. And, I spent a few nights on a beach in Phuket, Thailand, where a year later I would have been washed away in a tsunami.

I've also had the most magical nights of my life camping. Once Debbie and I were camped in the barren Thar Desert. The sun had just set, and the sky melded from red on the horizon through the spectrum to nothingness. The sliver of the moon, less than a day old, was cradled between violet and the black of night. The first star that appeared, the wish star, was actually beneficent Jupiter. (I could see the Galilean moons through my binoculars.) Then the Dog Star became visible and slowly the Milky Way curdled into view. The night was so clear that I could see the face of the moon dimly lit by the reflection of the Earth. Muslims see the name of Allah written in the moon. I wondered what Hindus see, and, suddenly it was obvious that Om, the sacred symbol for the sound of the infinite, is also written in the moon. (I find it ironic that Western people see a man in the moon.) The stark, glowing desert was not unlike the lunar landscape with the exception of the wispy silhouettes of trees. In the distance, I saw what appeared to be a donkey lost in the desert, but much larger with powerful shoulders. As it approached, I distinguished two short sharp antlers. Its legs were black as if wearing stockings, and its body was silver-gray, with white stripes on the back of its neck and rump. I had never even seen a photo of this animal that's reminiscent of a zebra and more so of a unicorn. The giant antelope stopped within 100 meters and studied us. When a smaller brown female arrived they ambled into the desert, nibbling bushes. It was an inspirational experience that I let sink deep into my being and become part of me, a moment that made the boredom of cycling worthwhile, a moment that co-created a grand gestalt to my life that I would never have been able to imagine or construct.

Contrary to my infinite-star campsite, this zero-star Kalyandurg hotel is the worst place I've every slept; however, I suppose any shelter if you're in dire straits is the Taj Mahal.

I'm taking a coffee break. I found some real coffee in the marketplace and covertly ignited my gasoline stove in the bathroom. I figure it can't get any dirtier. The room is slightly bigger than the bed, which is too small for me. There's no chair or desk. The bed is a tin table with a thin mattress, with one sheet and a blanket that I suspect have never been washed. I cover everything with my plastic tarp, and lay down my air mattress, pillow and sleeping bag; still, it's more uncomfortable and filthier than any campsite, even the garbage dumps. Like most hotels, I must also use my own towel, soap and toilet paper (other mandatory items for most hotels are bug spray, flip-flops for the shower and oil for the door hinges); however, the room does come with several varieties of complimentary mosquitoes and cockroaches. My bike is disassembled for repairs and maintenance and occupies the whole room, even the bed. Normally I hand wash my laundry in a waterproof pannier and string it across the room to dry, but here my clothes would just soak up more dirt and mold. (In Costa Rica, I dislocated my wrist while doing laundry, which gives me great admiration for the *dhobis*, laundresses that tirelessly wring and pound their wash along the riverbanks. Mark Twain commented that they could break rocks with their clothes.) The walls were once painted white in a generic chalky paint that rubs off on everything and is common in Third World countries. Now the walls are yellow and stained with water (possibly urine) and red spittle from chewing betel nut. (Harvested from the betel palm, the nuts are wrapped in a leaf with quicklime, used as a catalyst, and a sprig of mint for flavor. The nut turns your mouth blood red and the lime rots your teeth. The older addicts look as if they've just had their teeth punched out.) Old Bollywood posters covered in graffiti, shredded and burnt, decorate the walls and attempt to hide the flaking paint and cracks. A large crack has ripped one poster in half, not to mention the foundation of the building. In the hallway, the walls are streaked with monkey droppings. The bathroom door is a porthole to a dungeon. The first time I entered, I slipped, banged my head on the doorframe and knocked two tiles off the wall with my elbow. It's a dingy blue-black room illuminated by a bulb that flickers and dims when the voltage drops. [See photo page 88.] The paint, plaster and even the slime sloughs off and clogs the drain, a rough hole chiseled out of the concrete floor. The Turkish toilet is at an odd angle. I'm unsure whether to face the hole or not as there isn't enough room to face either direction, so I squat sideways hoping nothing splashes in the muck, and I watch the ants marching to the dripping faucet. Afterwards, I grab the slimy bucket and flush the toilet with the water that accumulated overnight. I must cautiously duck back through the porthole so as not to pop my eyeballs on the rusty nails. The ceiling has one small skylight where the hotel employees take turns spying. And finally, each room comes fully-equipped with iron doors that the wind bangs shut, echoing through the corridor so that no one can sleep. There's a bolt on each side of the door. I accidentally bolted Debbie in her room for an afternoon, and when she peered out the window to call for help a monkey

A common event—a group of people wanting their picture taken, probably for the first time.

jumped onto her window bars, giving her "a bad fright". It's reminiscent of some prisons I've visited. The funny part is that I'm imprisoning myself for most of the day because the outside world is even more chaotic. Dinner requires hours to track the individual ingredients from vendors while being followed by a dozen children who, I think, if rumors are true, should be in a sweatshop if not school.

Debbie feels worn out by India. "How have you managed so long? Aren't you tempted to get on a bus and skip all these places?" She suggests diplomatically that she's having a change of heart.

For some reason both mysterious and hypocritical, I find it easier to be optimistic in regards to other people's tribulations than my own, so I explain, "I agree. Most places aren't worth visiting, except that it's part of the journey. I remember in Guatemala the hillsides looked like a never-ending patchwork quilt of farms—no indigenous plants or animals anywhere. I used to ask Dennis the same question. But now, I have an appreciation for my cup of coffee every morning because, once, I climbed several thousand feet up a volcano covered in coffee bean plants. I thought I was in tip-top shape—I ached for days afterward—but peasants tirelessly passed me with baskets on their backs that climb the volcano every day harvesting coffee beans. The chaos of these industrial areas supplies the resources for idyllic vacation spots. We could skip ahead, but I enjoy watching the blend of geography—plants, animals, culture, industry, terrain, weather. I feel like I'm seeing how the world works."

Several weeks later, we take a train to Rajasthan near the Indian-Pakistan border. The train was patrolled by military personal. Fanatics on both sides are fighting over Kashmir by slaying trainloads of civilians to prove their determination—millions have been killed. We find a very nice bed in a hotel in the Golden Fort of Jaisalmer constructed out of golden sandstone and illuminated by a golden sun, which is as beautiful as the name suggests except for the early mornings when the sewage flows through the open gutters. One day Debbie did help me answer one of philosophy's great questions: "How do I know I exist?" It's a baffling question. I'm reminded of an ancient story about a Chinese Taoist: Once upon a time Zhuangzi dreamt he was a butterfly fluttering hither and thither, happy with himself and sipping nectar as he pleased. Suddenly Zhuangzi woke up and there he was, veritably and unmistakable Zhuangzi. But Zhuangzi didn't know if he was Zhuangzi who had dreamt he was a butterfly, or a butterfly dreaming he was Zhuangzi.

Am I a man dreaming he is God, or God dreaming he is a man? Whether life is a reality, dream, or *maya* (illusion) as the Hindus say, I had thought the question of my existence was a mute point—it's reality to me either way, that is until Debbie and I suffered delirium after being served an over-potent *bhang lassi* that I suspect was spiked. (A common occurrence in India, I'm told.) A few minutes longer and we wouldn't have found our hotel one block away and would've had to sleep on the streets like millions of Indians. Safely in bed, Debbie says, "I'm hallucinating. I don't even know if it's you talking to me."

"Of course, it's me."

"I could just be hallucinating you said that."

Not faring well either, I'm reminded of when I went to watch my debut in a Bollywood movie. The disclaimer read, "All people in this movie are fictitious." I thought, "Am I fictitious? Debbie's right. I could just be in her imagination." I notice the mirror on the wall. "That's not even my reflection. This is all Debbie's dream. Or, possibly that's the real me and I'm the reflection." I was caught in a nihilistic feedback loop and began to fall into the mirror, about to lose myself forever when it occurred to me, "Aha!" I exclaim, "Descartes was right. *Cogito ergo sum.* I think, therefore I am."

"What are you talking about?"

"A reflection in a mirror can't think. If I were a dream, I wouldn't think anything or feel anything. It's simple—"

"Stop. You're freaking me out."

Eventually Debbie and I would travel separate paths. She wanted to circumnavigate Annapurna, the tenth biggest mountain in the world, by foot. She asked me to join her, but I could barely entertain the idea of giving up my bicycle and walking around a mountain, much less the world. So, we had an amicable parting, but wherever I pitch my tent, it's more cold and lonely, and sometimes I wonder: "How do I *unboil* an egg?"

Buying some bicycle fuel at a Tanzanian market. **Page 112.** Frog, squid, fish, chicken and other unidentified meats from a Thai street-food vendor.

21   ◉   What do you eat?

My aching, malnourished, overtaxed body has been consuming itself to power my bike for days. Today, I cycled past a hundred food vendors alongside the road selling nothing but buckets of old onions. Yesterday, it was pyramids of half-rotten tomatoes. Occasionally, street vendors are selling *chips mayai* (a french fry omelet) in a fluorescent "tomato" sauce, *ugali*, beef soup, rice and beans, or bananas. Rice and beans are known as Poor Man's Food, because it's the cheapest combination of all the essential proteins. Eat only rice or only beans and eventually you'll die of malnutrition. In Latin America, I was told that recipes for rice and beans are family heirlooms, and that marriage proposals are made and broken upon the woman's ability to prepare a tasty dish; conversely, African rice and beans barely get the job done, simply boiled in salt water over a wood fire beside the road, giving them a smoky, smoggy flavor.

I eat whatever the locals eat, not because I want to submerse myself in the culture, but because there are rarely any supermarkets, and they certainly don't sell foods from opposite sides of the planet. (In my local supermarket back home, there are over a hundred types of olive oil from dozens of countries.) If I'm fortunate, there are some not-so-supermarkets with piles of vegetables on blankets on the ground, and butchered meat (including feet, head, brains, internal organs and intestines) hanging from hooks, piled on tables and swarmed with flies. I had little choice but to eat that stir *fly* rice, chicken foot soup, stray-dog noodle soup, and once I was even tempted by a bag of fried grasshoppers. Lately, as long as my food doesn't move around on my plate too much, doesn't contain too many germs, and I can chew and swallow it—I'm satisfied. I should add that I prefer eating herbivores, like cattle (salmonella is ubiquitous in chickens and the metabolism of pigs is very similar to humans possibly containing many diseases and parasites like trichinosis), and I prefer not to eat: dust, dirt, sand, ash, exhaust soot, flies, maggots and worms. But now I'm starting to sound finicky. Dennis once said while staring dismally into his bowl, "When an ant falls in your food and you just stir it in, maybe you've been on the road too long."

Judging by how many times people ask where I found food and the strange things I was forced to eat, rather than more useful and interesting questions like: Which country has the best food? (Every country has many special dishes.) Or, why are Americans so fat? (Processed food.) Most people, even if they have an overabundance of food choices and riches, seem to be stuck in survival mode. Most Westerners imagine that the world is starving, but—even to my surprise—there's food everywhere, especially in the Third World, even in Africa. The only exceptions in 50 countries were sections of India (too many people and over-farming) and Zimbabwe (corrupt government). For example, baking bread sounds simple but imagine everything needed: fertile soil; temperate weather; wheat and dairy farms; seeds (there are many stories of Zimbabweans that have been given farms, and then just eat the seeds); a mill, salt refinery, yeast factory; a bakery with plumbing and electricity; petrol to fuel the tractors and delivery trucks; and people with money to buy bread, which employs the people that make the bread. Mostly, baking bread requires, like anything, passion; and, in Zimbabwe the government has been "nationalizing" farms, essentially robbing society of the motivation to organize itself enough to bake a loaf of bread.

I've been cooking nearly the same thing everyday for three years. (It makes lugging my stove and pots up the mountains seem worthwhile.) My all-purpose recipe, kind of a Goulash minus the paprika, is to throw whatever I have in a pot, boil the bacteria to death, and depending on how rotten the meat and vegetables are, I add more or less chili powder and turmeric to kill the smell and taste. I learned that cooking tip in India. Eating rotten food never occurred to me as being possible. A medical student told me the main problem, besides flavor, assuming the

bacteria has been destroyed, is that some bacteria, like botulism, leave toxic byproducts that aren't destroyed by the heat; the secondary problem is that this process destroys many nutrients needed to rebuild my starving body.

I haven't gotten sick by my own cooking yet, but restaurants and street vendors are a game of Russian roulette. East Africa was under British "administration" for 40 years. The British, due to rapid urbanization and wartime rations, have developed a taste for corned beef, pickled foods and tinned mush. In contrast, the nomadic lifestyle of many African tribes dictated that they ate seasonal fruits and vegetables and whatever animals they happen to snare. There's a joke that circulates among tourists: What do you get when you mix African and English food? Answer: If you're lucky, nothing.

My general rule is to eat in the most popular locations. The locals know best, and there's a faster turnover, therefore, less risk of contamination. I ask directions to the finest restaurant in Iringa, which happens to be named "Restaurant," hoping to splurge on my favorite Tanzanian dish: creamed banana and beef soup. The décor is glaring white and the clientele is ebony black, except me, I'm mostly pink. The line cook, like an anatomy professor, shows me the menu by scooping various animal parts out of different kettles: pig's knee, goat's ribcage, cow bones. The fourth item on the menu looks beefy and tasty. "Is that beef?" I ask the cook.

"Yes. Beef."

Moments later, a sour-smelling waitress sets my dinner on the table with a thunk and a slosh. "God will provide for you today," she smiles. Most roadside restaurants sell the fatty broth at a discount until nothing is left but a desiccated hunk of meat in a bowl of salt water. I'm pleased to see a thick layer of grease floating in my bowl, but that's the only savory aspect. Unappetizing spongy bits float in a sulfuric yellow broth as if the chef scooped up a bowlful of roadkill entrails. I poke my soup as if dissecting a rat. There are rings of chopped intestines resembling calamari, gobs of fat resembling a pancreas and some other mysterious bits floating around. My neighbor tells me it's the stomach of a cow—tripe. I tentatively spoon a piece of tripe into my mouth. It has a feathery texture on one side and is slightly bitter. There are no spices. It's simply cow guts boiled in water. I sip the stomach juice and eat some intestine rings. They are rubbery and tasteless, but the gastric smell makes my bile rise.

A young man causes a ruckus in the restaurant, I ask him to speak English if he's going to talk about me, and he says, "Everyone outside is very surprised to see a white man eat African food."

The waitress laughs and says, "He is human, too," and shoos him away like a fly.

Feeling guilty for wasting food and money when I could've cooked goulash for half the price, and being watched surreptitiously, I try repeatedly, to wash each spoonful down with watery papaya juice, but I can't stomach my stomach soup. It's the smell, like a heartburn burp. I return to the chef with an apologetic smile and say, "I can't eat this. Can I have that one?" Without comment the chef takes my bowl, pours it back into the kettle and refills it with the goat ribcage soup. It disgusts me wondering how much human spittle is commingled in the kettle, but it tastes wonderful.

I settle down with a book to accompany my meal. I plan on eating for hours and storing enough fat to power me for several days.

My neighbor asks me what I'm reading, and I say, "I'm reading the Qu'ran."

Abruptly, his face scrunches in anger and his wife shrinks, and he asks what became of the rest of the sacred book. Throughout the world, though it saddens me, I tear the pages out of my books as I read them to save the weight on my knees. I lie, "I read it so much that it broke. The other half is in my luggage." He seems placated, but for good measure, I add, "It's not a real Qu'ran. This is an English translation." I'm told that many Muslims believe, and I think it's wise, that one can only properly understand the teachings in the original, undistorted, infallible, Arabic version.

He leans over and whispers authoritatively, "The *Bible* is quite mistaken about Jesus being God," and soon finds several passages in my Qu'ran to prove it. In addition, he elucidates, that the Qu'ran says Jews and Christians have forgotten (sometimes translated as *corrupted*) Allah's message.

"May I pay for your meal?" he asks. I refuse politely three times before accepting.

The Qu'ran dictates to feed ten indigent people for expiation. I wonder, "Are alms given under the duress of hell a charitable, soul-building act?"

The kind Muslim is the first person to buy my meal in Africa. Sharing a meal has a great social and spiritual significance in every culture. I think this desire is ingrained in humans on an instinctual level: inviting someone to your table to share a meal demonstrates trust and respect, and offers nourishment for ideas and friendships, as well as the strength to fuel the body and bring those ideas into the world.

I thank my host and prepare to convert my soup into kilometers.

"May Allah guide you," he says.

The waitress wishes me a safe journey home. "I'm a long way from home," I say.

"Home is not far away; heaven is far away."

Much further down the road, slightly closer to home, and as far away from heaven as ever, serendipity smiles upon me again. Immanuel (Hebrew meaning *God is with us*) escorts me to his office for selling bus tickets. He seats me at a small desk in the center of a small room facing the open doors and dusty road. There's a pitcher of water, soap and a bowl. Immanuel pours water, warmed on the stove, over my hands and into the bowl. Before me, prepared by his wife, is the standard meal—rice, beans, kale, stewed tomatoes and beef—all the dishes are covered, the food is perfectly cooked and doesn't contain one grain of sand. He tells me of the other cyclists he has met and of a man that has walked twice as far and through twice as many countries as I've cycled. "If you believe in God anything is possible," he says.

I ask, "Which God?" and he looks confused, so I rephrase, "Which religion?"

"Protestant," he says. When I acknowledge that I was raised Protestant, he leans back, puffs his chest and preaches in a baritone voice, "What is the *Bible*? It is a history written by men about God's creation. Most people must read the *Bible* and have faith. You have been around the world, and you have seen God's glory direct. You are a witness to God and his creation. You have a great opportunity: when you go home, you can tell people the truth about God. So, I encourage you, don't despair." And when I finish my meal, he says, "I want to give you a gift."

I begin to object. He doesn't have much; and, like a typical American, I don't want to be indebted to him. He pulls a book from underneath a pile of papers. "I want to read a passage from the *Bible* for you." He reads psalm 23, the same psalm that Jasmine gave me to safeguard my trip, which I carry in my wallet. (If my broken Qu'ran and psalm fail, I also have an amulet of the Viking rune for *journey*, another amulet of the Chinese character for *protection*, and an icon of Italy's Madonna del Ghisallo, the Patron Saint of Cycling. And if all those fail along with my charm and fast feet, I have a machete and ear-splitting whistle.) His voice booms off the concrete walls, "Yea, though I walk through the valley of the shadow of death, I will fear no evil: For thou art with me." He waves his hand indicating my surroundings. I've just descended into the Great Rift Valley—a hot, thorny, inhospitable desert; and, by coincidence, I just made a journal entry that reveals a shadow of fear: "One day I'll say this was the greatest adventure, perfect even in its imperfections. Yet, I'm greatly troubled by mundane problems, and hiding in my hotel room to stay out of trouble, trapped in my head."

As I leave, Immanuel says, "Remember God is with you." I feel reinvigorated with the belief that people must set aside fear and take responsibility for their salvation. Even days

later I'm feeling especially proud, as if God has given me a mission to bear witness, when I see an awkwardly constructed sign in the next village.

Certainly, if I know anything, I know God has a sense of humor.

Part II:
Questing

Learn from yesterday, live for today, hope for tomorrow.
The important thing is not to stop questioning.

~ Albert Einstein

22

Why don't you quit?

I've suffered a crippling bout of depression throughout Europe. I sequestered myself from Dennis for two months to save him from my whinging and preserve our friendship, while I cycled lackluster past castles and cathedrals, cried myself to sleep at night or lay paralyzed by my own thoughts. My depression was triggered by heartbreak and the fear that I will fail cycling around the world—as I've failed so many things. Dennis quit, and he's a stronger man. I doubt I'll survive the trip without him.

I'm in Oludeniz, Turkey. Hundreds of paragliders fall out of the sky like a rainbow blitzkrieg, and the English command the ground with their mushy food, smutty newspapers, footy games and English pounds (instead of Turkish lira). Worst of all, the Brits keep remarking, "What a bargain!" encouraging the locals to raise the prices, when, in fact, it's triple the price of Istanbul. This phenomenon, along with thousands of Australians, has followed me across Europe. (Technically, I just entered Asia.) At the risk of sounding cynical, even though I felt at home among my heritage, I'll be glad to leave Europe. Compared to the Latin Americans, I think Europeans are generally boring and unaffectionate.

Contrary to my ambivalence with Europe, I'm surprised how much I miss Dennis. He left a few hours ago on the minibus. If I didn't come from such cold-hearted German stock, I would've shed some tears. Perhaps, I'm tapped out. That reminds me of the saying: blood, sweat and tears. I think it should be reordered: tears are by the far the most challenging to endure, followed by blood and then sweat. Dennis has been the most intimate friendship I've had. For over a year, we've spent nearly every hour together. Most express amazement, "And, you still like each other?" I'm as surprised as anyone—I've fared much worse in my romantic relationships.

For the first time on the trip, in San Pedro, Guatemala, after the indigenous gauntlet of animosity—"Gringo. Gringo. Gringo. Gimmemoney. Gimmemoney. Gimmemoney."—roads too steep to cycle up or down, trucks without mufflers that made my fillings rattle, chicken buses that were invisible inside a black cloud of lunging-searing exhaust, and a another bad meal, probably a cow brain taco with diarrhea salsa, Dennis asked, "I think traveling is the best education one can give themselves; but, I have to ask myself, 'When will my life become more fulfilling and productive by going home?'"

It was only a month later, in Granada, Nicaragua—after a day of headwinds, hills, dangerous traffic, suffocating smog, crumbling roads that were like hitting a thousand tiny walls, and if I happened to be able to breath long enough to take my burning eyes off the road, there was nothing but the usual withered, dusty farm fields and garbage dumps—that my internal debate of "How am I going to make it?" switched to "When am I going to quit?"

In Ecuador, it was becoming obvious that there may never be anything alongside the road worth seeing when Dennis remarked, "Our guidebook says there are over fifteen-hundred bird species and three-hundred species of mammals. I saw a squirrel today. How about you?"

"I'm thinking of calling my book: *Cows, Chickens and Cars,*" I replied.

Selling beef and milk is the livelihood for many people. Forests have been razed to grasslands for fodder by the axes of men and the grasslands reduced to deserts by the hooves and teeth of cattle. I was hoping that India would be an exception because cattle, or cows as I like to call them, are holy creatures; however, there are millions of cows wandering the cities, clogging the roads and leaving cow pies and flies in their wake. Not only are cows reproducing helter-skelter, tribal people breed cows for the small amount of milk they produce, 16 liters a day per lactating cow. And, ironically, even though few people eat beef in India, the cows are the most unhappy in the world because they're often flogged and separated from the herd to wander alone eating garbage in the streets. I think some cows would be happier hamburgers. It has surprised and saddened me how homogenous the world can appear from the seat of the bicycle. I often lose my sense of self and daydream, or sometimes I even read a book while I ride my bicycle. Often I wonder if I'm really in some godforsaken place, or simply unable to appreciate the moment?

Atop mountains, in the bottoms of valleys, amidst rainforests and in deserts, pondering quitting was becoming a daily subject. In chaotic Puno, Peru, Dennis woke up and said with the same conviction that he announced he was going to bicycle around the world, "I'm not saying that I'm quitting, but I just realized I don't have to do this!" This seemed like an obvious epiphany, and I knew then, before Dennis himself, that he was going to quit.

I confess, "Cycling around the world sounds adventurous, but most of the time, I'm lonely, bored, aching and just feel as if I'm spinning my wheels."

Dennis replied with a glint in his eyes, "Sometime you're just spinning your wheels, or stuck in a rut. And if you go home, the same thing could happen."

"I'd feel ashamed to quit, because my friends think I'm living my dream, and I thought this was my dream. I mean, I do love to ride my bicycle, just not in the prevalent conditions. Yesterday, I received three emails from friends saying how inspirational my trip is and that they're jealous and all their friends are jealous, and that because of me my college buddies are going through midlife crises."

"I don't think people can relate to riding a bicycle in the Third World." Dennis said. "What's important to me is that I inspire people to follow their dreams. It doesn't have to be bicycling—but it could be. I just want people to know they can do whatever they set their hearts on—even being an office worker. But, I don't think I'm inspiring anyone if I'm not enjoying it myself. I feel I've mastered bicycling—I don't feel challenged. I know I can bicycle through the Third World. Now the question is how many Third World countries are enough? I wonder if it's going to be just the same with a different language and different food. India has over a billion people; I can't believe the bicycling conditions would be better than Peru."

"Even you admitted," I said, "Bicycle touring is like life—you have to persevere through the bad to get to the good."

"It's a question of balance."

A week later, in a smoky Bolivian drinking den full of a hundred men and only two women, Dennis repeats himself as if rationalizing a decision he has already made in his heart, "I feel I've mastered bicycle touring. I know that I can ride around the world."

"Maybe you should've stayed home."

"You're missing my point."

"What's your point: that you're quitting?" I said with irritation. I thought, "I'm the one missing a chunk of cartilage in his knee. I'm the one who dislocated his wrist. I'm the one who cycled for two months on bananas and Coca-Cola, because I was too sick to eat anything else. I'm the one who had ten times as many flats, a dozen broken spokes, sprung rim, torn tires and cracked racks. I'm the weaker one. If anyone has an excuse to quit it's me!"

"I don't want to ride my bike in the Third World anymore."

"If I quit, I'm afraid I'd regret it for the rest of my life." I was suggesting Dennis would regret quitting also.

"You might," he said, in his typically succinct and pragmatic manner.

"Any reason I go home will just be quitting."

"I disagree."

"I've committed to doing this for better or worse." I alluded to Dennis calling our trip "a marriage of sorts" because we agreed that two cyclists were needed to carry the gear and help guard each other against thieves and accidents.

"If I decide to go home because it's too difficult, that's a negative reason; but if I can make more of a difference by going home, I feel that's moving on with my life."

"If you quit the trip—you quit."

"I don't view that as quitting; I view it as reorganizing my priorities."

"Shouldn't we have thought of these things before we committed to it?"

"It's not a good idea to continue everything I start." It annoyed me when Dennis debated only from only his point of view. Of course, I do the same thing, which is why I find it an irritating reflection of myself.

"Maybe in theory, but how does one accomplish anything, like marriage? Marriage is a commitment in the community, so that the community may help each other through troublesome times. Feelings come and go. Words are abstract concepts. Power lies in deeds."

"I don't see anything wrong with trying. I can't always make the best decisions. If I'm not enjoying myself then I should try something else. Don't worry about quitting. Whatever will happen will happen."

"Are you talking about fate again?"

"Yes, if it's meant to be it will be."

"If there's such a thing as fate, I'd have no free will."

"God has a plan for everyone," Dennis said. "But that doesn't mean we have to follow his advice."

I don't agree that God planned my life, so I ask, "Do you know what your destiny is?"

"No," Dennis' answers are clipped when he wants to end a conversation.

"How will you know what your destiny is?"

"I don't know." He pauses, and I fear I've angered him. Dennis has a lot of patience, but he'd admit later, he was thinking, "Won't he just shut the fuck up with the endless questions. I don't have all the answers." Once he remarked, "You're trying to play God by asking all these questions and trying to solve the mysteries of the universe." But instead of voicing his annoyance, he said diplomatically, "You need a lot more answers than I do."

"If you don't know these answers, why do you believe in fate?"

"Whatever happens to me is God's will. He owns everything; we are merely shepherds of his creation."

"But this could be your destiny. No great person—Gandhi, Shakespeare, Einstein, Mozart—ever accomplished anything without suffering. They persevered until they achieved their dream—or destiny, if you want to call it that. Where would the world be if they quit?"

"The best bicyclists I see are just happy being wherever they are—enjoying the journey. They aren't worried about where they're going or if they're making a difference."

"I envy that. But happy people aren't necessarily great. Being happy doesn't change the world. Almost everyone I ask says the meaning of their life is to be happy. Why is being happy so important? What if happiness means abandoning your family for a drunken binge, having an affair, or kicking strangers in the shin? Remember that guy who said, 'I didn't come all the way to Machu Picchu to *not* smoke a joint.' Hell, why bother with that? If I just wanted to be happy—I would've stayed home and smoked a joint and watched a video about Machu Picchu," I spat my words out contemptuously. (In retrospect, I believed I was thinking outside of the box and trying to prove a point to Dennis, but I was just angry and rebelling against the Christian cultural belief that one must suffer to reach their goals, which I had subconsciously adopted wholeheartedly.)

"So, what do you want?" Dennis asked, "To be great? Or to be happy?" Dennis has a talent for cutting through crap; and this conversation wasn't about him quitting—it was about me quitting.

"I do think too much," I conceded.

"Thinking too much is only a problem if it prevents you from taking action."

An attorney Rodolfo, invited us to play a rum and dice drinking game with the only two women in the speakeasy, rescuing us from our tensest moment.

"I don't think life is hard, I just make it hard," Dennis confided.

"Ain't that the truth?" I said, and we laughed over our first rum and Coke. "Do I have to pay for this if I win?" I asked Rodolfo.

"You must pay if you win or lose," he said apropos.

From Peru to Germany, I admit being angry with Dennis. But now I realize that great people simply love what they're doing whether or not the world considers them great, and their suffering—if one can call it suffering—is a side effect, a necessary evil, a byproduct of following their passion. Dennis doesn't love bicycle touring. It's time for Dennis to move on and grow; for him, this means contributing to his family and building a community.

I will miss Dennis: Waking up to the smell of fresh brewed coffee every morning, chatting about world events over dinner, the fatherly and over-practical advice; for example, on a ferry to Greece, we watched the neon glow of the sun melt over a distant ship into the ocean. I said I was tired of going from place to place just looking at things as if I were watching television (this is how I've been trained to interact with reality) and Dennis replied, "If you can't appreciate this, you can't appreciate life. You might as well throw your bike—and yourself—off this boat." One day I was feeling sorry for myself, and Dennis said, "If you were an idiot, I wouldn't be doing this with you." Mostly I'll miss someone to share the moment with, like watching a gigantic full moon rise over a nearby mountain, silhouetting the trees, Dennis commented, "It's times like these that makes all the bicycling worthwhile." Does it make up for eight hours of torturous riding, I asked. "Yes!" He replied with unwavering conviction. I'll miss our hearty laughs, like when I bent over and farted, a quiet poof upwind of myself, I said to Dennis, before making the connection, "I think something died over here, maybe we should pitch our tents somewhere else." Or, when I said that to be interesting people need to have opinions even if they're wrong, and Dennis said, "I agree. I have many opinions that are completely wrong."

According to the self-help books and dime-store philosophy that I read in my tent almost every night: romantic love is just an illusion or a step on the way to true love. I believe, figuratively speaking, Dennis and I had our honeymoon period, or romantic love, then later we hated each other for awhile, seeing our own shadow-self mirrored in each other, and now, after developing some compassion and respect for each others quirks, I believe we've developed a brotherly love for each other. Only a true friend would jump out of an airplane after me and follow me around the world on a bicycle. "Good luck with your new life, Dennis. I've a learned a lot from you," I said when we parted ways.

As for me, what do I want: to be happy or to be great? Being great, In America, is epitomized by the bumper sticker, "He who dies with the most toys wins," whereas, in India being great often means getting off the hamster wheel of life. Being great is a cultural illusion—I want to be happy. Maybe I was wrong, maybe being happy does change the world. Maybe it's more accurate to say joyful. I want to be joyful—isn't that greatness? And there must be infinite paths to joy.

Dennis' impetuousness, passion, patience, stubbornness (only exceeded by mine) and strength were like rocket boosters that propelled me through four years of preparation and three continents. Now it's time to launch myself into truly foreign worlds. I don't expect I'll succeed, but I will go as far as possible, as long as I'm still enjoying the journey, or as Ali, my paragliding instructor said in pidgin English before I ran off a cliff, "You love mountain, mountain loves you. You love sky, sky loves you. You don't love sky, sky slap you into mountain." He laughed and amended, "Same with woman."

Same with life, I amend.

(Postscript: Dennis found and married, Alicia, the woman of his dreams. They opened an antique shop hoping to revitalize their community's art and economy. When I finished my trip, Dennis' compliment brought tears to me eyes, because no one but Dennis really knows what I experienced, "You should be proud. You earned every kilometer. Even if I had wanted to, I don't think I would have made it physically or mentally." Thanks, Deno, but I wouldn't have made it without you.)

23 ✳ How much did it cost?

Cairo was a gray city, its details and smells lost in a burning snow of ash. Drifts of dust were piled deep on buildings and imbedded deep in people's phlegmatic personalities. An airplane magically transports me to a new world where the air is clear, yet thick with moisture and swimming with a kaleidoscope of colors and smells, and the people's alien body language is as vibrant as the atmosphere—India. (It's shocking because while traveling on a bicycle the cultures and geography slowly, almost invisibly, blend from one to another like an artist's brush blends blue to indigo to violet—essentially there are no borders on a bicycle.)

I enter with no problem. My visa is good for a year and a half, but I doubt I'll endure one day of cycling. My cab traverses half the length of Bombay (now know as Mumbai because the Indians are de-anglicizing themselves) a city with more people than the Australian continent (an average density of one person per ten meters squared). The walls of tall apartment buildings, green with mold and black with smoke, have sloughed off revealing families still living in three-walled cubicles, cooking on open fires, colorful laundry flapping on clotheslines. The jumble of buildings is a mouth of rotten teeth, the road a ribbon of useless floss. The dilapidated decay spreads to smaller houses and to the shanties lining the road. My cab, a shrine on wheels dedicated to Ganesha, passes a mile of shanties devoted to bamboo furniture. Like ants, thousands of people pour from the holes of their nests to scavenge food and building materials.

Our cab is caught in a traffic jam of cows and rickshaws. Vendors at every door try to sell us kitsch. My driver rolls up the windows. The vendors are deterred but not the beggars. Crippled men, mothers and babies, and ragged children tap on the window. "Please, sir. Help me, sir. One rupee, sir. Half rupee, sir." I have 15,000 rupees in my pocket. I feel disgustingly rich, but how long would it last if I give every needy person half a rupee (one penny)? A few days? I put on my sunglasses and turn blind, deaf and dumb like my driver. I thought I'd seen everything, but India is proving shocking; hidden beneath my revulsion, as if a secret, I'm glad to still be shocked.

"Don't worry, sir. You will love India, sir." My driver says.

On my second day, as I reluctantly venture outside the haven of my hotel for food, I'm recruited as an extra in a Bollywood movie. "We'll feed you," they say, and I agree. A bus picks me up at my hotel and shuttles me through the pandemonium to the eroded iron gates of the movie studio. Along the way, I resort to using my teeth to penetrate an orange rind. My guide shakes his head, "That is very dirty. You will get sick." I spit the germs out the window just as a cyclist passes and hit him square in the face. I feel humiliated. I've been spit on, had fruit, cigarettes, rocks and bottles thrown at me. (Mostly in the USA, ironically, I've been safer outside my own country.) Now I'm one of those thoughtless bastards.

Bollywood is infamous for making even more tacky movies than Hollywood. We're filming the evermore-tacky music and dance scene set in a Bangkok nightclub with an iridescent foam cave décor. There isn't a single Thai person, but there are hundreds of idle Indian and Nepalese employees eager to assist. Bollywood can afford to employ many people. In one day, this small army accurately carved a life-sized dragon out of Styrofoam, modeled after a small bronze statue, the whole time surrounded by curious onlookers—staring is a major pastime here—and swarming workers whose job is to hold one tool for the sculptor. I've discovered the answer to one of life's big questions: How many Indians does it take to screw in a light bulb? Answer: As many as possible.

Three times a day, buckets of goulash appear—that's what it looks like to me, and the names sound like mumbo jumbo. There are also buckets of rice and boxes of bread. It makes my dining experiences in San Francisco's fancy Indian restaurants seem pompous, paltry and not nearly as tasty. There are four feeding stations, one for each caste. The caste system still exists in India though, in this case, it's a bit different: there are the movie stars, the foreigners, the Indians and the Nepalese. I attempt to dine with the Indians, but they, "Tsst. Tsst," and escort me back to the gringo canteen.

During intermissions of filming "You have robbed me," a Frenchman and myself practice juggling. The director's henchmen recruit us to juggle flaming bowling pins behind the dancers. Unfortunately, I can't juggle the unwieldy bowling pins that the Nepalese carved out of wood. (Our plastic pins would've melted.) So I'm relegated to being a backup dancer, although I can't dance.

Tomorrow, I have an audition to be the star of a shaving commercial. It pays an astonishing 1500 rupees per day (about 30 USD), 30 times more than the employees of my hotel earn, who work all day and night, though not very hard, and eat rice and peas two times a day. At least they have a bench inside the front door to sleep on. During the bus ride back to the hotel after a 14-hour shoot, we pass several thousand homeless Indians sleeping on the sidewalks in front of their closet-sized businesses or in the roads covered in rags, newspapers and mosquitoes.

I feel like a Maharaja. I have a room all to myself. Actually, the rooms are so small I purchased a double so I could put my bike in one bed, safe from the street thieves. Even though I only own a bicycle and camping gear, I'm a rich man and have means to work as a messenger or transport goods to the country. I calculated that even if the hotel employees spent their money on nothing but rice and beans, it would take them over eight years to purchase my bicycle (minus all the gear). I calculated it would take the hotel employees approximately 205 years to save enough money to cycle around the world or buy a nice car. Navdeep enjoys his job but says, "I go nowhere."

I'm impressed that Navdeep still dreams. Asking me how much it costs is a step in the right direction, rather than the more common, "How many times have you crashed?" (Dozens of times.) Or, the bizarrely common, "Aren't you afraid you'll never be able to have children from all that biking?" (More afraid of becoming impotent.) Now that I'm midway, the types of questions people ask have shifted from the doubtful "How do you survive?" into the hopeful "How can I do it?" Perhaps, now I'm a living testament that such things are possible, or perhaps I've just entered cultures that are more open-minded, optimistic, and curious about life's infinite opportunities.

I'm richer than at least 97% of the world's population; and I have to admit, it's not by my own virtue. I was blessed by being born into a country with a strong economy and a lot of opportunity; however, if someday I become wounded or sick, or the United States politicians become corrupt and the economy crashes, I could become the toothless old man on the street, who owns nothing but a pot for roasting and selling peanuts and an old newspaper for a bed and blanket.

On my day off from the movies, I explore the Colaba district. I have an entourage of beggars and all the rich Indians want their photos taken with me as if I really am a movie star. I've always been a celebrity in my travels, surrounded by awestruck boys, fraternizing men and single women swooning over the "rich" gringo with the blue eyes and American passport.

I pass a group of boney, semi-naked children sorting through the garbage in the gutter. India is so poor that people sell their garbage to those who either eat it, recycle it or burn it. Nearby, women are scooping steaming cow pies into baskets with their bare hands for fuel. Already India is testing my morals (external societal rules) and ethics (inner personal belief system). Every few meters the catalysts for a change of opinion bounce off me like pinballs, an infinite variety of: hawkers, touts, cons, thieves, beggars, drug dealers, addicts, prostitutes, transvestites, maimed, crippled and diseased people writhing, crawling and dragging themselves over the ground—and every variation in between—an endless stream of suffering and wanting.

"Please, sir. Help me, sir. I have nothing." A bashful, brown boy tugs on my pants. "Please, help."

"Where are your parents?"

"They die, sir."

"How?" I test him. Sometimes I can tell it's a scam if the story appears too elaborate as if constructed by an adult.

The boy struggles mightily with his English, "My father drink—" he holds up four fingers— "beers and someone push him off—" he gestures to the seaside wall— "My mother, she die on train." The second sentence seems sufficiently childish. "Please, sir. You rich foreigner."

"What makes you think I'm rich?"

"You have shoes. Look no shoes." He shows me his cracked, blackened feet and demonstrates the broken zipper and missing pockets in his shorts. "My pants broken. Already, I learn work. I shoe shine. But someone steal. I sleeping. Please fifty rupees for shoe shine."

Should I give him money for a shoeshine kit? I'm aware it's a common scam to buy boys shoeshine kits and mothers bottles of milk, which they sell back to the vendors, possibly using the money to buy drugs. I don't want to encourage parents to create miniature armies of beggars. It's rumored that to increase profits parents severe the fingers, hands or arms of their children or break their limbs. After ten days in Mumbai, compared to the other half of the world, I've seen an extraordinary amount of children with amputations and mangled limbs. And I've seen several mothers, thinking that I'm not looking and hoping to earn sympathy money, beat their children into tears as I approach, which enrages me as if their desperation is infectious.

How can I tell the boy that I worked my whole life for this money, and that I have no extra? To be specific, I've been spending 14 times India's average daily wage on my hotel, food and limited sightseeing. I'm worried that I'll have to make the decision between finishing or enjoying my trip. But is either one important compared to saving a starving boy? Is wearing shoes important when people are dying? However, how do I know the truth? I met a charismatic man who said he was just released from prison and needed enough money for clothes, a haircut and a shave so that he could get a job. "No one will give me a chance. They think I use brown sugar. [A cheap version of heroin.] They don't even believe who I am. You see—" he handed me his identification— "I lost forty kilos in prison." I was tired of feeling heartless, and I thought I'd test India; besides I had nothing to lose by donating my Bollywood earnings. Unfortunately, the next day I found him penniless and his boney frame still poking through his ragged clothes. I think his fascinating story was true except for one point: he was and still is an addict. "Brown sugar was the only way we could sleep—hungry, mosquitoes and people crying all night," he admitted.

It would be easy to become heartless and aloof. After one week in India, I ignore most greetings, especially in English because they're the most talented hucksters. As George Bernard Shaw said, "If you teach a man anything, he will never learn." Likewise, if you give a man anything, he'll never earn. Sometimes I've paid kids to help me fix a flat, but this also seemed like I was giving handouts, and sabotaging their desire to do something just for the joy of doing it—the beginning of a carrot-and-stick mentality. No matter what, I don't have enough money to hire every poor child that asks or even enough time to explain to them why not.

I tell the boy, "I have no rupees," and hope the boy will learn to provide for himself with an honest trade or his parents will be discouraged from sending him on the street. "Please..." his voice trails off with despair as he looks at me with watery eyes. What can I say to make him understand? So, I put on my sunglasses like a movie star spoiled by fame and wealth and patiently wait for him to disappear from my conscious. My heart twangs with empathy, but I feel helpless—or is it hopeful?—that he'll create a new life. Is this how Brahman feels looking down at all the suffering in the world?

An Indian street dentist extracting a tooth. Notice the pulled teeth on the carpet as an advertisement of his successful business.

24 ✳ Can I help you?

The Gran Chaco is a vast desert shared with Bolivia, Paraguay, and Argentina. When it rains in the Chaco, the paved roads are chewed apart and swallowed by a quagmire, and the gravel and dirt roads turn into mud that either sticks to everything or melts into the desert. During the rainy season, it's impenetrable.

Mist and mud spatter my face as I churn my bicycle wheels through miles of puddles and slime. I plow into a section of the road churned by feet, hooves, shovels and wheels searching for traction. The sticky mud spins up with my wheels, gets caught under the racks and in the brakes, coats my legs, frame and panniers, and submerses my drive train—my bike seizes and I slide to a halt, squishing one foot into the muck for balance. [See photo page 135.] As I push my bike towards more stable ground, the thick mud gathers on my feet and bicycle, increasing the weight until my limbs are too weak to move. The Chaco's muddy grip has reached to the top of my head, gluing me to the earth.

I'm averaging one kilometer per hour when I'm moving. Even at that rate, I won't reach the next village for several days, long after I run out of food and water. Dennis, camouflaged in mud, disappeared into the mist hours ago. Only one truck has passed me all day. The driver was too busy fighting the Chaco to notice me attempting to blaze a trail through the fresh, greasy mud and thorn bushes alongside the road. He's also caught in the rain and struggling to return home. That may have been my last chance to hitch a ride.

Maybe I'm congenitally or genetically unhappy, because when conditions become miserable it doesn't take long for my mind to sink into a figurative quagmire. I had entered Argentina dreaming of civilization: cold beers, hot showers, comfy and clean beds, the infamously beautiful women and, especially, the world-famous steaks, traditionally hanging over the edge of the plate, buried in french fries and accompanied by a bottle of Argentinean red wine to rinse down the grease.

I pin my hopes of steak and salvation on Dennis. Maybe he stopped the truck. So, despite exhaustion, I trudge forward. I must stop every ten meters to scrape the heavy mud off my shoes and wheels. I relieve some of my depression by focusing on the moment: Mist dampens the sounds of the distant desert. Except for the occasional flock of squawking, green parrots, only my breathing and the condensed mist dripping off my body vibrates the atmosphere. The waves of mud have splashed a raw, pungent odor into the air, smelling ripe with life only matched by a briny sea breeze. Judging by the footprints of birds, lizards and cats dancing among the sopping thorn trees and cacti, I'm surrounded by creatures alien to my experience. When I'm not struggling to tame it, the Chaco is a beautiful and peaceful land.

After an hour, I round a bend. Askew in the ditch, is the last truck that passed. With renewed vigor, I drag my bicycle sideways through the muck. I feel awkward having to trust my survival to strangers. They appear to be a family of three. Many families live and work in their trucks. "Nice weather. No?" I say in broken Spanish. The burly yet roly-poly father laughs, spewing coca leaves.

I introduce myself and answer the usual questions: The United States; yes, on a bicycle; very tired; 31; no children; single; haven't met the perfect woman yet; strong legs; 19,500 kilometers; 50 flats; eight tires; 14 months; for my education; almost everyone everywhere have been very kind; food poisoning; about a dozen, it's not how many times you fall, it's how many times you get up.

Romiro, the father, with his slight mustache, cherubic and charming face, reminds me of a Buddha figurine. On cue, he rubs his tummy as if for good luck. *"Muy loco biciclista."* (Very crazy bicyclist.)

Realizing my plight, Romiro doesn't just offer me a ride—he begins throwing my panniers into the back of his truck and easily lifts my mud-coated bicycle over his head; simultaneously his son, Diebe, throws down gifts of fruit and soda. Before we can continue, we must unglue the truck. First, Romiro shovels the mud from in front of the wheels, creating a semi-dry track to follow. Then, with Romiro in the driver's seat, the rest of us push the truck back onto the road, and we keep pushing—the Chaco sucking on our feet—until the truck reaches a section where it can stop without becoming bogged in the mire. All aboard: Romiro builds momentum slowly, spinning the oversized steering wheel one way, then the other, his legs braking, accelerating and shifting gears, his jaw chomping coca leaves to stay awake and his pungent breath fumigating the cab. All his seemingly frantic motions keep the truck cruising straight and steady through the slushy mud.

A few kilometers down the road, we find Dennis, *"Mi amigo,"* and another truck stuck in the mud. We slide to a halt and without words Romiro and Diebe grab a shovel and pickaxe and begin freeing the first truck while Romiro's wife, Yolanda, cleans the mud off Dennis and his bicycle. Romiro returns laughing, rubbing his tummy. "Another crazy bicyclist," he says, and introduces himself to Dennis.

The two trucks combine their efforts for the rest of the afternoon in a tribal instinct to cooperate and survive. The road is elevated above the desert, and the worn edges make the surface convex, so the trucks tend to slide off sideways. The other truck is empty and often slides into the ditch. For several hours, we shovel and push, and build bridges of branches for traction over small streams and slippery mud until we reach the nearest village.

Dennis and I offer to pay for lunch in gratitude but Romiro closes the debate, "You're my guests."

Currently, Argentina's economy is crashing. According to the news on our short-wave radio, the government has borrowed too much money and squandered it on poorly planned social programs meant to buy votes and make politicians rich. Argentina is considering defaulting on its loans and the international community is losing faith in the Peso causing inflation and devaluation. Romiro's pesos are only worth a third of their value three months ago.

Having gathered the local gossip, Romiro announces that the road to Juarez, where the pavement begins, is impassable. We must detour down sandier roads—wet sand makes a hard, smooth riding surface because the water drains easily through the large grains—to Romiro's house and ride a different route tomorrow. For the next 11 hours we drive a few kilometers until we get stuck, then we shovel mud from underneath the tires, or put chains on the wheels, or take the chains off the wheels. Mostly, we push and run, either from behind until the truck gains momentum, or from alongside to prevent the truck from fishtailing. "You must think it was easier to bicycle," Romiro jokes during a tea break in the middle of the night.

We arrive at Romiro's house on an "aboriginal community" and have an early morning dinner with the rest of the family—the sons Matias, Franko, Diebe, Andrés and Pablo, the daughter, Patricia, and her son. Romiro tells us not to worry. We'll try to reach Juarez tomorrow. He even offers to drive us to the bank in Corrientes, several hundred kilometers east. The banks have been shut down for a week because too many locals are emptying their accounts and converting their currency into the more stable US dollar. Romiro, Dennis, and I have very little cash.

"You're like my sons. Eat. Drink. No problem." Romiro speaks slowly and panto-mimes because the conversation is beyond our understanding of Spanish. In every country, we must relearn the basics because the accent changes and the most common words, especially names of foods, people and places, are mixed with the indigenous languages. In Argentina, the locals refer to their language as Castellano, the official dialect of Spain, though the Argentinean pronunciation has some idiosyncrasies. "Stay as long as you need to, or longer if you want to," Romiro says.

Everyone owns the land on the aboriginal reserve, or rather no one owns it. The land is communal property; however, Romiro and Yolanda, do own the house. They built it with their own hands. It's a ramshackle house typical of a developing country. The walls are constructed of concrete, brick or wood depending on the available materials when an extra room was needed. The floor is concrete, an improvement over the more common dirt floors. The roof is corrugated tin. In the backyard live fat, corn-fed pigs and chickens (normally pigs and chickens must root through the garbage and weeds), three dogs and two cats. There are no doors in the back of the house, yet the pigs and chickens never venture inside looking for food; meanwhile, the cats and dogs are always sneaking inside and dashing back outside when Yolanda reaches for the broom. The front of the house is a small store with storage space. This is Romiro's primary business. He transports staple products (meat, dairy, flour, rice, fruits, vegetables, toiletries and cleaning products) and some luxury items (candy, wine and soda) from the distant cities and sells them to the indigenous people. Tacked onto the house is Romiro's secondary business, a repair shop, and Romiro and Yolanda's bedroom. There are two more bedrooms inside the house for every-one else. Franko and Matias have given their beds to Dennis and myself. They sleep outside in the truck.

Romiro built his life in a similar ramshackle manner to his house. During his first few years he says he lived on the streets and owned nothing, not even clothes. At this young age, Romiro decided he wanted a better life. From the age of three until he was 14, he only owned one set of clothes and one pair of shoes and worked in his uncle's garage as an unpaid apprentice, watching and learning everything. At 15, he began to earn small tips and wages. Now, Romiro owns two businesses, two houses, four trucks, and provides for his wife, five children—two with plans to attend college in the big city—one grandchild and two ravenous bicyclists.

Romiro and Yolanda are very proud of the life they've built, although they're con-cerned about the community. According to them there are too many young males intoxicated on rum or coca leaves, too many pregnant teenagers, and, generally, the neighbors are too content to drink *yerba mate* (tea) and watch life pass their doorstep.

Going against the trend of drugs and social welfare, Romiro and Yolanda continue to build a life for themselves, their family and their community.

There doesn't seem to be anything Romiro can't do. He can shovel tons of mud, whereas I can barely sink the spade into the ground. With enviable charisma, he entices the local children to wash our bicycles. He fixes my bicycle rack, which three other mechanics couldn't fix. He studies English with his children. One afternoon, we go fishing in a small stream. In one motion, Romiro hooks a tiny piranha and sends it flying over his shoulder to land in or near the bucket. (Dennis catches a few piranhas. I only have nibbles, and nearly fall into the stream.) I think we're going to eat a bucket of piranha for dinner. Soon, though, we switch fishing holes to a raging, muddy river a few kilometers away from Paraguay and use the piranhas for bait. Romiro hooks two, large, feisty catfish, enough to feed the whole family. I desperately want to contribute a fish to the family, but I only succeed in losing my bait and hooking sunken branches. Romiro pats me on the shoulder, "Don't worry. Next time."

That night, as during every meal, Yolanda serves Dennis and me first—in this case, a pile of steaming, fried catfish, french fries and salad. *Yerba mate* and long conversations follow every candlelit meal. (At this time of day, the power is rotated to another community.) If the family doesn't ask us about our bicycle trip, Romiro jokes about how pathetic we looked drenched in mud. He also enjoys telling stories about the wild animals in the Chaco: pumas, piranhas, spiders and anacondas so big that a truck could run over them and they wouldn't even wake. According to Romiro, all the wild critters prefer white meat, meaning the crazy gringos that camped several nights in the Chaco.

Everyday Dennis and I entertain groups of visitors: On the first day, we meet the community elders, teachers and priests; the second day is filled with local businessmen and students; and the third day, a group of young, single women arrive; and the whole time we're surrounded by children. Some people, too shy to venture inside the house, wait outside for a glimpse of us strangers. We also have many appointments: running errands with Patricia to meet the community; participating in bicycle races with the kids; watching the local football game; giving a two-hour lecture for the high school students; and visiting a charity organization that is building houses for the locals despite what the locals really need and want are jobs. In Ecuador, I met a missionary who helped build latrines for the locals when they really needed storage houses. So, the locals ended up using the fields as toilets, and using the latrines to store their corn. The missionary explained that the indigenous population hasn't adapted their nomadic lifestyle to the sedentary lifestyle of farms and industry and the arbitrary political borders. Traditionally, these people worked hard to earn their food—hunting, gathering and trading. Nowadays, food is piled high on street vendor's tables; being farmed or growing semi-wild alongside the road; or running around the streets (many of the foods people eat come from the domesticated plants and animals the European settlers brought). Likewise, shelter and clothing are readily available, handed down through the generations or provided by international aid. In this modern age it's easy for people to meet their basic survival needs, especially if they have no ambition—we're told that the indigenous people have had the ambition crushed out of them, first by the Spanish conquistadors, then by the Western World and now by their own greedy and corrupt governments.

On the morning of the fourth day, the roads are dry enough to risk taking a bus to Juarez, though Romiro won't be joining us because the banks are still closed. Dennis and I profusely thank Romiro. Romiro, grinning as usual, says, "No, thank you for showing my village and my children that the impossible is possible." Romiro chuckles and rubs his tummy, *"Muy loco biciclistas."*

Weeks later, we reach Buenos Aires, "civilization," the land of convenience, where money can purportedly buy anything and solve any problem. I've found my steak that hangs over the edge of the plate, bought some new clothes and got a haircut; but, now what I think about is taking the bus out of Romiro's village and seeing his youngest son, Pablo leading the charge out of the classroom. The class must've been waiting for hours to throw themselves against the fence and chase us down the street to wave goodbye one last time.

25 ✳ Would you please visit my home?

Dennis and I awake hours before sunrise and hike 700 meters in elevation from Aguas Calientes, Peru to Machu Picchu. My knees grind as I walk up the uneven stone staircase that cuts through the road's switchbacks. We're the first to enter the park. It's dark and foggy. We can't see the city and the signpost has fallen over. We continue trudging up the mountain searching for the Lost City of the Incas.

"I think we're lost, too," I say.

Frustrated, we sit on some boulders and wait for the fog and rain to clear. "It's hard to believe the Incas built a palace to worship the sun here," Dennis says. Hundreds of years ago, as the winter solstice approached and the sun appeared to disappear more every day, an Incan priest would perform a ceremony tying the sun to a rock to keep it from vanishing forever.

After an hour, the fog begins to evaporate, and we're surprised to glimpse the Incan city far below us. We're given tantalizing views of Machu Picchu, as the fog flows over the ruins like a river and the sun spotlights emerald-green patches of grass and the jumbled-stone ruins. The mountains form the silhouette of a noble face lifted towards the sun, the city terraces resemble teeth, and Machu Picchu appears as if it's being born from the mouth of ancient Mother Nature. As the numbing fog dissipates, I feel born from limbo: the mountains cradle me in their nook; the sun tickles my skin; the hairs on my arm flutter in a breeze; a creek trickles; leaves rustle; and, in the distance some-one—maybe the mountains themselves—plays the pan flute.

I break our speechless awe, "Is Machu Picchu built here because this is a sacred site full of spiritual energy, or is it just the beauty of nature that's inspiring?"

"Many people believe they're closer to God on the top of mountains, perhaps because we can look down and see how small and insignificant we are," says Dennis. Indeed, the whole city occupies a tiny plateau, and the hordes of tourists and the llamas (Incan lawn mowers) are colorful dots.

A few days later, we cycle away from the tourists and their entourage of beggars. We traverse the Altiplano, a plateau at an average of 4000 meters elevation in the Andes Mountains. Soppy scrub brush carpets the ground and sweeps up the sides of the distant black mountains, their leaves turning from green to yellow as they struggle with the altitude. My body feels like a rusty gate. My head throbs from the thin air. I'm unable to eat cookies and cycle at the same time without gasping. My knees are weak from Machu Picchu. My lips are cracked and bleeding from the dry air. My in-testines have been burning for weeks. (Unbeknownst to me they're riddled with acute salmonella intestinitis that will mutate into irritable bowel syndrome and plague me for years.) I've lost over 20 kilograms. My heart aches with loneliness. And, I wonder if we've seen the only thing worth seeing in Peru.

After an emergency pit stop, we pitch camp near a creek and remain undiscovered until sunset. The owner shouts at us from across the creek. I reluctantly get out of my warm sleeping bag and push through the tall wet grass towards the creek. His Spanish accent is very thick, and Dennis keeps telling him that we'll leave—*"No problemo"*—that we didn't know it was his pasture. Finally, he conveys that we're welcome, and that he only wanted to invite us to breakfast.

I'm honored to have been invited to break bread with families in almost every country

I've visited, ironically, most often by the poorest of people. Their ostensible motivations vary: custom, honor, cu-riosity, friendship, pride, showmanship, even guilt or dishonesty; but, more fundamental than all of these reasons, people seem to value,

Photo courtesy of Dennis Snader

more than anything, sharing their lives. Back home, as I was preparing for my trip, I had doubt atop of doubts and felt I had to make a decision between the material world (career, house, retirement, stock portfolio) or living my dream; so, I thought to myself, "What would it be like to have all the riches of the world, but no friends, no lovers, no experiences, no memories?"

After a cold, wet night, I'm anxious for a warm breakfast to bring me back to life. Dennis and I push our bikes through the damp grass and drizzle towards their mud house. Most structures in Peru are made of mud and straw bricks with thatch roofs. I wonder how they don't melt in the rain. We're greeted by a smiling mother, her teenage son and a shy girl who falls over trying to hide her smile. The girl is barefoot and the adults wear sandals made out of old car tires and drive belts; their feet are gray and swollen with toenails falling out. It seems they've been waiting for hours. The husband has already left to shepherd some sheep to pasture. Their house—I nearly humiliate myself by referring to it as their barn—is the size of an average bedroom with small windows. An adjacent fence, built of stones with mud mortar, houses the sheep. Outside the fence, cattle are tied to rocks that break through the muddy ground.

To enter the small door, we have to stoop and turn sideways, step over an uneven dirt floor and past walls 30 centimeters wide. Inside it's very dark, and I can barely see the musty bed that our host invites us to sit on. As my eyes adjust, I notice the inside of the house looks similar to the outside. I expected it to be faced with plaster or paint, and full of knickknacks; instead the walls are "decorated" with farm tools hanging from wooden pegs. The roof has several holes, but their home is dry and warm, and smells comfortingly of moist earth and tangy dung. The woman wears the typical garments of the indigenous people: a bowler hat, stockings, and many layers of dresses and shirts, handmade from colorfully woven and embroidered fabrics. She prepares our breakfast in the steaming kitchen. We're soon given a bowl of soup that looks like tripe.

In undeveloped countries many people keep adding ingredients and reheating their soup indefinitely. Most soups are served lukewarm with soggy noodles and mysterious meats and vegetables. I am afraid my stomach won't tolerate a piece of tripe that has dodged the ladle for months. During lunch yesterday, the woman had a plate of gutted fish swarmed in flies on display for her customers. And when I ate some—it was either that or starve—I prayed that all the germs and larvae were fried dead. For dessert, I had some fruit. The vendors rotate the fruit only fast enough to give you one near—but not quite—spoiled, while perfectly ripe fruit is left for next week's customers.

I take a tentative sip, afraid to insult my host. It's a salty beef broth with dried potatoes. The starchy broth quickly soaks up the acid in my stomach. The second course is a cup of tea made from coca leaves, the same leaves used to manufacture cocaine. It provides a slight buzz like coffee and is very soothing on my intestines, and relieves my head of altitude sickness.

While we eat, the stout woman sits beside the bed on a pile of cow dung used to fuel the stove. She frequently stands and squats in front of us with impressive strength and agility and yells, as though the increased volume will help our understanding. Her accent is almost indecipherable, and I wonder if she's speaking a mixture of Spanish and Quechua.

They tell us that many people in the area don't have enough money to feed themselves. I doubt this family has any money, simply sheep and cattle for barter. Even an empty soda bottle is valuable to them. I've seen them used for anything from storing valuable papers to salt shakers with holes poked in the cap. We're flattered to receive their hospitality; they give us the only thing they have to give—food and companionship. Dennis and I are unsure how to repay their kindness; just owning bicycles it's obvious that we're rich men by comparison. We debate giving them money, pens or candy. But we don't want to nullify their hospitality, turn them into beggars or rot their teeth (they have no toothbrushes or dentists here). So, we settle for a simple handshake and, *"Mucho gracias."* Judging by their smiles, they're very happy. To me, they're more beautiful and inspirational than Machu Picchu or Volcan Parícutin, which we rode past in Mexico without even realizing it was a Natural Wonder of the World. Dennis says, "Just think of the story they'll have to tell their neighbors."

26 ✳ Are you married?

I know I'm going to love Thailand. The reputation of the beautiful, charming, smiling Thai women that embody all the classic feminine virtues, like being compassionate, nurturing and unconditionally loving, preceded my arrival as far away as Europe. The reputation of the Thai woman combined with the Chinese sinicizing Thailand with their brothels and the economic opportunity of the Vietnam War has transformed Thailand into the Sex Capital of the World.

Samuel, my housemate from DC, is now divorced and has been waiting weeks for me in Bangkok. I find it ironic that when he eloped it was one of the major factors that influenced my decision to travel, and now my trip is one of the major factors of his decision to travel the world.

Thailand makes me dizzy with the humidity, heat, flashing lights and sexy women; and I'm drunk on oxygen—not long ago, I was suffocating on the slopes of Everest and drinking slush from my water bottles. We venture south with a flock of backpackers to the idyllic islands. After two years of sleeping on the ground and eating tuna fish, Samuel treats me to a "vacation from my vacation" in a luxury resort on Koh Phi Phi. (I always tell people, "If you think riding a bicycle around the world is a vacation, why don't you do it?") We spend our time at the breakfast buffet, pools, beaches, restaurants and bars attempting to relive our college years. Two weeks in a luxury resort goes faster than one hour in the Atacama Desert without water, and too soon, Samuel is gone.

During my return to Bangkok, I cycle to Malaysia to renew my visa, and thinking of getting Thai citizenship, I make a side trip to Burma to renew my visa again. A large sign reads, "Welcome to Myanmar. Drug trafficking is punishable by death." And, ironically or not so ironically, a mere hour later, above a café, seeking a toilet, I stumble into an opium den, a dark, musty, ramshackle room with comatose men sprawled underneath mosquito nets, illuminated by smoky shafts of light.

Back in "civilization", in an Internet café, my computer goes blank, and I struggle with the wires until a Thai woman with sparkling eyes and dancing dimples rescues me. Samuel's ghost echoes in my head, "She smiled at you. What're you waiting for? If you don't talk to her, you'll regret it when you're an old man. You're crazy if you don't stay in Thailand as long as possible and get a beautiful Thai girlfriend while you still have a chance. Soon you'll have prostate cancer and no amount of Viagra will make a difference. What's this number you're chasing, anyway?" He was referring to my goal of cycling the circumference of the planet. "Enjoy your life while you can. Trust me—you have no idea how lucky you are. I work with executives that have misspent their lives to earn millions, and now they don't have a life—they've never actually done anything original—and they don't even have their health anymore."

I invite Pi to ice cream. She walks beside me like a runway model trained to jackhammer her legs into the pavement and wiggle her flesh hypnotically. In the restaurant, she sits straight and proper with legs crossed modestly. Her poise seems to be a coquettish act modeled after movies and magazines because her motions are too theatrical and performed too fast and strong for such a delicate woman. I'm reminded of Samuel's pep talk, "You're going to love Thailand—the women really know how to treat a man. I'm so sick of aggressive, angry, manly Western women whose idea of a relationship is more like a business deal—and all that *soulmate* bullshit. True love— that's bullshit, too. It's like saying you believe in true hate. Have you every truly hated someone with all your heart forever and ever? Do you know how many women have fallen out of *true love* with me?"

"I agree. There's not much yin in America."

"Forget America. There's a couple things you need to know about Thai women. First, you have to make sure that she's a real woman. Don't laugh. I'm not joking. I hate to say it, but it can be hard to tell." He's referring to the *kathoey*, the lady-boys, ranging from transvestites to transsexuals. Many *kathoey* believe they're women that have been unfortunately born in the bodies of men (possibly due to a karmic transgression in a previous life). Since it's a Buddhist country, I'm tempted to say, "Better luck next lifetime," but because it's a Buddhist country, Thailand is an open-minded culture and identity is a matter of preference. This idea is imbedded in Thai culture;

for example, in every country I've visited the formal greeting is translated as, "Hello, sir," or, "Hello, ma'am," whereas the Thai greeting identifies their gender preference: "Hello, I am a man," or, "Hello, I am a woman." (It took me weeks to realize this and stop telling everyone that I preferred to be a woman.)

Pi's voice, though high-pitched, is still half an octave below the normal chirpy voices of Thai women. I've been warned by the backpacker grapevine: "If you can see an apple up here, there's a banana down there." But she has no Adam's apple. Her hands are smooth and delicate and taper into long glistening fingernails. (In India, men often inspected my hands for their strength and calluses—clues to my status.) Her shapely legs are sleek and silky, never mowed by a razor, and her breasts appear glittery and jiggly, not hard silicon balls.

I consider Samuel's second piece of advice, "You need to learn what type of woman she is: is she a real Thai lady, a bargirl, or a prostitute? Remember what my dad says, 'Treat a lady like a lady and whore like a whore but never confuse the two.'" (Samuel's father was forcibly indoctrinated into the Hitler Youth, and when the war ended and the tides reversed, he barely survived an Eastern European concentration camp, and witnessed some of his family executed; consequently, he has spent over 30 years training Samuel to be cynical of human nature. Samuel says, "I'm not a cynic; I'm a realist. You should hear my father's stories—you'd be surprised what people will do if they think they're going to die." Samuel has been keeping me real for years.) I'm suspicious Pi is a bargirl. "A bargirl," according to Samuel, "will trade sex for a lifestyle upgrade, or, if you're really unlucky, she'll hold out for the gold medal—three years of sex in trade for half your money and a one-way ticket to America." Samuel's still bitter about his divorce.

After ice cream, Pi spends all my pocket money on dinner and a nightclub. I begrudgingly think, "Doesn't anyone like anything about me except my wallet and my passport?" I didn't bring much money to prevent myself from getting drunk and bringing a woman to my hotel. Temptation is everywhere. "Despite what a Thai woman says," Samuel cautioned, "if she's the type of woman to sleep with you, she's the type of woman to ask for money the next day. A real Thai lady will never ask for anything, and she'll never date you unless you meet her parents first."

Once three Thai women insisted on buying me dinner—as many do. Afterwards I thought I was being kidnapped as we passed my hotel despite my protests; they couldn't speak English, so they took me home to meet their mother, who translated their desires into English. The matron welcomed me, offered me a drink and an hour later said, "I have three single women. Which one you like? Pick one."

When she kept pressuring me to choose a "wife" I said, "I can't decide. I like them all same, same but different."

I've had eight wedding proposals. One family, in a small village off the beaten path, offered their daughter as if she were their golden ticket; she was only 16 and the most beautiful woman in half the world, she was hypnotic and I realized that it was indeed possible that a war was fought over Helen of Troy. I asked if she wanted to move to America to test her.

"No, but if my husband wants," she answered with a bashful smile that dissipated the day's tribulations. My heart panged and I fantasized about running to the cathedral with her—I must've been on the road too long.

"Your daughter is very beautiful and nice," I said. "But, Thailand is much better than America, she would be very unhappy. Besides, I'm a poor man in America."

Pi's tour of Bangkok is like a Vegas casino, even if you lose all your money, they make sure you enjoy it. However, I just want a friend; but what does Pi want? Underneath neon lights surrounded by scurrying geckoes and buzzing insects, she puts her arms around me for the first time. Pi is drunk on one bottle of beer. I'm tipsy and pliable, but vow she won't get one baht for sex. I place my hands on her wasp waist, just above where her figure blossoms into an abundant bell-shaped bottom. She kisses me with plump—very plump lips. "I want to tell you something," she says. "Promise you won't be mad."

I stare at her with dread.

"Do you know about *kathoey* women?" she asks.

"You're a man?" After years of living in San Francisco, the Gay and Lesbian Capital of the World, I thought my *gaydar* was finely tuned. I should be panicking, but I'm shocked as if I've been merrily cycling along one second, and the next I'm somersaulting over the concrete.

"No, same, same you, but different. I am a woman." Her English is very good, but often she lapses into Thai idioms. (I'm using the feminine pronoun to be polite.) "I want to tell you sooner, but I want first you give me chance. Do you like kissing me?" Her shapely lips dance around the words. "You see. You like. It is not bad."

I feel no pain, but, as if I crashed my bike, I tenderly prod my psyche for damage. Obviously, some moments ago, when I thought she was a woman—a woman that I liked but felt no particular heart connection with—it was pleasant except—"Your lips feel funny."

"I had the doctor fix them."

"What else did the doctor fix?"

"My nose. I wanted a nose like a *farang*." Having a straight nose, like a Westerner, is considered very beautiful. The bridge of her nose is straight and sharp like an Egyptian, not the cute Thai button nose. It seems very obvious and tacky now.

"What else?"

She heaves up her bosom until they bubble out of her shirt. "Made in Hong Kong. You can touch them if you want."

I press my thumb into one very firm breast.

She laughs, "Are you afraid to touch me? Most men like it very much."

"Is that all?"

"Yes."

Samuel and I talked in Pig Latin or very fast so the English-speaking locals wouldn't understand. His voice rat-a-tats in my brainpan, *"Whatareyoudoing? Getthefuck-outofthere."* But I feel I must abide by the Thai culture and smile and "save face," meaning *not to dishonor us*. I tell her I had a wonderful night, feign that I drank too much and send her home in a tuk-tuk.

The next morning, I analyze my maps of South East Asia planning a route out of Bangkok. "Ugh!" I sweep the maps off the bed and lie down. "I'm in the middle of the most exciting city on my trip and I'm bored." On cue, the phone rings. I'm startled. I haven't had a phone call since London a year ago when my pseudo-girlfriend loaned me her mobile. The whole double-decker bus was ringing and it took me ages to realize that it was my phone. Just like now. "Hello."

"Sáwàt-di khâ." (Hello, I am a woman.)

"Sáwàt-di khráp." (Hello, I am a man.)

"Do you know who this is?"

My breath catches, "Pi?"

"Are you surprised?"

"Not really."

"Do you know how I found you?"

"Yes."

"How?" she's disappointed.

"I told you the name of my hotel." A classic traveler's mistake.

"Do you want to meet me?"

"No, thank you."

"Why not?"

"I'm tired." Maybe I should tell her the truth: I don't want to because you're either a man wanting to be a woman—which is weird—or you're a man who thinks he's a woman, which is really weird! And—worst—you're beautiful and I'm disgusted with myself for finding you attractive. And, either way, I feel like a naïve, close-minded, arrogant jackass. I wonder if my gay housemates were right when they said, "It's not a matter of black and white. Life is rainbow-colored. It's a matter of being open-minded and loving a person for who they are."

"It will be fun. I'll show you Bangkok."

"No, really—"

"Wait for me. I am coming." She hangs up either to save a couple baht or giving me no more excuses.

I decide to move to the hotel next door and begin packing. I'm assembling my bike when the phone rings again. I ignore it and stuff clothes into my panniers when someone knocks on the door. It's Pi, a simple but complicated number. She's wearing a tight top that contrasts her big bosom and tiny waist, cinched like a purse with strings, and her leg juts from the split in her miniskirt as if threatening to sunder her clothes. "Why didn't you answer your phone?" Her voice is husky because she's perturbed and has accidentally dropped her feminine mask a notch.

"I was in the bathroom."

During my world travels, I've seen some really bizarre things, like a leper describing his life to me and showing me how his foot is falling off while I'm eating lunch. In comparison Pi seems relatively normal and harmless. In fact, I find it admirable that she lives in a culture where she feels comfortable expressing herself. America is very prudish and insulated from the world of wonder, which must create a lot of angst in people that fall outside the cultural norm, and I suspect that angst mutates into harmful perversions, anger and even violence. It would be difficult to ditch Pi without hurting her feelings, possibly resulting in a dramatic backlash in my hotel,

besides she's fun and my curiosity to delve deeper into her psyche overwhelms common sense.

She's brought her scooter. "You drive," she instructs me in Bangkok's tuk-tuk jam.

"I don't want to."

"You have to. You're the man."

"I don't know how."

"If I drive everyone will stare."

"Everyone already does stare."

"It's easy. Look."

"Well... it's gotta be easier than riding a bike," I say. Pi sits sideways, ladylike, behind me. I give the scooter gas, but I'm stuck in neutral and the engine revs loud enough to explode. My heart sinks when all my acquaintances turn around and stare. I console myself thinking they don't know. Pi is a very convincing woman: the only giveaway, paradoxically, is that she looks and acts too feminine and sexy. When I find first gear, the scooter gallops forward and Pi wraps herself around me, poking her breasts into my back.

At the end of the day exploring Bangkok's parks and temples, though I feel like I'm entering the lion's den, we visit her fashionable high-rise apartment. Her room is decorated in pastel colors and stuffed animals, but it's cluttered as if a small earthquake shook everything. There's an expensive entertainment system and piles of pirated movies and music.

"What's this?" I refer to one of the numerous photographs decorating the wall, a photo of fifty *kathoey*, none are nearly as attractive as Pi.

"I work with them."

"You're a prostitute?"

"No, I'm a bargirl," her voice is becoming husky again.

"Do men pay you to have sex?"

"They give me money if they like me—not for sex. I never ask."

She confesses she's the "number one girl" and entertains one to two clients per day, plus earns tips and commission, adding up to a small Thai fortune. It's obvious she spends all her money on modern gadgets, not too mention make-up, clothes, plastic surgery and hormones. "Pi, you should save some money. You won't be beautiful forever."

"That is why I need a husband."

"But you're a bargirl."

"I make a lot of money. What do you want me to do?"

"Why not work in an office?"

She sidles up closer. "I will quit if you marry me and take care of me."

"It is illegal in the United States. Can you cook?" I'm just curious: Thai food is some of the best in the world.

But she latches onto this as a dim hope. "Take me to America. I can be good wife to you. I do everything. I learn to cook for you and care for you." She nudges me and wraps her arms around me as I backpedal. She bats her eyes seductively. "Don't you think I am beautiful?"

"Yes." She is beautiful, but it's luck, hormone treatments and plastic surgery. I suspect her personality is also wrapped in plastic. All day I've felt hunted by a wolf in sheep's clothing. The irony of being homosexual, which I learned from my housemates in San Francisco, is that usually gay men are much more attracted to straight men because they embody the masculine ideal. I feel Pi wants to appease her ego by seducing a straight man thus proving her femininity. I politely turn away. "Can you show me your balcony?"

She follows me outside. Eighteen stories below mice run the maze of Bangkok. "I will turn off the lights. You will never know."

"I find that hard to believe."

"Please, I want to show you that I can make you happy."

Pi hasn't been demure, nurturing, compassionate, wise or full of the unconditional love for which Thai women are famous; in fact, she's been aggressive, cruel and critical, one minute calling me "the cycling Gump," the next saying she didn't believe I rode anywhere. Is it really me who she wants to be happy? She may be aesthetically beautiful, but she's full of too much yang. Her forceful personality irritates me, and strangely she makes my skin crawl when she's too close. Perhaps, it's her over-powering perfume that attempts to disguise her masculine odor. "Maybe tomorrow. I'm tired," I use my all-purpose excuse, but think, "Tomorrow, I'm getting the hell out of Bangkok."

"Mâi pen rai." (No problem.) She grumbles the classic Thai catchall phrase. "Up to you. No one complains yet."

Maybe I'm old-fashioned or close-minded, but I happen to prefer feminine females who are my opposite but equal—same, same but different. I think relationships need a balance of yin and yang so that a couple may walk down the middle path and use the complimentary combination of their energies to create a future.

"Okay. First, one more kiss. Then you can leave me. I only ask for one kiss...."

A Thai scooter gas station.

27 ✳ Do you have children?

I spend Sunday afternoon in Vienna, Austria with an Egyptian woman. We listen to a quintet play Strauss in the park and eat giant pretzels. I drink *weiss bier,* and Lily drinks soda water—wine is specifically forbidden in the Qu'ran; she extends this to include all alcohol. Lily has a long neck, high cheekbones, a strong nose, eyebrows that arc over the brow bone, shaded underneath in lavender, lips like sparkling purple gumdrops, and hair tinted the color of forbidden wine and coifed neatly around her angular features. She looks remarkably similar to my imagination of the great Egyptian beauties, Cleopatra and Nefertiti. She further charms me with stories of her houseboat on the Nile River. "You will love Cairo. It is one of the world's great cities. You must come." However, before making plans, I should've taken her seriously when she said, "If you are using me to move to Cairo to get a job and an Egyptian mistress, I will kill you. I mean it. I will kill you. I will get you drunk and poison you. I've done it five times already."

Months later, when my bicycle trip is stonewalled by the tension in the Middle East, Egypt Air, the mechanical version of the Egyptian god Shu, wings me around Iran and Iraq, and over the golden deserts of the Sahara—more so for the smog—and deposits me among the pyramids and cubes of Cairo, where I hide my bicycle amongst the dusty garbage on the roof of my hotel.

The next day the male receptionist comes to my room, "Your friend is here. She is beautiful woman. You did not tell me she is woman."

"What difference does it make?"

"Is she Egyptian woman?"

"Yes, of course."

"Your friend, Egyptian woman," he muses. "Where did you meet? What do you two do together?"

"The same thing any man and woman does."

The shocked and awed receptionist escorts me to the lobby, an underwater scene of the Red Sea, just in time for Lily to overhear our conversation and see his astonishment. She admonishes me in the elevator, "Don't tell anyone I'm Egyptian. Tell them—"

"Why not?"

"They won't understand. Tell them I'm... Italian—"

"Italian?" My inflection oscillates up and down in a wave of disbelief. "You're obviously from the Middle East."

"Then tell them I'm from Lebanon. My father is Lebanese." On the street, she says, "Don't walk so close to me." In the cab, she gives me more instructions, "Don't hold my hand. Don't touch me. He's watching." Sure enough his dark, baggy eyes, as if disembodied, bulge out of the rear view mirror.

"Who cares? You weren't like this in Vienna."

"I don't want him to know I'm a Muslim woman." She's wearing a blouse, slacks and sandals that expose bunions and cracked soles from walking through Cairo's dust. I have a small foot fetish: I certainly didn't notice this in Vienna. She's also straightened her lovely curls, thinking it's more modern and professional. To me, it looks like a wig.

The Qu'ran gives many "commandments" for a woman's moral conduct, including how *not* to display her beauty. My favorite verse in the Qu'ran: "Women should not strike their feet in order to draw attention to their hidden ornaments." (24:31)

"You didn't care in Vienna; everyone saw us together."

"It is different here. I hate these people. They have such small minds. They know nothing about the modern world."

"Why don't you teach him? No one will learn otherwise."

"Egypt is different. Women of Islam are forbidden to be with a Western man." The Qu'ran cautions against the coupling of a Muslim and an infidel (nonbeliever). Furthermore, I'm told Egyptian law requires a Muslim man to have written permission from the police to "accompany" a Western woman; however, it's never possible for a Western man to accompany a Muslim woman. In all cases, public displays, like kissing, are illegal. I haven't been able to confirm these to be actual laws; however, I've been told these rumors so many times, that if they aren't true, they're still effectively acting as an Egyptian cultural law.

Lily slumps in the seat, "They will make problems for us."

I stare out of the window as the ancient statue of Ramses II slips underneath our flyway, wrapped in a bow ribbon of modern highways. "I'm colossally naïve," I think. "We can't even be friends. I should end this now."

She takes me to the largest bazaar Khan Al-Khalili in the old city. We jostle past the veiled women and turbaned men to Egypt's reputedly oldest café, Fishawi. We sit upstairs, in a long narrow room with two rows of circular tables and two rows of chairs built into the walls. It's full of young modern Egyptians, yet they all stare as we squirm our way into the café; there isn't enough room for a falafel sandwich between us. The crowd becomes bored with us or remembers their manners and resume smoking their *shisha* (water pipes). Lily doesn't smoke—though it seems nearly all Egyptian Muslims smoke—so we drink apple tea in a cloud of apple tobacco smoke. I'm afraid to violate more cultural taboos, so I sit facing the opposite wall, feeling like a granite statue of a pharaoh watching his progeny perform strange rituals. Egypt seems to have gone downhill in the last 5000 years. Afterwards, she admonishes me, "Most people love this place. You didn't like it: I was watching you."

"Too many people," I justify, but think, how can I enjoy myself when I can't act or speak freely.

On our third tour of Cairo, Lily says, "Come. I will show you my houseboat and cook you a traditional meal." I'm reluctant, especially after she tried to convert me to Islam during tea. "We believe in Jesus because it is written in the Qu'ran, but not like you. Think about it logically—" she tapped her head, pursed her lips— "You crucified Jesus. You tortured and killed your own God. How can you live with yourself?"

"Well... I didn't do it." I'm not sure if she was missing the point, or making an excellent point. "Don't you have a major in comparative religion?" I asked.

"Yes, that is why I know what I say. What kind of God is that? What kind of people does that make you?"

For a few Egyptian pounds, another bug-eyed cab driver delivers us to the houseboat. Lily instructs, "If you see anyone, tell them you are German. My housemates are German. They will think you are visiting them. First, buy pita at the market across the street. Don't pay more than a pound." She refuses to accompany me because I suspect she doesn't want to be seen with me.

After a semi-successful trip to the market (I only get overcharged 50 piastres, about 8¢ to me and about 8% of her average daily profit) I tiptoe onto the houseboat, the servant sees me. *"Gutentag,"* (Good day) I say.

"Gutentag."

"Wie gehts?" (How are you?) He just smiles. We have both reached our limit of German and I haven't blown my cover.

Inside the aroma of sautéed chicken mingles with the smell of wet rice and cucumbers, and fills the rickety, dilapidated building floating on drums in the stagnant Nile. The deadwood disintegrates as my footfalls sway and creak the boat. Stacks of books and papers are piled in the corners as if left in the eddies of a great wind. The walls are covered with chipped paint, peeling wallpaper, varnished wood, even shag carpeting: it's beyond eclectic to ramshackle. She leads me to the bedroom: warped furniture and piles of junk illuminated by a dim bulb. She flips the switch and the room changes from yellow to blue with a flickering neon light trickling in the window. She grabs my hand, pulls me towards her, kisses me, rubs my shoulders, arms, back and hips. Hands sliding lower she whispers, "I can do many things with my mouth. Egyptian women know how to make their men happy." She inflames my lust by placing my hands on her breasts. "Do you like that? You can kiss them. I give you permission. Do it," she orders.

My mind and body throb with lust. Against my better judgment, I begin to remove her shirt. "It's okay to love someone even for short while. Nothing is forever." I think.

"I'm a virgin," she whispers, as if it's a great prize.

My jaw slackens, "Your twenty-five years old."

"I'm saving myself."

"Until you're married?"

"No, for someone special."

"I understand." I pull her shirt down and backpedal.

She grabs my hand pulls me into bed. "Don't worry. I know how to satisfy you."

"We should wait." My lust is wilting. "We don't know each other well enough."

"Please, I want."

As I feared, the evening has gone as sour as my camel driver's armpits in the Saharan sun. I stand. She grabs my hand and won't let go until I feign needing the toilet. In the bathroom, I formulate a plan. I'll change subjects and appear disinterested until I can leave without raising suspicion. "Let's eat dinner on your swing," I say. We watch the lights on the opposite bank of the Nile and nearby a fisherman casts his nets with a slipslop noise in the purple moonlight.

The Nile casts an enchanting spell, until I return to the bedroom to gather my belongings. Lily corners me, "You can't leave. You must give me a baby first."

"You're joking!"

"Are you a married man?"

"No."

"Do you have a mistress already?"

"No, of course not."

"Do you have children?" American women have never asked me this, but while traveling women have asked hundreds of times, as if screening me as a potential mate.

"Not that I know of," I jest to diffuse her *amor*.

"Give me a baby with blue eyes, then you can leave." She's stroking her belly and when she sees me looking slides her hands down her hips. "Yes, you like. See I can make a good baby—a strong baby."

"I'm not going to sleep with you. No Muslim man will want to marry you if you lose your virginity."

"I will get my husband drunk on our wedding night. He will never know. All my friends do this."

"What will people think if you have a Western baby?" I'm trying to convince myself; my body is beginning to burn with lust again, and I find her desire to have my child very erotic.

"It will be my baby. They will never know. I don't even know your last name. I will never see you again."

But she does: It's written in my email address. I suspect a trap. "Maybe tomorrow. I'm tired."

She grabs my backpack containing my money, debit card, camera and passport moments before I reach it. "This is mine," she says. I grab hold of the strap and yank her halfway out of bed. Stuffed animals tumble onto the swaying floor and she moans in pain. "Go if you want. But, you have to give me something."

Her father owns half the docks in Alexandria. Once, she told me spitefully, "But I don't need his money." I suspect she ran away. Traditionally, men control all aspects of a woman's life: who she marries, whether she works or goes to school, even walking down the street she must be accompanied by a male relative following like a shadow.

The Qu'ran states: "Men are the protectors and maintainers of women, because Allah has given one more than the other.... As to those women on whose part ye fear disloyalty and ill-conduct, admonish them, refuse to share their beds, beat them...." (4:34) Somehow from passages similar to this, the tradition of Honor Killing has arisen. Though it's illegal, it's not an enforced law. If she disgraces her family, her father may perform an Honor Killing and murder Lily to restore his family's honor. The United Nations estimates over 5000 honor killings occur in Muslim countries per year. And—who knows—I may suffer the same fate, the Qu'ran also states repeatedly: "Fight and slay the pagans wherever ye find them."

(9:5) Though it does caution that it would be better to seek peace and let Allah be the judge. At the least, if caught, I'd be imprisoned.

"What will your father think?"

"I'm a modern independent woman. I can do what I want. No one can stop me." She sees my shock. "Yes, it is true. Do you *not* believe me?"

"Of course," I mumble. The equality of women (or humans in general) is a truth so ingrained in me that I rarely think about it unless confronted with someone that has differing opinions. In my experience, when someone becomes adamant or easily enraged by a particular topic, it's because on some level they believe (fear) it to be true. I'm shocked because I realize Lily, despite appearing to think and act like a modern woman, fights everyone to prove to herself she's worthwhile. I grossly underestimated the influence of her cultural upbringing and feel saddened that she's been emotionally burdened with such nonsense, that it's become the campaign of her life.

"What's the matter? Am I not attractive to you?"

Suddenly, she seems like an old woman. Once she told me, "I want to build a life and grow with someone special. Maybe that is you. Let us plant a seed and see what grows. I will tell you something for the rest of your life: if you are looking for beauty, you'll never find it. Beauty is everywhere. Just decide what you want and go for it." Where's this Lily now? I feel foolish to have been wooed when I was weak with heartache by a Western woman that spoke of being soulmates and eternal love, but in retrospect, like Lily, seemed more interested in defying her father, religion and culture in an effort to prove her self-worth. If like attracts like, what does that make me?

"What is the matter, you Europeans do it all the time?"

"You watch too much television." Does she simply want to lose her virginity? I doubt she'd enjoy sex. One of the hot topics in Egypt is clitoridectomy, or female circumcision, a bizarre tradition originating in Egypt during pharaonic times, which has spread across many African and Arab countries and is still performed millions of times per year. In the extreme form, the clitoris is sliced off, labia docked and then sown together so the vagina heals with a very small opening. Disregarding senseless taboos and vague religious claims, I've been told this procedure is meant to guarantee virginity (the husband must rip open his bride on the wedding night) and temper the woman's lust and infidelity. I personally can relate to the horrors of genital mutilation. One Kenyan woman, with her flirtations still intact, told me she narrowly escaped the procedure when her grandmother rescued her after hearing her screams.

"You flew all the way here to see me," she says. Should I confess that it was just the cheapest flight to my real destination, Mumbai, India, with a free layover in Cairo? I feel very immature and guilty for not having considered her feelings or the consequences of my actions. "You must give me something to remember you."

I sit on the edge of the bed and think, "Does she really want a baby. Why do so many women keep telling me they want a baby with blue eyes? Or, does she want to upset her father? Or reject her religion? Or blackmail me for money or a visa or a passport?" Lily is not her real name. She's chosen her name after the national flower of Egypt, the water lily, considered by ancient Egyptians as the god of the Resurrection. When the bulb of the lily is planted it decays and dies, fertilizing the soil, from which is reborn the lily flower. (Ironically, in the West, the lily symbolizes the chastity and virginity of Mary and the resurrection of Christ.) I suspect the most plausible explanation is that she's rejecting the Arab culture hoping to be reborn as she says, "a modern Western woman."

After an hour-long Mexican standoff, where she holds my backpack ransom for my seed, I formulate another plan. I sprawl on the bed, "Okay fine. You can sleep with me."

"You must kiss me first."

"No, no. Just do what you want to me. I give you permission," I echo.

"Kiss me."

"If you want my child, you must take it."

"Bwah! You are a coward. You are not a man—you are a boy!" She slams my backpack into my stomach. Woomf. "Go."

I wrap my arms around my backpack and trot out the bedroom.

"Auf Wiedersehen."

Preparing for an outback adventure. **Previous:** Vienna, Austria.

28 ✳ Don't you miss your family?

I've been sitting in Glen Helen Gorge, Australia all day waiting for the full moon to rise before beginning my night ride. I've been waiting weeks for this moment. I needed special permission from the Aboriginal Land Council to cycle the Mereenie Loop, the back road to King's Canyon and Ayer's Rock, now known as Uluru, one of its aboriginal names. I had to convince them that "I'm experienced in riding in remote and difficult conditions, and that I'm fit and competent in all respects," in other words, that I wouldn't make myself a nuisance by dying in the Outback, and as evidence I presented, "I haven't gotten myself killed so far." Then I signed a three-page indemnity and waiver form agreeing that if I do anything stupid or fate frowns upon me it's my own damned fault. I particularly enjoy 1.6: "The cyclist acknowledges that they have been advised that at certain times of the year the road can be quite busy. This traffic may constitute a hazard to cyclists, as travelers may not be expecting cyclists on the road. Less busy periods may also constitute a hazard as the cyclist may find themselves without any source of assistance if they are in difficulties." The last thing the lawyer said before issuing my permit, "Please don't die on me, and try to come back in one piece." It's surprising how many times people have said this. I'm reminded of skydiving with my brother, sister and Dennis to christen our trip. The instructor said, "First, you're going to sign your life away. Second, we're going to take all your money. And third, we're going to throw you out of an airplane. Sounds fun, hey?"

It's my third day from Alice Springs. (When I left Darwin, I asked some locals for directions to Alice Springs, they laughed and said, "Go straight fifteen-hundred kilometers, turn right, can't miss it, mate.") I've traveled 157 KM through the McDonald Range to Glen Helen Gorge at the end of the paved road. If I don't make another 226-261 KM (depending on which map is more accurate) over a gravel road to King's Canyon by the seventh day, people will come looking for me.

I'm losing Scrabble to my German friend, Lars, who I found trying to hitchhike to King's Canyon, but no one has room for his bike. "Aw, mate, that road is bloody fucked." Lars affects an Aussie accent. "I'd never cycle that road."

"I'm sure I've ridden worse," I say. As long as I can keep pedaling I'll be happy, and life isn't dire if I'm able to walk my bike or hitch a ride.

Some locals stop to fuel their car and after hearing my story say, "I hope you know what you're doing. There're skeletons everywhere in the Outback. Not long ago a German girl died 100 meters away from her car with eight liters of water inside." Sometimes there are eight liters of water, sometimes eighty; sometimes she dies over the hill, sometimes just out of sight of her boyfriend that, for some inexplicable reason, is waiting in the car—but, the moral is always the same: if you run out of water and do anything stupid, like walking to the main road, you'll die—you'll probably die even if you don't do anything stupid. I've been told a hundred times, accompanied with a vague wave, "People die all the time out there." And the perennial, "Only an American would be so crazy to do something like this." All day I'm pumped full of horror stories until the juices in my intestines gurgle, my arse is brimming over and I'm distracted enough to lose Scrabble to a non-native English speaker. (To my credit, he kept changing the rules saying, "This is how we do things in Germany.")

I stuff myself with junk food (the only food available) and water until I'm bursting with indigestion and head into the sunset. I'm carrying 17 liters of water. I've duct taped six soda bottles to the frame of my bike and put another six liters in a backpack to take the weight off my racks. At the last moment, I add two liters to recuperate the sweat needed just to carry the extra water. If a rack were to snap from the extra weight or attrition of the bad roads, which has happened several times, I would be screwed. I don't like having my life depend on someone else, but I arranged for a friendly Dutch couple that seemed very mature and intelligent, to drop 15 liters of water alongside the road about halfway to King's Canyon. It's fortunate that I met them because I didn't realize my six-liter jug had a hole. I wouldn't have made it. I figure I'm carrying the minimum amount of water, 11 liters per day, which is one more than I use on paved roads. I hope riding at night and sleeping in the day will compensate for the extra sweat lost from riding a dirt road. I can't carry anymore if I wanted to. I should be able to top off my water one last time at the next gorge provided it's not too muddy for my water filter, and I hope to camp there so that I'll have a supply of water until morning.

I hit the gravel road at 13.80 KM. Mark. I should reach my water drop in 126 KM, unless the Dutch couple forget or measure wrong. The skies are like the inviting yet perilous red lights in *Rosse Burt,* Amsterdam. I have a slight tailwind and the temperature has fallen from being able to cook me alive to simply dehydrating me. My overweight bicycle rattles and flexes over the corrugated surface, skips over some rocks and slides through the sand until I find a smooth track. It's a typical gravel road run ragged by the speeding motorists, better than riding down a Bolivian riverbed used as a road in the dry season (everyone stays home when it rains), and much better than a Vietnamese dirt road churned to foamy mud by the monsoons or a Guatemalan mountain road at 36% grade with air black with exhaust. "I can do this," I think.

An hour later, I look down at my odometer to estimate my arrival at the next gorge. My velocity reads double goose eggs and my total distance 13.81 KM. It appears a water bottle that I duct taped to the frame may have torn the wire in half. The wire was already damaged from an accident in Vietnam. I halt and dismantle the odometer and splice the wires. A car stops while I'm kneeling in the dirt circled by panniers and bicycle parts. "Are you okay? It's hot out here, and the road is really bad ahead," I'm told for the hundredth time. "Do you have enough water?" There's camaraderie among strangers in the Australian Outback because the environment is so dangerous that no one can survive alone. I assure them I'm okay, and reassure them that I'll turn around if necessary. As I strip the odometer wires a second time and separate and insulate them with electrician's tape, the rangers stop: "Are you okay? The road is really bad. Do you have enough water? Wouldn't want you dying out here."

"Australians love to exaggerate."

"Yes, but the truth is people die out here every year. Just last year a German girl...."

I begin to wonder if it's my turn.

When the rangers leave, I continue trying to fix my odometer for a third and fourth time. I rummage around in my packs for more tools when I find a letter from mom. This is unusual because I never carry extra weight, even a piece of paper. I hadn't seen my mom's handwriting in three years and must've been feeling sentimental to have kept it. The letter informs me that my grandpa died a month ago. I didn't have a chance to say goodbye. I hadn't seen him for over three years, since before I left. I remember worrying I may never see him again, and I think he knew because he said, "At my age, I only regret what I didn't do." I hadn't thought about my grandfather much, but now that he's gone, I surprise myself by crying. I almost never cry, even though at times I sure wish those negative emotions would just flow out of me and disappear into the earth.

One of the main things I've noticed that America lacks more than any other country I've visited is a sense of family and community. We're so conditioned to be independent and unique, material people in a material world, that we compete with everyone even, if not especially, our parents, siblings, romantic partners, friends and next door neighbor, to prove ourselves better at the expense of their pocketbook, self-esteem and future welfare of society as a whole. In America, you're either a winner or a loser. The idea of cooperating with your community to build something for the greater benefit seems lost, unless there's something in it for you. In fact, I'm doing it right now, my trip, my personal hoorah to the world, proving that I can do what hardly anyone has even attempted, and I can do it by myself, and that makes me unique and, therefore, important. This theory may explain why one of the more common questions on my trip is, "Do you miss your family?"

Mom's letter reads, "Now you have another guardian angel."

Do I need another one? There have been many bad omens for the last few weeks: my migraine, malaise, rumors, warnings, broken water jug, broken odometer and now grandpa's ghost, or at least, an overwhelmingly bad feeling. I contemplate continuing. My water drop should be obvious and there should be plenty of tourists on the road. But one kilometer could seem like ten, and what if my water is stolen or "borrowed" and there are no tourists? I wonder if grandpa is telling me something.

I've never turned around—I'm not happy. I find Lars, but he won't sell me his odometer at any price even though he can buy another one tomorrow. So, the next morning I hitchhike to Alice Springs (Lars invites himself along) and buy a new odometer and tires. I could return to the Mereenie Loop but it feels unsafe, so I cycle 459 KM over four days in the cancerous sun to Uluru. Instead of an Outback adventure, I get the generic, blue-hair and backpacker's tour, with highlights such as a private piano performance by Dinky the dingo, and followed by someone I'd rather never see again—Lars, whose idea of fun is to scribble graffiti on road signs, or wake up in the morning and say, "Punch me in da nose. *Ja*. I need a challenge. I vill svim vit da sharks, vit a nosebleed." Perhaps, Lars reminds me too much of myself: a strong, stubborn, logical, selfish, inconsiderate, immature, hound dog.

I roll over the sand dunes with a limited view of the Outback: red and orange sand, green and silver bushes, and the bright blue sky dappled in wispy white clouds. Then I summit a small hill atop a hundred small hills and, in the distance, Uluru pulses like the heart of Oz. I park my bike and hike up a dune full of burnt bushes with charcoal black trunks sprouting vibrant green shoots. In the sun, Uluru is a peachy-rose color, and when shadowed by a cloud, it's purple and lavender, luminescent colors as if there's a light bulb inside. The amazing thing about Uluru is not that it's the biggest boulder in the world; what's amazing is the thousands of kilometers of nothingness in every direction, excepting a few of it's immediate neighbors like Kata Tjuta [see photo page 155], and unlike most tourists, I've seen and felt every hot and dusty millimeter, which makes Uluru like a cool pool of water to my thirsty eyes.

The next day I cycle the remaining 26 KM. Up close Uluru is a rusty-ochre color from the iron oxide. It's so massive that its undulating shapes create rivers, ponds, valleys, chasms, mini-ecosystems of flora and fauna. I hitch my bike to a post and investigate a crevice, running my hand across the boulder from light to shadow, hot to cold. Aborigine culture is approximately 65,000 years old, making Uluru one of the oldest sacred sites in the world. During Dreamtime, the time before time, aboriginal myths tell how their ancestral beings emerged from the void and created everything in the world. Most of the myths aren't revealed to *Piranypa* (non-aborigines); so, I'm left to wonder if the crevice was formed when a giant ancestral being missed a giant emu, and accidentally lodged his boomerang in Uluru. When I return to my bike, I notice my tracks in the sand. Aborigines believe that every action leaves a vibrational echo of its creation in the universe.

Uluru seems magical; nonetheless, I feel detached from the significance. I'm weary of scenery, besides all day planes and helicopters buzz around Uluru like Outback flies on a dung heap. I had hoped, if not for an epiphany, for peace. On the contrary, I find myself wondering, "If Uluru is sacred, why are other places godforsaken?"

That night, I see my first Aussie brown rabbit, a big fellow, hopping around my tent. He'd be an easy target for my slingshot. I could make rabbit stew if I wanted, but it's a 55,000 Australian dollar fine to interfere with an animal, which, I assume, includes eating it, even if it's only a rabbit, which are a plague upon Australia. Also, I would be fined $3,300 for illegally transporting a hunting weapon into the park. There are two rabbits now, doing what rabbits are renowned for doing. Afterwards, the male falls backwards on his cottontail with his feet splayed in the air. The female turns her head around as if to say, "Is that it?"

I catch myself feeling peaceful and think, "How strange and ironic that I'm more calm and content here and now then during my visit to Uluru. Why? What's life telling me now? Should I be grateful that I didn't roast to death in the Outback? Did grandpa have something to do with this? Should I be enjoying the moment before I'm dead and buried? Am I so egotistical and intent on feeling good about myself that I can't appreciate one of the most famous spiritual places in the world? Should I learn to love life whether it be a giant rock or a fluffy rabbit or angst-ridden self? Am I lonely? Do I miss my family? Do I wish I could belong to a community and create a legacy?"

"Yes," I think, "All of the above." Then I laugh as my epiphany finally occurs: one of the steps to enlightenment includes being enlightened about how ungrateful I am.

29 ✳ What is your tribe?

I zoom down the Poroto Mountains; from Tanzania into Malawi; down the Rift Valley; alongside Lake Malawi; up a strenuous road onto the Nyika Plateau, where progressing 30 KM consumes a day and hopes to see animals reap no rewards; down the mountain and into the valley again; along the lake; and, instead of going the scenic route through Mozambique, I decide to go the *unscenic* route, inland with the wind, 1580 KM down Zambia's Great East Road towards Africa's second premier tourist trap—Victoria Falls.

One morning, I awake from something squirming against my side. "Oh no, not another scorpion," I think. I leap from my bed that stinks of African body odor, but it's only a small, striped lizard. An old injury has broken off his tail and crippled his hind legs, but he's still agile and dashes over the edge of the bed and goes ass over teapot—plop!— onto the floor. Seeing the paraplegic mosquito eater makes my heart pang: survival in Africa is like cleaning your hands with a greasy rag.

Yesterday's road had a corrugated surface that rattled my brainpan with potholes big enough to hide inside: one crippled the hinges on my rear panniers like the lizard's verte-brae, and a second, flung off the front set, and like a sparrow who lost its wings mid-flight, and while tumbling over the pavement, I realized depression is a lot like a pothole. If I look at it, I become hypnotized, and it sucks me in like a blackhole. The key to averting disaster is to look where I want to go. Many times I've nearly ridden my bicycle into a bone-breaking pothole or off a cliff because I was mesmerized by the imminent danger and too afraid to pay attention to the solution.

Packing my gear this morning, I discover a brazen is cracked. In the fashion of Third World countries where you can get anything, anytime, anywhere, the brother of the hotel manager is a welder. Within minutes of discovery, he's dripping hot brass on the top and bottom of the crack. It seems a simple procedure. The only problem I've had getting my bicycle welded was in New Zealand. New government regulations, essentially mandating common sense—you break it, you fix it—somehow stymied the welders in paperwork and fear of liability. Finally, I said, "So, this is the civilized world? Just give me the torch and tell me what to do."

Today the road surface is perfect and it rolls through the colorful *miombo* forest, between the distant hills of Mozambique to the south and a vast game reserve to the north. During the heat of the day, the hills appear as if they're evaporating into a haze of autumn colors. My ears delight in birdsong, freed from the packs of children, spoiled by years of tourists and foreign aid, chanting, "Gimmemoney," and chasing me through Malawi.

In the outskirts of a small village, a group of women wearing sarongs with clashing colors and patterns that I'd be reluctant to use as a picnic cloth, see me and break into song and dance. They gyrate in circles, trilling their tongues and pressing their hands to their heart and then holding their hands towards me cupping love. (I'm reluctant to believe they're begging.) This is what I enjoy most about the culture, just when you think Africans are happy to watch maize grow, they suddenly begin singing and dancing, drums appear out of nowhere and their impromptu music spreads through the hills and into neighboring huts. Their blessing follows me over the crest of the hill. Zooming down the next hill, my hat aeroplanes atop my head, then flips off, like a parachute connected to my Adam's apple. Around the switchback, bushes lay uprooted across the road as if a twister blew through, but they're only warning flags. Up the next hill a kingpin truck is stuck, braced with rocks, it's clutch burnt out. My clutch is nearly burnt out, too. Over the next hill, I see an opportunity to rest in a hut, a *banda* with a conical thatch roof, minus the mud-brick wall. A group of men appear to be playing checkers. I park my bike against a pole. "Hello. How are you?" I ask. Pleasantries are very important everywhere; and, almost everywhere, except big cities, people actually care.

"Fine, sir. How are you?" A man with thin lips and the shape of his bones pressing through his skin appears to be the ambassador of the banda.

"I'm fine. Thank you. Are you playing draughts?"

"No. We are playing a card game."

"Poker?"

"No. It is named Casino." It's a simple game: if your card comes up in a pair even, you win, odd, you lose. Their deck is ragged and, despite their fingers being thick and callused and nails worn to the root from using their hands as shovels and hammers, with an impressive flourish they snap the cards down. Their feet encroach the game, at times having a card dealt atop it. Their elephantine feet are dull purple, dusted in gray and cracked like a mudflat in the dry season. One man is missing a toe, but the others have swollen to accommodate the space. Some men wear flip-flops, apparently as a fashion statement or sign of wealth, as their tough soles are accustomed to treading broken rock.

A pile of thousand-Kwacha bills are in the pot. "You're playing for big money."

"Yes, big money. Do you want to play?" Often people want me to join their games, even if it's tossing rocks into a ditch to build a road or singing songs while harvesting sugarcane.

I decline. Either I'll lose a small Zambian fortune, or I'll win money from people that appear impoverished and unscrupulous.

"What is your tribe, sir?"

"I'm from America. We don't have tribes." But on second thought, we have a much more complicated tribal system, like an invisible, nameless caste society. Given enough time, people ask many surreptitious questions to determine who I am: age, nationality, race, status, income, politics, religion, family, career…. In fact, I could say that all the questions people ever ask me boil down to one thing: "Do I want to include you or exclude you from my tribe?"

"What is that you're drinking? Maize beer?" I gesture towards a man pouring a shot into a sawed-off soda bottle from a greasy wine bottle with a worn label. I've seen trucks with tankards several thousand liters in capacity roam between villages selling maize beer. Villagers walk, hobble and cycle to the road and wait for the hose to fill their plastic bucket with a beige, chunky liquid.

"No, no. Made from cane."

"Sugarcane? Rum?"

"Yes, rum," my newfound compadre rolls his head back and smiles as if this were a joke.

"Are you finished with the harvest?" I assume they're farmers with a pocketful of cash and three months until the rains. Though the farmers could sow their seeds now and reap a harvest year round, there's not enough water to irrigate the crops and termites would eat the seeds. He looks confused. "Are you farmers? Are you finished harvesting?"

"Yes, yes. We are farmers."

"What crops do you grow?"

"We grow maize and groundnuts and yams."

"Are the people near here safe?" I'm questioning the safety of bush camping.

"Oh, so safe. People here, so, so friendly. Near Lusaka, people very dangerous."

Once Dennis summarized this us-versus-them tribal mentality, or fear of the unknown,

"Did you notice in every country someone says, 'Everyone here's very friendly; it's those people down the road you can't trust. You must be very careful.' And then down the road, they say, 'Everyone here's very friendly; it's those people up the road you can't trust. You must've been very lucky.'"

"Are the animals dangerous?" I ask.

"There are no animals near the tarmac."

"Where are the animals? There's only forest here, a game reserve; there are hardly any people."

"We like to eat the wild animals: antelope, buffalo. Very nice."

"So, if the animals come here, you eat them?"

"No. We go to the animals. They are over there." He gestures behind a small mountain. "About five kay."

"Is this ill… I mean is it against…" my voice falters as I realize I'm broaching a taboo subject. "Can you—"

"It is not illegal."

"No problem," I say and he echoes me. " What about elephants?" I know this is illegal game. "Do you eat elephants?"

"Yes. We eat. Elephant is the best meat. Especially this part." He lifts his foot, toes clutching the strap of a broken sandal, and pats his crusty and cracked sole. "Very tasty. So, so tasty." His expression is like the cliché of a French gourmet.

"You're not farmers?"

"No. Our business here is not farming," he smirks.

My realization illuminates the world in a dastardly light: aside from birds and lizards, I haven't seen any animals, dead or alive, since Tanzania; a pile of blood money is in the pot; the holes in the road signs are from rifle shots; they aren't poor farmers, but spendthrift drunk poachers; the man in the Yankees' cap, rolling on a rusty barrel, is no longer gnawing on a goat bone but a poached antelope or possibly even—"Do you eat lion?" I ask.

"No. But some like lion very much. Farther down the road—"

A malnourished slim-jim with teeth worn to the root by chewing a cud of sugarcane his entire life, looks up with one watery, bloodshot eye, "We can not discuss." With a flourish of his hand, he zips the conversation shut.

The nape of my neck prickles with the instinct to survive clashing with my curiosity. "Don't worry. I'm just a guest in Zambia. I'm not here to cause trouble. *Hakuna matata.*" My Swahili is useless now, "No worries." I smile my celebrity smile.

"We are not worried. We pay the juju man—do you know juju?" says Slim-jim.

The man with the lion on his shirt elucidates, "The traditional medicine man."

"A witch doctor?"

"Yes. Witch doctor. The juju man makes a crocodile to eat our enemies." It's illegal to perform witchcraft and even to buy charms against witchcraft.

"A magic crocodile," says a man with bubbling sores around his mouth and forked side-burns. Mid-sentence his chewed and burnt matchstick drop from his lips and tumbles into the pot. Statistically, three men of this small group have AIDS, or more if you con-sider this a high-risk group—I do.

"He do voodoo," the honchos boom in an up and down pronunciation that I don't initially recognize as English.

The rum bottle is passed round, the cards ruffled, and some men roll tobacco inside newspaper to smoke. I shuffle my feet, feeling a quick get away would incriminate me. My companion isn't deterred long; from his trouser pocket retrieves out a handful of transparent blue stones. "Do you know what this is?" He hands me a nugget resembling a piece of glass worn in the surf. I expect he'll say it's a diamond in a prelude to a gem scam, but he says, "It is a blue sky gemstone."

"I've never heard of this," which is true but also disarms his sales pitch.

Meanwhile a pickup truck makes a U-turn and two fancy fat cats with sunglasses and shoes as shiny and black as their truck cause a hubbub amongst the gamblers. The cats pass me, the first Zambians to never greet me or inquire my mood, instead they scru-tinize me with shifty eyes. The game ceases and half the men disappear down a track parting the dry, parched elephant grass.

"What do they want?" I whisper to my rummy friend.

He doesn't whisper but heaves breathless sentences, "They are here about the business we discussed, sir." English is one of the seven official languages in Zambia (there are 66 unofficial languages) so communication is never a problem, but the formal grammar amuses me.

"How do they know your business?"

"People know," he replies mysteriously. "I am a miner. I have two mines. The problem is capital. I need a sponsor."

A dozen people have asked me to fund their restaurants, bars or schools, even a hospital, as if the money will flood back to me when half the population can't afford a Coca-Cola. I hear murmuring from the *banda*, "Where is the *mzungu*?" The one red, rum-soaked eye of the honcho swivels in its socket, pinpointing me. With a few words, his henchman, the man with the forked sideburns, sidles up beside me, watching what I'm writing. I slide sideways and he shadows my movement.

Mzungu is the derogatory Swahili word, which has migrated throughout Africa. I find it interesting that the most common words and phrases I learn in every country are: hello, goodbye, how are you, thank you, please, excuse me, one, two, three, good, bad, and foreigner.

I feign interest in the gems to convert my identity from a potential threat to a customer or partner, from a 'them' to an 'us.' "How much is this worth?"

"Six to ten dollars per gram depending on the quality." He prints his name and address and the type of gems he's mining, in my notebook, everything misspelled beyond identity.

My main interests, the tubby Zambian government employees, have returned with a bamboo mat. I whisper, "What did they buy?"

"They bought the buffalo and warthog."

"How much?"

"It is ten to twelve thousand per kay-gee." (About a dollar per pound.) "Do you want to try? Very tasty."

"No, thank you. I can not bring it on the bicycle." Actually, my malnourished body is craving a pound of buffalo meat, maybe even warthog; and, my hunger begins to rewrite my ethics.

The fat cats conspicuously hide the bamboo mat with the meat rolled inside by tying it to the roll bar of their truck, and without any wasted pleasantries their wheels churn dust into our faces.

Vice versa, I waste some pleasantries and vamoose with false promises to research his proposal, and that we would make excellent business associates. I'm saddened that the life force of the majestic African wildlife seems to have been converted to rum, cigarettes and a few rich, fat-bellied Zambians, but I don't blame the poachers: they've been eating game animals long before they were considered games, and only so many Africans can make a living selling grass hats and wicker baskets to tourists. There are too many people with too little food; consequently, people will eat every animal they can catch. I've even seen men selling skewers of field mice to passing cars.

I wonder if it were my hunger versus a lion's life, what would I do? Or, what if it were the survival of a species versus the survival of my family? Or my tribe versus another tribe, such as the current "War on Terror"? What would I do if the war involved more than watching TV? And, what would I do if I understood the other person and their point of view?

(Postscript: I've seen three crocodiles, none appeared magical. My only curse is this contagious African body odor. The bacteria have burrowed deep into my moist armpits. Even after four hot showers and scrubbing my body raw with anti-bacterial soap, still I stink.)

30 ✳ Who cares?

I went 929 days without having to pitch my tent in the rain until New Zealand's gale-force headwinds (gusting up to 125 KPH), stinging rain and gravel roads like grinding paste. My body is being iced by the wind, yet burns with pain. Water streams down my legs into my shoes stealing my warmth drip by drip. The icy-fiery pain spreads the numbness, creaking and popping, tendonitis of my knees through my whole body. I make faces like a Maori warrior: tongue wagging, eyes scrunched and roaring voice to scare away my demons. I see a sheltered spot in a tree farm, hop the fence and pitch camp. As I feared, by the time I pitch camp, my tent is soaked and full of puddles of muddy water. I strip off my bicycle clothes and pull on all my soggy winter woolies and warm myself with two cups of coffee that I make from rainwater running off my tent. Pinpricks of pain signal life is returning to my extremities, and my feet turn beet red and swell to twice their size.

According to a scientist that I met in the Invercargill museum, "It's the worst weather on record, probably the coldest weather since the last ice age one-hundred-fifty-thousand years ago." He was caressing an indigenous lizard with a crocodile-like tail. "They are more like dinosaurs," he coos. "The fossil record suggests that New Zealand was much warmer in the past."

For four long days, I've averaged a walking speed as I battled my way to the southern end of New Zealand—the subantarctic, a word that sounds much colder than antarctic—I prefer snow to cold rain. This region lies in the southern latitude between the *roaring forties* and the *furious fifties*. The nicknames refer to the winds, which blow perpetually from the west. (In the olden days, ships sailed the long-way round from Europe down the west coast of Africa, circumnavigating Antarctica, using the trade winds to propel their ships to Australia and New Zealand.) The gale-force wind prunes the branches of trees leaving only half a tree on the leeward side shaped like a windsock; and rocks, called ventrifacts, have been sandblasted into fin and sail shapes. Two weeks ago, a woman was killed when the wind caught her tent like a kite and blew her 27 meters through the air, into a pile of rocks, smashing her skull.

The next morning, I make coffee from a bowlful of slush and hail then prepare to leave. I can't wait for the weather to clear, because I have no food or water. When I'm finished packing, my hands and feet are like blocks of wood and I've gone from shivering and pain back into numbness.

I'm struggling: I walk up the hills and coast down, jettison all the pages out of my books that I've read, throw away my pillow, some clothes and my slingshot, and I'm still crippled by a burning pain below my knee.

A few days ago, just as I was regretting not buying a hat, I found a colorful wool hat in perfect condition alongside the road. The next day, I prayed, "Don't think I'm ungrateful for the hat: my head is warm, but now my feet are cold." Soon, I found one wool sock, and one prayer later, I found the other sock. Now, I pray to my guardian spirits. "Not my knee again, please. You can take back the hat and socks." Almost five years ago, a pink-haired hippy ran a stop sign, knocking me off my bicycle onto my kneecap. After arthroscopic surgery and two years of physical therapy and chiropractics, I still hadn't fully recovered as I began my trip despite chronic pain, and feeling like the cartilage in my right knee had turned into gravel. My stubbornness, one of my strongest virtues, has been battling the pain ever since. Many times, I've even pedaled one-legged, and now it seems I've worn out my left knee. My knees had benched me in Christchurch for weeks. I visited a doctor and after performing various tests she announced in medical terms that I have overdeveloped thighs and a flabby ass. She poked me in the bum and said, "You see." She gave me some strengthening and stretching exercises and ended my session by saying, "If it hurts too much, don't ride so far the next day." Shortly thereafter, despite her recommendation, I rode up the World's Steepest Hill according to the Guinness Book of World Records, in Dunedin, a 35% grade [see photo page 173]. (I've ridden up much longer and steeper unpaved roads.) I amazed everyone, including myself, by cycling up the hill fully-loaded, and I made a pleasant discovery, that when I stand on the pedals, my knees don't hurt.

A dozen kilometers later, my knees literally come to a grinding halt at an intersection where I can take the short road to Invercargill but turn into fiercer winds, a black cloud, with no indication of a bed, shower, food or water; or, I can turn left, the long way towards a café and supermarket. It seems foolish to continue, so I pedal to the café. While standing beside the coal fire, I ask a local if there's a bus to Invercargill. "Don't hold your breath, mate. Better watch yourself." He gestures to my smoldering clothes.

Two hours and two cups of coffee later, after my body temperature stabilizes, I'm sitting outside a supermarket eating day-old bread on the concrete among the potted plants and whitewashed walls moaning, "I'm not going to make it." An old man sneaks up, suddenly putting his overgrown eyebrows in front of mine and says in a thick, trilling accent, "Where's your hat, lad? I was going to put some money in it."

I slide my bicycle helmet over, "Here you go."

"Oh, well—" he gestures with his shoulder shrugged high and shorts tugged low— "I'm a Scotsman: short arms, deep pockets." He pats me on the shoulder. "Don't worry. Ya probably think I'm a crazy old arse; I'm not. I just say what's on my mind, like everyone should. Life's too short to take seriously, to be sitting around like this—" he yanks the loose skin of his face down like a bulldog pout— "One day, cancer will be knocking on your door, 'Are ya having a g'day, mate?' I'll be pushing up daisies soon enough. (If they cremate me, I'll burn for three days from all the whiskey I drank.) I remember during The War—" he pantomimes marching with a sign— "everyone saying, 'The end is near.' Ha! I'm still here." He kneels on one creaking knee. I feel obliged to stand, and we both stand. "I've done everything: I've been all over New Zealand. I've been to America. I have a family: I love my family. I've been parachuting and bungee jumping." He notices my distracted gaze tracking a couple of beautiful lasses. He crouches low, jabs his fist and trills, "I've done my fair share of rooting, too, mate." He sees me laughing. "I have, mate. Why not? That's what we're here for. I know people who haven't done any." He places his fingertips on his chest and mocks, "'Oh no, not me.' It's a bloody shame. I'll be seventy-five next March and I can still do everything."

With a smirk, I ask, "Can you still root?"

His forehead furrows in disbelief. "You'd better believe I can. Well... I should let ya go. Ya probably think I'm mad but I wanted to put a smile on your face. That's the problem today—no one talks to each other. I talk to whoever I want; I don't care. Where ya off too?"

"Auckland," which is on the opposite end of New Zealand and a different island. "Then Africa... if my knees don't give out."

"Africa?"

I'm reluctant to mention my bicycle trip. It's tedious to explain to naysayers and nonbelievers, but the bothersome thing is that many people, especially those close to me, enjoy holding my trip against me, saying such things as, "For someone who's managed to go around the world, you're not too worldly." Or, "I don't care what you've done. You're no better than me." It seems they expect, or my arrogance pretends, that I'm some kind of superman, and they become jealous and vindictive. I don't deny being naïve and foolish and dozens of other things on occasion, but I do wonder why it bothers me so much what people think of me and my trip, and why some would rather see me fail. "I'm going round the world on my pushbike," I tell the Scotsman.

His caterpillar eyebrows leap halfway up his brow. "You're jokin', mate! That's bloody fantastic. I know many people who haven't done anything their whole life except make excuses. Now they're my age wondering, 'Where'd my life go?' It's a bloody shame."

"Days like this, I wouldn't miss."

"But if ya quit, ya would, wouldn't ya? Where ya from?"

"Milwaukee."

"Well, ya can always go sit on your arse in Milwaukee, can't ya? Or ya can roll the dice. Have some fun." Then he makes a comment that I wish I would've told to the thousands of people who confessed to me they wanted to make an adventure but instead made excuses, he gestures to my bike, "It may take ya all day to get somewhere—but who cares?"

I cycle into New Zealand's emerald hills with renewed inspiration. One of the benefits of the pissy weather is that I see rainbows almost everyday. Rainbows only occur when it's raining and sunny at the same time, and only visible when I'm cycling the path down the middle. Billions of raindrops, tiny prisms, fall out of the sky, and as if they're observing the world, perfectly reflect and magnify their surroundings, revealing the nature of light, and colorizing mountains, pastures and skies. I find it curious that as the drops are born, fall and die, that the rainbow barely moves. Perhaps my being is like a rainbow broadcast by my DNA or my soul; and, perhaps humans are like drops of rain in the rainbow of humanity.

"Bad" weather sculpts world-class scenery.
Previous: More road sign graffiti—"Beware falling sheep".

31 ✳ What are you trying to prove?

After three hours of tramping up New Zealand's Franz Josef Glacier, through rubble and streams, following yellow-tipped poles, and climbing up staircases carved out of ice, our tour group is approaching the icefalls where the top of the glacier has cracked along numerous faults as the bottom, remaining solid from the pressure, cascades in slow motion over a cliff, ripping the rocks off the wall and grinding them into silt. We cross five bridges—aluminum ladders topped with a sheet of wood, with rope handrails—the chasms deepen from a frosty white to a cool blue to a cold, bottomless black. Distant ice tunnels thunder as they collapse. Just past the bridges, we lunch on a slope overlooking the toes of the glacier hundreds of meters below us on the valley floor where ribbons of silver streams braid themselves into the Waiho River, which disappears through a notch in the horizon into the Tasman Sea. "Does anyone suffer from claustrophobia or fear of heights?" asks our guide.

"It's a little late for that," I laugh.

"This is your last chance to—" the wind freezes his words in midair— "isn't raining yet." In fact, a black cloud is forming around the tops of the mountains and the mist is slowly globing into a pissing drizzle (Kiwis call this fine weather). Our guide has a beaming smile and animated eyebrows that I imagined make women swoon;

however, I lose faith in his wisdom, especially when he refers to the greywacke sandstone as "terminal moraine" as if a jeweler were referring to a pile of diamonds as glass. On second thought, that sounds incredibly arrogant—what exactly am I trying to prove to myself playing word games?—that I can outwit and out-survive my guide?

As lunchtime ends, our guide gives us more death-defying advice, "Don't cover your ears with your hood so that you can hear me yell. Don't cover your mouth so that I can hear you squeal when you fall. And don't trip over your feet." We enter the seracs, towering pillars of ice, as if the subantarctic sea were breaking on the shores during a gale and flash frozen. The deeper into the crevasse labyrinth we climb, the more the ice vacuums away my body heat, and the cleaner and bluer the ice becomes—blue as the bluest sky. I reach out and chip off pieces, intrigued to find the ice clear or white from a frozen effervescence of air. I lose site of the group and hurry forward, but a spike on my crampon catches a strap on the opposing foot and I topple near the heels of Chris. I bloody my hands and knees but Chris isn't impressed; he's an emergency medicine specialist, "I find bullet wounds and drug overdoses really interesting," he says. "I love the ER."

The trip climaxes when we shinny down a narrow passage using footholds on each wall, spreading my legs wide to wedge myself into the crevasse. At the bottom, I shuffle my crampons across the ice on either side of a pool until it fills the entire passage. I dip my ice axe by its cord into the pool unable to touch the bottom. Unsure how to proceed, I push aside some mini icebergs until I locate a small foothold just below the surface. I take one long step, search the pool for another foothold, find it and hop across imagining one slip will plunge me into a subterranean river. The crevasse narrows, so Chris and I have to remove our backpacks to slide through sideways. The walls are canted so I lean back and shuffle forward like an inchworm.

The Pacific and Australian tectonic plates are colliding, flowing uphill, creating New Zealand and the Southern Alps, forming a cold wall that condenses the moisture out of the perpetual subantarctic trade winds. The equivalent of nine meters of rain per year falls atop the Alps as wet snow. Franz Josef glacier is one of the fastest moving glaciers in the world, spilling out of the glacier's basin, or *névé*, at 2.5 meters per day. I think, "I only have centimeters to spare should the glacier suddenly shift."

I pause. My crampons plugged into the glacier, the electric cold flowing up my legs, seizing my knees. I watch the grey sky roll past the seracs. I'm reminded of Everest's Khumbu Icefalls—the most treacherous section of the ascent to the summit—and Goran Kropp. I met Goran in San Francisco and he told me he's the only man to summit Everest beginning from sea level, in addition without using bottled oxygen or the Sherpa's assistance. He bicycled from Stockholm, Sweden (sea level) to Nepal where he began a long trek by foot through the Himalayas to Base Camp, carrying two backpacks, and sometimes only able to carry only one pack up the mountain and having to return to the bottom for the second. This was during the famous disaster in 1996 that Jon Krakauer detailed in "Into Thin Air." Nine people died; one of them was Goran's close friend, another man named Scott. Nonetheless, the next day the song of the mountain lured Goran past the bodies of his friend and acquaintances to the summit of Everest.

"C'mon, Scott. You don't have time to reminisce." I inhale deeply, expanding my lungs, as if I can use the sky to wedge open the crevasse—or is it my spirit? After a moment, I slide one foot forward but my jacket is frozen to the glacier. Leaning sideways, my jacket pops loose; suddenly, as if the walls are buttered, I begin falling. I am barely able to reposition my heavy boot and crampon to prevent wedging myself in the bottom of the crevasse where it would've been nearly impossible to get my feet underneath me. I would've been trapped like a rabbit in a three-walled cage. (Rabbits can't walk backwards.)

Goran told me he intended to quit mountain climbing. "It is not good for the head," he said referring to the lack of oxygen. But the call of the wild was too strong and he was killed several years later in a mountain climbing accident, during a "moderately difficult" ascent, which seemed to me an anticlimactic end to his adventures. I'm sure he could have done so much more. I admired Goran's contagious enthusiasm, charisma and accomplishments; in fact, after I met him and explained my dreams, I knew I could do it. But was Goran caught in a psychological three-walled box? Or, like a fish unaware of the ocean of possibilities? Did Goran die for the sake of exploration, to expand the frontiers of humanity? Or was he simply a thrill-seeker, an adrenaline junkie? What's the difference between an explorer, adventurer, traveler and tourist?

Often people ask me, "What are you trying to prove?" Or, "Is this some kind of world record?" I've often been told that either I'm on a fool's quest to find myself, or just a selfish thrill-seeker, even somebody too lazy to get a real job. If I could open my eyes and see that I'm a rabbit in a three-walled box or a fish in water, would I be able to escape? Is my box pride? Or, its alter ego, low self-esteem? Am I making a difference?

Or, am I trying to prove something to myself?

I mumble, not loud enough to distract Chris, but loud enough to give my prayers resonance, "I promise. I'm going to retire in Cape Town. Just let me survive with a sound body and mind. I don't want to end up like Goran: I've had my adventure. I don't need to set a world record in order to feel accomplished. I could feel satisfied just planting a garden someday."

When handed an ice axe in the beginning of the day, I joked with my current cycling companion Stefani from Switzerland, "I bet we won't need this but for a photograph." However, throughout the day I discovered many uses for my axe: as a hook to pull myself up; a wedge to lower myself; a brace against an opposing wall; in the end, my knees weak and feet blistered, I use it as a cane to hobble back to the bus, last out of 50 people. New Zealand must be laughing at me: "Do you think you're special Mister I-bicycled-around-the-world?" Perhaps, I can use my axe to chip away my need to prove myself better than others.

Cycling fully-loaded up the "World's Steepest Hill" to prove that I am who I think I would like to be. Note: the camera is angled down about 19° making the road appear flat. Several cyclists have been killed while showboating down this hill.
Opposite: A group of hikers appear like ants upon New Zealand's Franz Josef Glacier.

32 ✳ How did you get so lucky?

Dennis and I passed 86 roadside memorials today—86 carloads of people killed. I stopped to investigate one Greek shrine that resembled a glass birdcage atop an iron pole, with wooden plaques of various saints, a faded photo of the deceased, an oil lamp and matches. It was windy, but I managed to light the lamp and say a prayer. Most shrines were clustered around the curves. If the cars couldn't negotiate a turn, I wonder how they've managed to miss me.... On second thought, I've been nicked many times and knocked off my bike a few times. Many people outright state, "You should be dead," or ask, "Do you have a death wish?" And judging by more innocuous questions, most people reckon we should've perished long ago: succumbing to microscopic monsters, thirsting or starving in the wilderness, stoned by fanatics, beaten by overzealous bandits, or, most likely, crushed underneath a truck—there are a million ways to die. A million to one odds, yet we survive. I wonder—and many people ask—what motivates me to keep cycling when I've been inches from death so many times?

I feel I have nothing to lose. I'm more frightened of dying from boredom back home.

We're camped halfway up a mountain. There are shanties and goats everywhere. I think we have a secluded spot until two sheep dogs discover us. They bark sporadically, unsure to interpret us as friend or foe until I feed them bread. Nonetheless, an old Greek woman arrives in a black dress and shawl and relying heavily on her cane searching for her missing dogs: they have a job to do. I hate being discovered. No one has made us move yet, but I fear that when the gossip spreads thieves will ransack my gear, or children will wake me in the morning wanting to be entertained. I seem to have a parade of children following me around the world. *"Yasou,"* I say hello in Greek. She's friendly and returns my informal greeting. We pantomime the rest of the conversation. I gesture with my open hand towards the ground and then rest my face on both hands clasped like a prayer and close my eyes.

"Ne, ne." (Yes, yes.) She gestures as if dribbling a basketball, meaning I'm welcome to stay. Then she points towards the dark clouds.

I reveal the location of my tent, my rain shelter.

Her eyes widen, and she picks up an imaginary pannier as if it weighs a ton, then grasps an imaginary steering wheel.

"Ochi." (No.) I pedal my arms and show her my bicycle.

She places her hands on her chest, looks towards the sky and murmurs a prayer.

I bow slightly.

She returns my bow.

Then a man wearing a black suit cut from thick, coarse material approaches looking for his wife and dogs. *"Halo. Deutschland?"*

"Hello. No, America." I'm considering hanging a sign around my neck: *"Ich bin nicht Deutsch."* (I am not German.)

He turns to his wife, "American!" He gestures towards his sheep and accompanied by elaborate pantomiming says, "America."

He must mean his sheep are going to America, and I try to convey that they must be very fine sheep, indeed. They give Dennis and me a blessing. We thank each other many times before they leave, wishing us a good night. I feel lucky, indeed, to meet such kind, interesting people.

After dinner, I sit in the entrance of my tent atop purple slate crushed into purple dust by hooves. I'm getting cold despite two layers of clothes. I hope it doesn't rain because I lost my ground sheet and mattress. I wanted to write about quitting, but I shouldn't consciously indulge myself; it's challenging enough—I call it the Flaw of Attraction—automatically and subconsciously thinking pessimistic thoughts. I'll postpone my worries until India. I've mastered denial. The benefit is: I do things I wouldn't normally do, like go to India alone before I can over think it. The con is: I'm often being slapped in the face by reality, even so I've been lucky.

I watch nightfall. Nearby trees, like stalks of celery in colored water, soak up the winter chill. The roar of distant trucks climbing the switchback is soothing. Thousands of years ago the Greeks must've cut down most of their trees and replaced them with crops, but here, in the mountains, they appear safe in their precarious perches. Knolls of limestone break the mountains, covered in conical pines, spherical thorn trees and cubic bushes. Pine trees cover even the tippy-tops of the mountains. How did they get there? Does the pinecone grow into a towering evergreen with far-reaching limbs that drop another pine cone a few meters further up the mountain and so on...?

I'm reminded of cycling a Mexican mountain, back when I bitched all the way up a hill and daydreamed all the way down, missing the whole point of touring. It was a steep, rutted dirt road full of rubble the size of oranges and grapefruit. I was pedaling hard enough to risk ripping the tendons from my bones to maintain my momentum. (If I had stopped, I wouldn't have been able to start again, and I would've had to walk my bike.) I hit a stone and nearly fell, but I zigged right, steering into the fall, to recover my balance, yet couldn't regain control before hitting another stone and zagged left. (One of the tricks to riding a bike is letting the bike decide where it wants to go.) At one point, I nearly zigged off the cliff, but a square rock caught and held my front wheel. Some say it's only blind luck, but if it was only luck, as if I kept doubling down my life on a roulette table, I would be dead a dozen times over. Feeling lucky leaves me wondering if I could do it again—a victim of luck. Others call luck being in the zone, the synchronous signs that reveal you're traveling your true path. Deep inside me, I believe a force greater than what I'm aware of as myself, propels me forward despite the odds. And so zigzagging, bouncing off rocks,

spinning my wheels in dust, caught in ruts, I realized I was falling—falling uphill—falling all the way to the top of the mountain. And when I crested the mountain, my epiphany must've rewired my brain, because my attitude changed. Coasting down the other side of the mountain—creatively falling—I felt as if I grew wings and could soar off the cliffs, and seemingly I gracefully flew all the way to the valley floor.

The French call an orgasm *le petit mort* (the little death). To live a little, one must die a little. *C'est la vie, non?* (Such is life, no?)

A rainbow and sunny skies in Mexico.

NEXT
20 000 YEARS

33 ✳ Are you crazy?

Yester evening an Australian windstorm blew in from the south plastering me in my tent like a vacuum-packed hotdog. Today, bicycling into the remnants of the storm, the wind is shredding my sun-bleached jacket and my morale.

"If it's not the sun, it's the flies. If it's not the flies, it's the wind. If it's not one thing, it's another. Ugh, I sound like my parents. I'm never going to make it." As a child, I must have learned by example that mumbling and complaining, like a teapot whistling hot air before it explodes, was a method to cope with life's "injustices".

"You'll make it, you always do," I reply. Now, I have entire conversations with myself. Maybe I've ridden myself crazy—too many hours, days, even months on a bicycle pondering problems and paradoxes.

"My saddle sores are eating me alive. My knees are grinding. And, even if my penis didn't snap in half—deep down in the 't'aint—from the potholes, I'm so lonely my heart surely has cracked." I've come to identify this aspect of myself as Primitive or Poor Scott. He's the guy concerned with survival—the less pain and the more pleasure the better—basically a hedonist. Primitive Scott was trained (conditioned) by the world to feel like a helpless victim, who enrolled in the continuing education program as a way of blaming others rather than taking responsibility and an honest look at the "ugly" side of himself, who if not causing the problems was expecting and participating in them. He's a very insidious character, eroding my confidence from the subconscious.

"Bicycling around the world is a flawed concept. There are too many ugly places and dangerous people. And, when I meet magical people and travel through beautiful places, I'm too busy racing the weather and visas to stop or visit the *now*. I've reached the point of diminishing returns in my travels. I've mastered bicycling; there's little payoff. Nobody will blame me for quitting." This is Logical Scott. He's excellent at manipulating the outer world to attain pleasure. Logical is difficult to recognize because he's my dominant personality and loves to think of himself as my true self. Logical even conceptually understands that he's only a small aspect of myself like a monkey in control of a starship, but not willing to give up control, and constantly attempting to overrule my emotions.

"I will regret it. I'm not a quitter. This trip is bigger than myself. I'm doing it for my friends and family and the dozen people I meet everyday who've never imagined it's possible, and the hundreds of people who write saying they wish to but never could. I'll never quit. Maybe I'll re-prioritize my goals; but, currently, I have no other priorities. I have to keep going while I'm young, strong and healthy. Finishing this trip will create the foundation for me to do something even better." This is Spiritual Scott, the most difficult aspect of myself to identify or define. He's that nagging angst that says, "There's more to life than this," an ideal or true self, god-like, a Platonic form, my superego. He's the creative inspiration that strikes when I least expect it, the man who can effortlessly bicycle 100 KM, the smile induced on a passing stranger, it's the serendipitous coincidences, like the string of friends that have joined my adventure as if to guide, protect, teach and carry me when I couldn't carry myself, it's the feeling of being a human molecule in an ever-evolving crystal. Spiritual Scott seems to go beyond mind and body into the universe. Perhaps, he's my soul speaking and it has taken most of my life to identify him.

"You're not so young anymore. If you want a family you'd better get busy. Women my age are either married, divorced, have children or such a bad case of the baby bug that they can't see straight."

"Besides, I don't want to."

"Life isn't about doing what I want. If I sat around drinking beer and watching television I'd never get anywhere. Life is a gift. I have an obligation to myself and society to live up to my potential."

"Since when is life about going somewhere? Where am I going? Who cares? There's no prize at the end of this road. It will be the same as any other day."

"Life, love, wisdom, most importantly, my self and my soul. These are my prizes. To change the world—change yourself."

"I can have these things at home. I'm not a couch potato. Besides, how can you change the world, if you can't even change yourself?"

"I can always go home but I'll never have this opportunity again. Correction: I'll never create this opportunity again. I never want to leave my friends and family again."

"What about now. Grandpa's been dead for two months. And, Grandma just had a heart attack on top of Alzheimer's disease. If I'm not careful, I'll be dead, too. I've been lucky, so far."

"Don't be melodramatic. I'm not going to die. I can feel it. And, Grandma understands. She was the first person I told and she said, 'You gotta do these things while you can because when you're my age you won't have any knees left.'"

"Do you think another country will make a difference?"

"It's the cumulative effect, the sum of the parts being greater than the whole, the Gestalt."

"Forget all this nonsense. It comes down to one thing: Am I willing to live with the regret for the rest of my life?"

"No."

"If you quit anything, quit your damned belly aching. Quit deceiving yourself. Quit focusing on the negatives. Quit walking on the shadowy side of the street, and your other ten-thousand bad habits. Watch the scenery. Live in the moment. You're going to have ridden around the world and not experienced anything. Look at that desert oak. That's a miraculous tree. See how the sapling grows without any branches until its roots find water. That's amazing. You'd have to be an ungrateful bastard not to admire that tree."

But, it's too late for sightseeing, I've arrived at the next source of food and water, a roadhouse 119 KM away from the last, and Australia has scrolled past almost unnoticed. My skin is flushed from the heat and wind, ghosted white from my sunscreen and speckled with gnats like a flycatcher. "You must be mad, mate," a road train truckie tells me. His ropy muscles are mostly covered in heaps of blubber and wrapped in a wrinkly brown skin that's daring melanoma with Aussie pride. Road trains are semi-trucks with four trailers and 56 wheels, hauling freight from the one end of Australia to the other smashing aside, so I'm told, 100 kangaroos a night.

"How would you know if I'm crazy? Has it occurred to you that maybe you're crazy and I'm sane?"

"Mate, you've been in the Outback too long."

I've been told I'm crazy a few times a day for five years—thousands of times. I'm beginning to suspect that I am crazy. I ponder this for some months. Am I bonkers? *"Muy Loco."* Or, is it the rest of the world that's bonkers?

In Melbourne, I meet a haggard Scotsman (generally too drunk and stoned to be coherent) who spent five years trafficking drugs in India, growing marijuana in the mountains during the spring monsoons and summer heat and then taking ten kilograms down to Goa in the cool, dry winter to sell to the European holidayers. "If I came to a police barricade, I'd slow until they lowered their bamboo poles and then I'd gun my motorcycle. When they hit you, it doesn't hurt—" he shrugs— "not much. If you go fast, the bamboo will break you. The police have bad motorcycles and no radios. They are like tramps."

I'm reminded of my Malaysian acquaintance who was imprisoned in India on charges of marijuana possession. He had lost half his body weight, suffered from malnutrition, dysentery, malaria, drug addiction and, since these medieval gulags require prisoners to provide for themselves, like the London Clink, he was forced to deal heroin, to feed himself and his cellmates. "There are more drugs in prison than outside," he said. If caught, the Scotsman was facing 12 years to life—a shortened version. If this isn't crazy, surely Logical Scotsman went AWOL. "It's not the drugs that are a problem for the police, it's the rich Westerners," was the extent of his reasoning. "Never flash any money or wear nice jewelry or clothing."

I mention my trip to him, and after he prods me for information, declares, "Mate, you're mad!"

"You're calling me crazy," I laugh, "How do you know I'm crazy?"

"Your problem is that you appear normal. You may even think you're sane. But, take it from me, I know, you're completely mad." Seeing my shocked countenance, he consoles, "Don't worry. You have to be mad. What're your options? To stay home? To live a normal life? What would happen if everyone did this? The world needs crazy people."

This concurs with my conclusion a healthy dose of angst combined with the whims of insanity is my *raison d'etre,* the sacred fire under my ass, the burning itch to get off the couch and cycle around the world. Life thrives on the mystery, the x-factor, the wild card, because one in a million, even one in a billion crazy people, or random mutations, will succeed and life will evolve beyond imagination.

A few days later, against all logic, against all hormones, for indeed it is magic, for the first time Spiritual Scott is attracted to a spiritual woman, the X-factor. It's an attraction as mysterious as spinifex grass competing for a view of Uluru in the scorching desert. (If I were spinifex, I'd shrivel to dust and blow to a faraway land to be reincarnated as a giant redwood slurping the Pacific fog.) I'm having drinks with our friend, Michelle, and she says, "Jane deserves to be loved. She's fantastic. You should fall in love with her. It would be great."

The noisy, smoky bar and all the people disappear from my awareness. My thoughts catalyze, "Jane is fantastic; she deserves to be loved. Maybe that's the reason we met—to love." The truth of this thought sends tingles through my skin. I've no desire for myself. No thoughts about survival. For a moment my mind is free of contradictions and ego-importance. Then a loud thought, like a voice in my head, booms out of the nothingness, "We are here to love." And another says, "Life is love." And the two sentences echo off the inside of my skull and I digest them word by word—words from God?

Logical is quick to analyze the event: it's interesting to note that the voice said, "We are here to love," not, "to love each other," not an exclusive, romantic love but, simply love. And it said, "Life is love," not, "The meaning of life is love," but, as if life (time, space, matter, energy) is animated if not constructed out of love, another dimension.

Then my reactive Primitive and Logical selves share a common fear, "Oh no. Am I falling in love?" Then Spiritual realizes, "No, not falling. I don't know how to qualify or quantify love. I simply feel love." My equation for love becomes reversed from judging myself by who loves me to judging myself by who I love. I think, "What I desire is to love and be loved. Jane is everything I wanted or expected in a mate." I feel as if I blink in and out of existence and realize I do love her.

This realization, to use Aussie idioms, leaves me shattered and knackered. I brave the rest of the evening and then slog back to my noisy, smoky hostel called The Coffee Palace, which is more like The Pancake Shithole. Early the next morning after restless sleep and troubled dreams absorbing this hokeypokey stuff, I awake not simply believing—implying faith—but knowing and feeling that love drives the universe and that love is the universe, the Holy Grail, and that I love everything and everyone.

I lift my spoon, affectionately referred to as my shovel, and admire the metal, the craftsmanship, the shape and the tingle of the spoon in my mouth. Very subtle, like the remnants of a dream, energy from the spoon flows into me. I'm not feeding off this energy. It's more like the ebb and flow of the tide, the circular breathing while playing a didgeridoo, a cosmic, quantum dance. "I love my spoon, or the spoon loves me," I think and laugh. "It's true. I'm one-hundred percent, certifiably insane."

Outback sunrise.
Previous photo: Riding through the edge of the Maralinga atomic bomb testing site.

34 ❋ Why cycle around the world? (Part 2)

People have asked me why I'm bicycling every day for years now. And everyday I have a different answer. I've notice that the intention behind people's questions has changed from disbelief to wonder and curiosity, still some more hopeless people ask, "Why bother?" Or, "Do you know what you could do with all that money in Thailand?"

I'm on a deserted back road in Zimbabwe—many roads are deserted because of the crashing economy and rising cost of petrol, which suits me and the wildlife. A few hundred meters ahead, a monstrous wild bull elephant, where supposedly there are no elephants, weighing about six tons and big enough for me to cycle underneath without even tickling his tummy, strolls across the road with slow, plodding footsteps. Elephants and ants are composed of the same-sized cells, and I wonder why the elephant, as if it were a six-ton pile of ants, doesn't crush the life out of itself.

The hazy, blue, silhouette, back lit by the morning sun, disappears into the forest. I reengage my pedals and sprint to the spot. I imagine ancient Africa: herds of elephants trampling grass, overturning trees, creating arterial paths through the fleshy bramble of the most impenetrable and mysterious continent, driving even lions and humans before them. I peer intently for the elephant amidst the trees. Not even a leaf rustles. My ears perk and strain for the sound of cracking branches. I hear nothing but my own panting; and, nothing moves but a trickle of sweat down my temples.

As the thrill subsides, disappointment seeps into my blood and weakens my muscles and mind. All the years of preparation, all the years of cycling, all the thousands of dollars, and one of the highlights of Africa is a dim view for scant seconds. The nagging thought, "Why bother coming to Africa?" saps my enjoyment, dissolves the memory before it's firmly fixed. Why bother cycling around the world if all the experiences are going to be lost in time like waves against the seashore? Perhaps, I should have retired on a beach in Thailand.

I'm disappointed, still those few seconds were more magical than an entire day on a guided safari with over-wound tourists with cameras, guidebooks and checklists. When they saw the first elephant, they *oohed* and *aahed*, cameras clicked and whirred, but soon we were off to hunt another animal. I never heard the elephant snuffle or even birds singing because of all the talking. I was further blinded from my enjoyment when a Dutch woman said, "Even giraffes run away from the American." As we passed many animals, the tourists were unimpressed unless they could make a new mark on their checklists. It's a shame when elephants become as ordinary as cows in India, and it would have to wear a tutu and perform circus tricks to be noticed. I believe the key to the mystery of life is locked in the flower that is trampled in the rush to go somewhere new and novel, or in a candle snuffed in quest of the bigger and better huff and puff of life. There's a whole universe ready to explore in everyone's backyard. So why bother going to Africa in quest of elephants, especially when there's a minimum of 1000 times more photos of elephants on the Internet than elephants in Africa? Why go anywhere or do anything? Why: a profound question in life, a question that I suspect many people don't ask until it's too late—a deathbed conversion from what their life was to what it could've been.

I contemplate this as I cycle through the dusty African wilds. Perhaps, a partial answer is because the elephant's true nature isn't the one I saw as a child in the zoo with dull eyes and ragged ears, trapped behind a concrete trench, standing in a pool of piss and a pile of dung, neurotic with nowhere to hide. In a zoo, the elephant ends at the fence and its outstretched trunk snuffling for peanuts. However, in Africa, the elephant isn't contained between the tusks and tail. It's the leaves that the impala are too short too eat, and the leaves the giraffes are too tall to eat; it's the troop of baboon sentinels; it's skin is the pattern of dappled African sunlight filtering through the multi-colored leaves; it's the elephant dung nourishing the sandy soil and maggots, which mature into the flies that swarm me, and the song of birds that eat them; it's the dust in my eyes from its passing; the thrill of placing my barefoot in its sandy spoor; most of all, the elephant is the reflection of myself in his eyes as he ruminates on whether to trample me, embrace me or ignore me.

Just being in Africa for six months—I realize this is the reason why I bother—Africa has shaped me. I can feel the dark, ancient, beat of evolution drum in my veins—it's exulting. In Africa, there's no end to the elephant and beginning to me. We share the same quest for food. We compete for the same space and water. We're both hunted by the same men and burned by the same sun (even elephants can turn pink and freckly). I've even begun to think like an African. I see a cool coke as a great luxury I can't afford and a diet drink as a waste of money and resources. I'm happy as long as my bed is safe and food is clean. I rest when the sun sets and rise when the sun rises, and if the mood strikes, why not drop my bike and pick up some bongos? As I cycle through the villages, I see houses sculpted out of mud and sticks and decorated with colorful designs. I think, perhaps, I could live there and start a macadamia farm. I wonder how many wives I could afford, and if I would have an army of children to tend the fields while I chat with the elders about ancient magics.

Often I joked with locals, pointing to my freckles, "Ten more years and I'll be the same color as you." Maybe not in my lifetime, but in several hundred lifetimes Africa would mold my descendants. Life evolves forwards, backwards and sideways filling every niche (the bacteria is still the most successful organism on Earth). Conceivably in a million generations, my descendants could have necks like giraffes or noses like elephants or maybe they'd turn back into hairy apes—I do seem to be getting more hairy throughout the years.

I also realize that my experiences aren't lost in time, they will always exist within me; and that the world isn't just full of logic and material things, but that somehow meeting the elephant, even for a few seconds, was full of an emotional energy, call it magic, ebbing and flowing back and forth like my spoon in Australia, and that we imparted a piece of our essence upon the other, like a gift, and we are both indescribably more than we ever were.

A shaky photo of a bull elephant crossing the road in Mikumi National Park, Tanzania.

35 ⊛ Are you on a spiritual journey?

Debbie and I cycled from Mumbai to Bangalore mainly to get a new rear cog. In Goa, some Indians were fiddling with my bicycle gears—it appears, being foreigners, we fall outside Indian taboos against groping—and when I cranked the pedals mightily up a steep hill, the chain caught and snapped my easiest gear. We're weary of sticky-fingered India and heading towards Nepal. We just boarded the train to Delhi (2100 kilometers, 41 hours).

I left our bicycles unlocked and unencumbered on the other end of the platform, leaning against 100 cubes wrapped in burlap and twine next to the desperadoes in general class. All the train platforms, warehouses and vast storage yards are stacked full with crates. I paid two men to wrap our bicycles in brown paper and twine—it's the law—but they only wrapped the cross bar, seat and rack. I was required—or so I was led to believe—to pay another two porters to walk our bikes to the end of the platform, and I paid yet another man to watch the bikes. I thought he was a porter, but he just grunted as he walked away with my money. I'm attempting to be mindful and not worry about my bike, but my new Buddhist philosophy, inspired by Asia, is ruled by years of Western cultural conditioning, emphasizing being logical, in control and wary of the unknown. Meanwhile, Debbie walked up and down the length of the train, about 800 meters, several times searching for our coach. No one, not even the station manager, seemed to know or had desire to inform her that the coach numbers aren't pasted onto the train until one hour prior departure—the Indians are masters of inefficiency.

The trains are pre-World War II relics leftover from the British Raj and aren't constructed with much more elegance than a sardine can padded in vinyl. I've stowed our panniers and tents underneath the seat and shackled them with my bicycle lock, two pounds of steel that everyday I begrudge carrying. I have the top bunk of three, which is barely big enough for me. I use my handlebar bag full of valuables as a pillow and stare out the window. Colors swirl past: the maroon togas of the Buddhist monks, the saffron robes of the Hindi sadhus, pastel colored shirts and trousers of modern businessmen, blue jeans of the affluent youth, the police in desert-colored khakis, the navy blue of the vendors, the dust and sweat stained dungarees of the porters, and the ever-present rainbow hues and peacock patterns of women's saris.

The air is thick with fragrant curry. Only now am I thankful for the Hindu's vegetarian and over-spiced menu. The Indians say Westerners smell horrible, like moldy cheese. The train lurches forward through the slums of Bangalore, parting the smoke of burning garbage and cooking fires, past thousands of piles of human waste, and hundreds of Indians using the track as the path of least resistance. All the doors and windows are open, and when the train enters the country, a fresh, gusty wind scours the train and passengers.

Day two: the train ride has become a feat of endurance and patience. I'm suffering from claustrophobia, but fairing much better than some bus trips where I had minus eight centimeters of leg room, couldn't move, couldn't sleep, and spent the night chanting, "I'll be okay. Everything's fine. Don't think about it." Now I chant, "I promise I won't complain about bicycling anymore." My upper bunk provides a retreat from the madness in the stations; and while we're moving, I prefer to ride outside on the running board of the train, occasionally ducking inside to avoid signposts and brick walls.

The train's full of beggars and vendors that stowaway for several ports then hop on the last train home. For the first day, the piercing cry of the vendors made my skin prickle, but now I drool when I hear the cry—which has ruined the voices of some men—for *chai* or *samosa*. The handicapped ride free and make a business out of begging for money in the names of god, panhandling pity or simply annoying passengers. It's like a macabre parade: A man without a hand just passed, followed by a man hobbling on a bloody (probably make-up), dirty, bandaged stump. Various cripples scoot past either dragging their legs behind them or balancing their gimp legs atop their hands in a variation of the duck walk. Now, three blind men pass, one with no eyeballs and a bicycle bell attached to his cane. The *hijras*, a caste of eunuchs, a third gender, which also includes transvestites, transsexuals and hermaphrodites, threaten passengers for money with the sight of their mangled genitals or their touch (one gropes my inner thigh). They're considered bad luck say my cabin mates, who risk their curses; yet, others who want to pay for their blessings say they bring good luck. And, I see one man forcing a sloth bear, an endangered species, to dance on the train platform for coins. It's the boy with the sad eyes and beautiful, heart-wrenching song that wins Debbie's money. I think most are honest beggars, but I've heard stories of crippled people that wipe the floor clean for tips and rifle through your packs, then miraculously find their feet and run away. I've caught a few eyeing my panniers until they see me watching. The police and train personnel do nothing. So, Debbie and I alternate guarding our luggage. In contrast to the lame beggars on the train, the handicapped people in the villages I've cycled through are self-sufficient and amazingly happy, much more than most Americans who still have their feet, eyes and a full stomach.

Day three: I hang outside the train, despite the spittle and garbage flying out the window. The wind frazzles my hair, and feeling as if I'm bicycling down an endless mountain and flying over chasms, I marvel at being able to risk my life. One slip and I'd be gone; maybe one less person, like me, doesn't make a difference in India. The train passes through a small village, with boney women beating clothes on the riverbank, men setting fish traps, and several gnarly, grey-haired sadhus standing spiritual watch. Sadhus are holy men (considered dead unto themselves) who've renounced the world in pursuit of enlightenment and liberation from the Wheel of Life, which seems sad and antithetical to being alive. Sadhus are infamous for their ascetic practices intended to purify (or deny) the body in favor of the soul, many become grossly deformed: standing for years, even while sleeping; or not sleeping for years; flogging their flesh raw; crawling instead of walking; holding one limb in the air day and night; and some sadhus of mythical status apparently never ate or drank; but, generally, it seems to me, their path to enlightenment consists of begging, never bathing and imbibing a variety of drugs to awaken their god-consciousness—seemingly in pursuit of a life of appeasing their self-importance or unimportance, not unlike Poor Scott.

The sadhus, clad in saffron and ochre, seem to awaken from their spiritual world and wave to me. I've attracted the attention of many sadhus. Perhaps, because I'm clad in a saffron-colored bicycle jersey (saffron is the color of renunciation). Or, perhaps they can see that I, too, am a lost and wandering soul seeking enlightenment. I've been told that gurus can see the auras of others and that enlightened souls shine the brightest. Supposedly, the aura of a person with a clear purpose and intent looks like a Christmas tree with rings of colored lights and sparkles. (I suspect mine looks more like the unkempt shrub in my parent's yard.) In India, people often ask if I'm on a spiritual journey or vision quest, some have even called me the Cycling Sadhu.

Sadhus remind me of peacocks. In the Thar Desert, 31 peacocks, sounding like kazoos, passed through our camp early one morning. I was surprised that they could find enough sustenance in the barren, dusty land to support their extravagant plumage. Likewise, among India's crowded, deformed cities, where simply surviving consumes the entire day, occasionally a spiritually extravagant sadhu strolls past. Is India's spirituality a byproduct of witnessing death and decay as part of daily life?

The reason I consider this a spiritual journey—a *bikeabout*—rather than a simple adventure is because I want to live the best life I can, and to me that meant traveling the world to answer the fundamental questions of philosophy: What's the meaning of life? Is there a God? What's the nature of the universe? Where did it all come from? Who am I? Do I have a soul? Do I have free will? How do I know what I know? What is good and evil? What's my moral and ethical duty? How can I find peace, love and happiness? What happens when I die?

I've been told by one of my teachers (anybody can be a teacher) that stopping self-conflict is the first step to becoming a beginner; and, I thought if I answered these questions that I would be able to flow with reality instead of struggling blindly upstream seeking a fairy tale dream. According to Hindu tradition, I've been following the path of knowledge, one of many paths to enlightenment.

Debbie often says that I think too much, ask too many questions and make myself unhappy; however, I think the plethora of questions people everywhere have asked me proves that everyone, to some degree, is a philosopher, because our world constantly

presents us with a multitude of challenges and experiences, and the mind instinctually sorts through this mass of information, questioning and creating patterns, some sense of life, so that we may survive if not thrive. Our philosophy is our interpretation of the world, our meaning of life, our survival strategy, and the more accurate our philosophy, the more fulfilling our lives.

Unfortunately, I recently learned that Hindus consider the path of knowledge the *least* effective and efficient. It's like reading a book about cycling around the world and never riding a bike, or spending years writing a book about traveling and never leaving the house. I've been told, albeit after I spent over a decade of my life, that philosophizing (intellectualizing) almost always leads to more confusion, because most likely you're adding more layers of cultural garbage atop the simple truths of reality.

However, I've surprised myself by discovering answers to questions I thought unanswerable; and, as I grow my answers evolve. For example, I adopted my parents meaning of life, which meant to suffer, be good and go to heaven, then I thought life was meaningless, then I thought it was to be a happy hedonist, then it was to discover faith in myself, then find atonement with God, and eventually I will realize that, effectively, the meaning of life is whatever I create it to be, and that at any moment, if I had enough skill, I can create a new meaning. I always seem to be seeking new meaning to my life (learning), which leads to endless questions. Conceivably life is the paradox of always seeking to know the unknown.

I haven't found any ultimate solutions yet, but every set of answers to life's great questions has brought me to a new level of awareness. However, when I told this theory to a guru, he knocked me off my steel horse by saying: "Just because you have a realization, doesn't mean you're getting promoted. It doesn't make you more or less than anyone else. You believe the goal of self-improvement is to fix yourself. The reality is you're not broken. The point of self-improvement is to learn how to become a better and more joyful creator."

Suddenly, disturbing my philosophizing, Debbie's windblown hair tickles my face as she leans out the door. "Are you going to come inside the train? You've been out here for hours. I was beginning to think you got scraped off the side."

Watching my bicycle disappear into the Indian bureaucracy. **Opposite:** New Delhi.
Previous: Saddhu.

Part III:
Oneness

[A human being] experiences himself, his thoughts and feelings, as something separated from the rest [the universe] — a kind of optical delusion of his consciousness. This delusion is a kind of prison for us, restricting us to our personal desires and to affection for a few persons nearest us. Our task must be to free ourselves from this [self-imposed] prison by widening our circles of compassion to embrace all living creatures and the whole of nature in its beauty.

~ Albert Einstein

36

What gods do you worship?

I'm atop the roof of my hostel in Istanbul, Turkey, playing chess with one of the kindest people I've met, an Iranian Muslim. We're sharing tidbits of our life, such as our religions. Moments ago, a thunderstorm washed the smog out of the atmosphere. Behind me, a double rainbow spans the surreal orange sky. Perfectly centered below is a twinkling lighthouse, and ferries shuttling to and fro across the Bosphorus Straight, from Europe to Asia. In front of me, the silhouette of Istanbul's most famous monument, the Blue Mosque, hides the setting sun. Above the dome of the mosque, hangs a single neon-red cloud like a halo, and hundreds of circling seagulls, their bellies illuminated by the setting sun as they soar between the minarets.

As I near the Far East, one question has become increasingly common: "Do you believe in God?" Sometimes the question is phrased as: "What is your religion?" Or, as an Indian boy innocently asked me: "What gods do you worship?" I explain to my friend that I was raised under a Christian God, but I found more problems than solutions in the Bible, such as the war in heaven, which resulted in God casting the troublemakers down to Earth to tempt and torment earthlings, so I declared myself an atheist. However, my spirit grew restless with the meaningless, mechanical life of an atheist, so I went on a quest bicycling across America in search of answers. I'm reminded of a stormy day in Kentucky.

It had been raining on and off everyday for 28 days; yesterday, I got caught in a torrential thunderstorm and was fortunate to be near a motel. This morning it's still pouring. According to the Weather Channel, the only cloud in the whole country happens to be right above me. My eyes are bleary from watching too much television; my head is foggy from too much sleep; I've eaten myself sick; a soiled towel is crumpled in the corner; I've showered, shaved, and satisfied all my physical desires. I wonder, "What do I do now? Is this all there is to life?" I've heard free time called the curse of my generation.

After contemplating my options, I have an idea, "If the Buddha can become enlightened starving himself underneath a tree, why can't I become enlightened over-indulging myself in a hotel room?"

I refill my Styrofoam coffee cups in the motel office, turn off the brainwashing machine, wedge the door open with my cleats, so a fresh, misty breeze keeps me from becoming too comfortable and begin my thought experiment:

I theorize that if God exists, and I could deduce the nature of God, I would discover how the universe works, and find the meaning of my life and happiness, and if I get run over by a Kentucky coal truck it's not, literally, the end of the world. What began my spiritual quest was the realization that underlying all the religions and myths were remarkable similarities; I discovered coincidence upon coincidence, until I realized that it was more like serendipity pointing to the true nature of reality. However, after several years of studious examination, I couldn't find any conclusive answers; so, I concluded it wasn't the simple fact of God that I wanted to confirm, but a real heartfelt experience.

I speculate that whether I am the product of billions of years of evolution or God's creation, the answer to life must be ingrained in my body, mind and soul, as a fundamental truth, the common denominator between all the different religions. I call it the General Theory of Spirituality, and I'm convinced I can unlock the answer.

As a starting point, I write in my notebook, "If God existed what would He be like?"

Assuming God exists, either I'm not hearing Him or He can't or won't communicate. Does God choose not to answer? Is He a personal God, meaning a separate entity that exists in a different dimension, called Heaven? Is God the universe? Or a creative fundamental force of nature like gravity? If God is omniscient and can see the future until the death of the universe, if He knows every step I will make, do I have free will to choose my path? Can God stop the planets in their tracks anymore than I can stop the blood in my veins? If God is omnipotent, why didn't He create a more loving, faithful Scott? Why not skip this world of suffering and create a bunch of perfect souls in heaven? Though if God is immutable, what difference would a few quintillion souls worshipping Him make? Is God omnipresent? If God exists, He must encompass the entire universe and beyond. He must be the everything and nothing of the universe. "Aha!" I find this thought interesting enough to break me out of my dogmatic Christian loop, remove my *Bible* goggles and seek a new answer.

When I was a child, I remember asking, "How big is the universe?"

"The universe goes on forever," my uncle told me.

"You mean it never stops?"

"What, do you think there's a brick wall at the end of the universe?"

That made me think, "If there's a wall, wouldn't there be something on the other side? That means it wouldn't be the end of the universe. What if the wall was really thick, so thick there wasn't another side?" Even then, I made myself dizzy philosophizing.

It still intrigues me. The universe has been shown to contain hundreds of galaxies in a pinprick of the sky and there are probably billions beyond those. To get an idea of the magnitude of God, I lean back in my chair, close my eyes, visualizing myself sitting in my motel room. I zoom out to visualize the hotel, followed by Irvine, Kentucky, the Appalachians, my entire ride from DC, the Earth and its oceans. I imagine airplanes tracing an arc in the sky, perhaps five miles high, at the outer limit of life, and somewhere beneath me, perhaps another five miles, is the inner limit of life, a layer not even paper thin, relative to a basketball. Such a small percentage of the solar system reserved for humanity. If the sun was a little closer or father away, life on Earth would be disintegrated in fire or frozen in ice. If the Earth was the wrong size or force of gravity was a fraction bigger or smaller, life would be crushed out of existence or fly apart. Perhaps, it takes the whole solar system and precisely balanced forces of nature to support Earth's fragile skin, and conceivably it takes a galaxy to support our solar system and a universe to support our galaxy.

I imagine the planets, solar system, galaxies, trillions of galaxies all around me. I'm reminded of an illustration of the Hindu god, Vishnu, the Preserver, floating in a void with a lotus flower growing out of his navel. Born from the lotus was Brahma, the Creator, and when he opened his eyes the universe was born, and when he closed his eyes the universe was destroyed. In this illustration there were dozens of Vishnus floating in the void, with lotus flowers, and Brahmas being born and dying. Perhaps, there are as many universes as there are drops in the ocean; and, maybe, there are as many oceans as grains of sand on the beach.

My mind tries to encompass all of space. It's bigger than that, I think. No, bigger. Bigger yet. Then inevitably, no matter how many times I try, the universes looks like a handful of sand being washed by an ocean surf of nothingness, and my vision folds back on itself, like a colossal four-dimensional möbius strip. I end where I started, in the motel room with an aching body and a nagging mind.

I try a different approach. I imagine the beginning and end of time. Common sense seems to dictate a beginning, middle and end to all things. Science's Big Bang theory and religion's numerous creation myths, like Genesis, confirm that once the universe and time never existed. Hindus believe that eventually Shiva, the Destroyer, will recycle everything, including Vishnu, Brahma and himself. Shiva fascinates me. Unlike Western religions which view the devil as running amok ruining God's plan, Hindus view death and destruction as a vital force, not only does it create the space and fertilize new life, when you die you're given the chance to be reborn on a higher spiritual plane. I find it a pleasant thought to reincarnate over and over until I get it right and my spirit returns to Brahman to live blissfully ever after in oneness.

Hypothetically, if life is a coincidence of random events, assuming we're dealing with infinite amounts of time, space and matter, plus the fact I'm here to talk about it, and you're hear to read about it, life is not that much of a coincidence—it's an absolute certainty!

One thing boggles my mind: instead of matter and energy, which are really the same thing, there could just as easily have been no-thing. I play the Big Bang backwards in my mind until it winks out of existence and there is not even nothing, the endless, immutable perfection of a void before time, but my dualistic mind thinks that by the very fact that there is nothing creates the potential for it's opposite—something—and the greater the nothingness the more the potential for somethingness. And then through some quirk in time-space, like a simple idea, something was born. Then something realized there was a possibility of something more.... And with that thought, I have a vision of the universe after a quantum hiccup of self-realization exploding into a Big Bang of being, as if I looked up at the storm outside and saw rainbow drops pouring out of the black sky.

From a thought, the body of God, the universe, was born, and with it the endless, ever-changing possibilities of something combined with nothing.

The thunderstorm breathes out a gust of wind and rain, blowing my room door open; I realize, simultaneously, the storm breathes in the humidity of the atmosphere and ingests the energy of the sun, channeling these elements through itself like a living being. Isn't everything the children God? I'm not the food I eat, the water I drink, the air I breathe or the fire of my loins, or even the thoughts I think; I'm more than my elements; a million times more concentrated than the spring storm—I am an incarnation of the consciousness that creates life—I am both a part of God and I am God.

My vision swims and I swivel in my chair to regain balance. Whoa, maybe I drank too much coffee.

⊙　✳　✲

Many years later, here I'm in Turkey still intellectualizing that experience. Despite trying to fit God into a box—my life is full of paradoxes—I've come to believe God to be an ever changing, ever evolving force. Yahweh told Moses, "I am the becoming of that which I am becoming." And, I believe we're created in God's image, mirroring God's evolution, essentially asking the questions: "What am I?" and, "What am I not?" meaning, "What could I be?" How can God not evolve when my soul is born like a candle in the heavens, as my candle burns brighter, doesn't it illuminate the glory of God evermore? Hindus essentially believe in one god, Brahman. The other 330 million Hindu gods are manifestations of different aspects of Brahman. Hindus also believe people are incarnations of Brahman, which makes another 6.8 billion gods. If we're each unique manifestations of Brahman, each describing a fraction of the infinite, like a word in a dictionary, then together humanity is a great novel written by the universe—the Book of Life.

I lose my chess game by intellectualizing my past rather than focusing on creating a new future. I thank my friend for teaching me to play. He returns the compliment and says it's unfortunate that I can't visit his home in Iran. (I probably wouldn't be granted a visa due to the tension between our two countries.) Later, I dance with a gorgeous Australian lass for half the night, sweat commingling, another simple, heartfelt experience that defies rational explanation.

Istanbul's Blue Mosque. Also see the cover, lower left-hand corner. **Previous:** Hindu temple.

37   What did you learn?

The wet "upfront" as opposed to Australia's arid Outback has been a shock to my system. I'm cycling down a mushy gravel trail through turbulent winds and frigid pelting rain. On either side, rows of grape vines scroll past; in the distance, paddocks on the rolling hills are an unearthly purple from a flower called Patterson's Curse, one of Australia's many curses, like rabbits, cats and European settlers. Beneath my wheels a billion legs of a million millipedes crackle and snap. We're in the Clare Valley, a world-famous wine region, so read the tourist pamphlets. I've consumed my share of wine (I get about 20 KM to the liter). I ask several winemakers how Australian wine compares to French and Californian wine? Of course, they all say, "Australian wine is the best in the world."

I've been traveling with Matt, an Aussie bloke from Melbourne that I met in Kathmandu. Matt's bicycled overland from Scotland excepting the ocean. So, when Matt saw the first sign that read "Melbourne" he said, "It really does exist," and swaggered over to the sign and gave it a lippy kiss. I fumbled for a photograph as the startled expressions of passing motorists distracted me.

Afterwards, I say, "Okay, my turn."

Matt laughed, "Well, yeah, mate, pucker up."

"I meant for a photograph."

It's been a pleasure touring Oz with Matt. He's embodies the Australian virtues of being ruggedly handsome, open-minded, good-humored and seemingly impervious to tribulations. He's very proud of his country and its hospitality; he's given me a good tour, for instance, he spent days looking for a koala bear and eventually spotted one of the slothful creatures napping in a tree. The koala bear woke, stared at me for a few seconds then went back to sleep. It was very exciting.

We arrive at the cellar door of the Sevenhills Winery; we're riding from vineyard to vineyard to coax ourselves along. We enter a musty, dark, sour-smelling warehouse filled with 500-gallon barrels of fermenting wine that appear as if they came with the first boatload of prisoners. We pass through a sliding door into a museum and wine tasting room. It's a small, polished-wood room with a log fire in the corner, a fat, surly cat curled on a bench, rows of wine bottles along the back wall, and I'm shocked by the sommelier, the most beautiful and charming Australian women I've seen, not that I've seen many women wandering around the Outback; 100 meters off the Stuart Highway, I'd be dead for years before anyone would find my body. Once I lost my own tent.

I love to ring my bell every time a beautiful woman passes and watch them smile; and, I'm so excited to see women again that, after a few weeks in South Australia, I've inadvertently trained Matt to salivate like one of Pavlov's dogs. Sometimes I ring my bell just to watch Matt whip his head from side to side scanning the streets for pretty women.

This winery was founded by Jesuits, their motto is: "If God didn't want us to drink wine, He wouldn't have invented it," which, I think, applies to everything.

After a few tastes of "Heaven on Earth", working our way down the list, from simple to complex flavors, from tipsy to knock-you-off-your-bicycle, we reach the fortified wines, formerly known as port wines and sometimes called dessert wines. The wine business is doubly confusing. Due to a World Trade Organization Agreement wines are being relabeled. For instance, a wine can't be called *champagne* unless it comes from Champagne, France, otherwise it's called a sparkling wine. However, I think the real confusion comes from highfalutin wine aficionados that insist wine drinking isn't just a matter of taste.

"What do you think of the tawny?" asks the sommelier.

"It tastes like raisins."

"All the Americans say that."

I'm still haunted by the perception of America as the Goliath, and it seems human nature to throw stones at giants. I hope to salvage my country's dignity with a humorous twist on the obvious question, "Is this wine vitamin fortified?"

She laughs politely. "No, it's fortified with extra spirits."

"What kind of spirits?"

"Ethanol, distilled from byproducts, such as grape skins, and added back into the wine as a preservative. Sailors discovered that it stopped the fermentation process by killing the yeast and that fortified wine tasted better after long trips. And, being a Catholic-owned winery, we fortify it with a few other spirits, too."

We all chuckle politely and I ask, "Where do you get the spirits?"

"We buy them."

"Isn't that just like the Catholics—" I guffaw— "you buy spirits." The curves in her face straighten and I feel like an idiot. "Like confessional... forgiveness of sins... mumble, mumble...." I avert my eyes from her unforgiving stare and cast about the room. "Nice cat."

I buy a bottle of tawny as penance. Matt consoles me, "Don't worry, mate. Did you see the size of the rock on her finger? Somebody already got to her." We venture into the blustery weather to Stephen John Wines, a 'high-profile boutique winery,' where Stephen himself serves us. I'm confused with all the new naming conventions and information spinning around in my head: *To cork or not to cork?* This is one of the consequences of getting older, one must relearn the same subject per se the whims of science and fashion. (For that matter, traveling is like relearning who you are, sifting the facts of life out of the cultural garbage heap.) Currently, wines can be named after the region the grapes are grown, the chateau that produced the wine, the barrel the wine came out of, even, the tax and duty numbers. Apparently, whether one prefers a wine corked, screwed or in a box is only a measure of snobbishness or tradition, not the quality. I ask a basic question to get my bearings, "What kind of grape is the merlot made from?"

"The merlot," his accent, a silly mixture of English posh and Australian drawl, makes it difficult for me to determine his inflection.

"Right, the merlot wine. What kind of grape is that?"

"The merlot!"

A bit frustrated I backtrack to familiar ground, "The pinot noir wine is made from the pinot noir grape, correct?" He nods. "The shiraz wine is made from the shiraz grape." He nods again. I've sunk myself and know what's about to happen, "And, the merlot wine is made out of—"

"—The merlot grape."

I feel about as tall as a fly on a kangaroo dunghill. I've just contributed to the myth of the stupid American. People love to tell me stories about the stupid Americans they've met: "So this American says: What happens if the windmills use all the wind?" or, "Where does Australia get its koala bears?" or, "Where's Australia's North Pole?" or, "Is Australia part of the European Union?" Apparently, Americans easily confuse Australia with Austria.

I often think of my trip as earning my master's degree in life. I've been learning a lot in Australia, like horse racing. I bet two to win and two to place on the favorite of the Melbourne Cup. My horse held the lead for most of the race. I thought, "This is so easy. Why doesn't everyone do this? C'mon on Frightening. C'mon." Then 100 meters from the finish, Frightening choked and millions of dollars changed hands. I've also had a two-hour lesson on the didgeridoo from Herman the German, some coaching on the rules of rugby and cricket, and I met one man walking through the forest who showed me many varieties of flowers. He was a wise man. "Some lessons you learn in an instant; some lessons take a lifetime; some you learn while traveling; and some lessons you only learn when you go home," he said prophetically.

Many people ask me, as if there's a secret to life: "What did you learn?" And, I've asked hundreds of people all over the world the same question, and the consensus seems to be that Earth is a soul school with one droll lesson after another, and if one receives high marks, they can graduate to their version of nirvana. For at least 12 years, possibly my whole life, I've thought if I can find the meaning of life, I can live happily ever after here and now—I didn't plan on waiting until I was dead to find heaven, but what if there's no meaning to life?

Once I asked myself the reverse question: "What is a meaningless life?"

Suffering seemed meaningless to me for a long time. The most commonly bizarre question people ask me is: "Doesn't your ass get sore?" meaning, "Why do you endure so much pain because I never would?"

But how boring would life be if we knew everything and had every comfort we ever desired? As Victor Frankl, a psychologist and survivor of the Nazi concentration camps suggested, there is meaning in suffering. Although, suffering implies being a victim with no influence upon the world, perhaps it's more accurate to refer to suffering as affliction, discomfort or *dukkha*, the Buddha's first Noble Truth. I can imagine Buddha explaining his philosophy to his disciples, "You know, I was sitting under a tree one day, and I realized—shit happens."

Now that I've survived unscathed I have many fond memories of suffering. As Dennis said, "It's funny now." He referred to these moments as *menudoes* after purchasing a can of *menudo* (like minestrone but with beef tripe) that was so old the label was faded blue and the can rusted. That was the first time Montezuma gave us a swift kick in the guts. Other *menudoes* include: Dennis pitching his tent in our hotel room because there were more mosquitoes and creepy crawlies inside than out; camping in a swamp during a storm, a tree falling beside our tents, nearly crushing us; awaking in ten centimeters of water, floating on our air mattresses like rafts; being eaten alive by a swarm of fire ants; crawling into bed with a scorpion; getting caught in a riptide, nearly drowning and bumping into a shark while surfing in El Salvador; being so exhausted, that I fell asleep three meters away from the road and didn't wake until the next morning; rotating in the shade of a saguaro cactus like a sundial; making a rain suit out of plastic bags and duct tape to survive the icy rain and wind; being stoned out of a village in India by some children; waiting for a bus in Nepal alongside a corpse (still wondering if that counts as baggage or if the relatives had to buy an extra ticket)....

Sometimes I wish I could bottle and sell my *menudoes,* like a happy pill: jamming my chainring into my calf and telling the Mexican children that I was bitten by a shark; my salmonella sandwich, a guaranteed weight loss program and reason to stop and admire the scenery (from behind a bush); the burning pain of cycling up a mountain, and the exhilarating descent; being so hungry and thirsty that rice tastes like ambrosia and water seems like nectar; camping less than 100 meters away from a plantation that was burned by the farmers during the middle of the night, and listening to their eerie Hindi music while watching a firestorm sweep through the banana trees like an orange tornado; over-exerting myself chasing some fishmonger bicyclists, and racing through a small village, being cheered by a hundred people as if it was the Tour de Tanzania; being startled awake by the haunting rhythm of African drums; hearing the gut-wrenching caterwauls of two women groveling, sand running through their hands like an hourglass, as they mourned their relative; sliding through gravel, around a curve and nearly off a cliff, and grateful for a simple sunset; being heartbroken, and spending a morning giving coins to every homeless person, who didn't and may never have anyone....

Moments like these made me feel alive. Perhaps suffering is a small taste of the possibility of success. Certainly, an absence of pain does not make a meaningful and happy life.

Once I made a potentially major *menudo:* In Nepal, I had to cross a river. There was no bridge, only a shriveled Nepalese man in a dugout canoe offering to ferry Debbie and me across for a few pennies, but there wasn't enough room. The man offered to take our gear across the river and come back for us; however, it felt foolish to let my bicycle or Debbie get on one side of the river with me on the other, besides I've always wanted to swim across a river. So, I told my guide, "Ask him if there are any crocodiles in this section of the river." It's running fast, clear and deep; crocodiles prefer calm and muddy waters. After consultation, my guide and ferryman agree there were no crocodiles. So, I swam across, not letting the boat get away from me.

One of my teachers said that you can only truly make one mistake in life. Had I let the ferryman get across the river and steal my bike that would have been an error in judgment or an unfortunate circumstance—live and learn to laugh, so to speak; however, if I had been eaten by a crocodile, that would have been a mistake—no one lives to regret true mistakes. Mistakes are matter of perspective. From one side, you've lost something expected; from another side, you've gained something unexpected. Some mistakes have led to the world's greatest inventions, like rubber and ice cream cones. And conceivably, one can turn making mistakes into an art form, meaning consciously taking actions that result in unforeseen consequences creating things never imagined.

I have to admit that I'm ashamed of how often the fear of making a mistake and suffering has kept me on my cushy couch, assured of a perfect, mistake-free life, which I'm sure is a recipe for dying of boredom.

I suspect that the answer to the meaning of life is actually in the question. Simply the act of questioning —what does this mean?—and risking an answer. In other words, curiosity is a reason for living, and that life is not meant to be one lesson after another, but discovering one mystery after another.

The word "culture" is derived from the Latin word *cultura,* meaning *to cultivate.* For example, wine is cultivated from a culture of yeast (fungus), which breeds off the surrounding material (sugars), until either there's nothing left to eat, or it dies in it's own excrement (alcohol).

Perhaps human culture is like a fermentation process, the artificial culture sometimes beneficial, sometimes detrimental; and, as I travel around the world, I pick and choose what I want to assimilate, because unlike grapes, people can choose whether to become wine or vinegar. And, even if we reach enlightenment, most likely, we'll still be afflicted with illness, suffer and die like the Buddha; so why not enjoy it while it lasts?

Meanwhile, Stephen's probably saying, "So, this American walks into a winery and says to the winemaker—"

Southern Indian Family living and working alongside the road carving tombstones for people who make their one true mistake. Notice the variety of reactions to me.

What was your favorite?

I spend two days climbing a mountain in Nepal to glimpse the Himalayas and Mount Everest over 500 KM away but saw nothing but clouds. On my second attempt, I cycle to the top of a mountain outside Kathmandu and climb a lookout tower. I see 2000-3000 meter mountains disappearing into a band of clouds along the horizon. "They don't look very big to me," I say disappointed.

"No. There," a man points, "above the clouds." Above the horizon of mountains and clouds, a powder blue pyramid of ice emerges, like a half-moon rising, a rooster tail of vapor curling off its peak. It's so gigantic it defies my perception of space. I'm reminded of the story of Kenge the pygmy. When Kenge left the African jungle for the first time and saw animals grazing in the distance, he asked, "What insects are those?" And when he was told they were buffalo he laughed and said, "Don't tell me such stupid lies."

Thamel, the Kathmandu tourist area, is a bubble of modern civilization unmatched since Bangalore. Like most cities, I'm surrounded by a ring of poverty, followed by a ring of industry which blurs into a dead zone, and surrounded by a giant outer ring of over-farmed and overgrazed lands, but in the "civilized" center with my water buffalo dumplings, hot shower (it took three showers to get the dirt off) and whisky, it's easy and preferable to forget about the rest of the world; at least, until I recover my strength.

Fifty years ago, Nepal's borders were closed to foreigners. When the first mountain climbers entered the country, they spent months locating specific mountains, like Annapurna, because few maps or roads existed. Imagine losing mountains 7–8 kilometers tall. Now, Kathmandu is a climbing and hiking mecca with maps and photos of the Himalayas around every corner.

Tomorrow, I leave on an expedition to Lhasa, Tibet (claimed by China) with a side trip to Mt. Everest Base Camp. Even the old-salts say this "is no vacation" with freezing temperatures, scarce food, water and oxygen. The slopes should be full of climbers acclimatizing themselves for an attempt to summit Everest in the next few weeks. It's the 50th anniversary since the first summit by world-famous New Zealander, Edmund Hillary, and the Sherpa, Norgay Tenzing. Tenzing's grandson is attempting to summit the mountain this year. Most climbers drive or fly to Base Camp and then climb 3668 meters to the summit at 8848 meters. I intend to cycle from sea level to Base Camp at 5180 meters; in other words, I will climb 1512 meters more than almost every mountain climber. (Actually, I began -0.25 meters below sea level, because while disembarking the ferry in Mumbai, being shoved by 200 impatient and unhelpful Indians, I dropped my bike overboard, and if the boat hadn't swung ashore and pushed my bike onto the pier, it would be on the bottom of the ocean.)

From Kathmandu, it takes eight days to summit the World's Longest Hill and four more days to approach Base Camp. By three in the afternoon, katabatic winds fall down the flanks of Everest and funnel through the valley at 35 KPH average (according to Edwin's gadgets) with gusts almost double that. The wind steals every calorie of energy my overtaxed body can produce.

Tibet, the Roof of the World, is a high-altitude desert similar to the Bolivian Altiplano but more harsh. The Sahara desert is three times as humid. Here, nothing grows but moss and tufts of grass. The blood vessels have burst in the faces of the locals and color their cheeks rosy and bruised-purple. The children's hands and feet are blackened and wrinkled prematurely. Likewise, the elements have exposed veins in the marbled cliffs, warped boney rocks, pushed aside folds of Mother Earth's flesh, revealed colossal liver-colored boulders and pancreatic outcroppings with ribbed steps, and channel rivers of cerulean-colored blood.

Gigantic whirlwinds that appear a kilometer in diameter vacuum the dust off the plains and tint the atmosphere orange. I've seen as many as three at a time.

The illnesses, dust storms, freezing wind, and bumps that rattle my brainpan and vibrate the pants off me cause seven members of our group to resign themselves to the truck. "It's only a side trip," they rationalize.

"Life is a side trip," I rationalize. This leaves only Edwin and myself, and I admit: if it wasn't for Edwin blocking the wind and his undying optimism, I too would have fallen alongside the road.

We've cycled about 5% of the distance to outer space, but the air is half as thick as sea level and the oxygen level about 40%. If you were suddenly teleported from sea level to Everest Base Camp you'd die of asphyxiation. Still, after several weeks of acclimatization, my heart beats double-time as I churn through the loose rock and sand. Suddenly I lose my breath and begin gasping for air. All my muscles are on fire and my lower intestine and anus spasm from the exertion. I feel as if I'm drowning in a vacuum. To open my lungs, I crouch alongside the road coughing and gasping, flashes erupt in my eyes and an ensuing migraine obscures the vision in my left eye—altitude sickness. Lacking oxygen, my body has begun to digest itself to survive. Lactic acid builds up in my bloodstream, compounded by dehydration from the dry air and water too cold to drink. And I've lost my appetite because oxygen and water are required for digestion. It feels as if the lump of food in my stomach lags behind the rest of me.

Tibet is like two countries in one: the Chinese cities and the Tibetan villages. In 1950, China, for various political reasons invaded Tibet. I suspect the real reason either involved building the Chinese version of the Iron Curtain or, of course, money. The Chinese call it the Great Liberation, but the only things liberated were 1.2 million Tibet souls. Then as the Chinese began their socialization and cultural cleansing of Tibet, they destroyed thousands of monasteries and monks because China believed "religion to be an opium for the masses." In recent years, due to international pressure, China has ceased most of its aggression but has devised an even more insidious plan: The Han Immigration Policy. This policy, through economic incentives, encourages Chinese people to move to Tibet in the hopes they'll outnumber and outbreed the Tibetans. Politically, economically and militarily the Tibetans are excluded and their national culture is slowly being extinguished. According to our books and guides it's illegal for tourists to bring pictures of the Dalai Lama to Tibet, and it's rumored that there are undercover monks lurking in the monasteries keeping an eye on subversive foreigners. The Chinese are so dastardly there's even a word for their dirty business: *sinicize*, meaning *to modify by Chinese influence*. Rather than free Tibet the Chinese would prefer to keep Tibet free of foreign influence. Our group of cyclists banded together to tackle the Chinese paperwork for nearly two months, before finally obtaining all the visas and permits.

Even if it's half true, it's a sad story, but from the point of view of a bicyclist without borders, the Indians have slowly morphed into the Asians, making it obvious that this ebb and flow of cultures has been washing the land for millennia. Tibetans have been relegated to mere servants of the Chinese machine. Still, the Tibetans appear happy to live a simple life, and have an indomitable spirit, bred from the harsh climate—it's a marvel to see them laugh, sing and dance. For instance, one monk was having the time of his life losing all his money in a card game. His karma caught up to him because earlier he made me get off the rock in front of my tent (we were camped in Rongbuk, the World's Highest Monastery) to burn a pile of dung where I was sitting. I was dumbfounded to be displaced by a pile of crap since there were plenty of other rocks. "An offering to God," he pantomimed with a smile; or was he laughing at me? I bet in the end, it will be the Tibetans that morph the invader.

One strange thing about the Tibetans is how many of them have a fossil of a nautilus shell in their pocket ready to sell to any tourist that happens along. And, the weirdest thing about Tibet is that the most popular beer is Pabst Blue Ribbon. Everywhere, even on the slopes of Everest, cans of Pabst lay alongside the road labeled, "Established in Milwaukee in 1849." Several times I'd tell the locals, "I'm from Milwaukee." They'd stare at me perplexed. "You: Tibet—" I'd say pointing to them— "Me: Milwaukee—" pointing to the word on the can. I went through this routine several times but never conveyed anything but: "I'm a beer can."

The Tibetan method of road construction and repair is to scrape the nearby scree onto the road and let the traffic crush it into gravel and compact it into potholes, but usually it just blows away or creates a dry, tire-eating quicksand. As my burning and frostbitten body labors up the mountain, one indomitable Tibetan road worker grabs my bike and begins pushing me up the hill with all his formidable strength, despite my cries, until my bike jackknifes and I plunge to the Earth painfully—gravity is a wee bit stronger up here—I twist my knee and get a mouthful of dust. His cheeks form rosy, purple balls as he laughs at me. My emotions also seem to beat double-time on a bicycle—I lose my temper. I'm still riled from some Tibetan highway bandits that tried to knock me off my bike when I skirted their highway tax. As if watching myself from afar, I witness myself calmly grab his shovel and throw it, with all my formidable anger, off the cliff. "That will teach him," I think, but immediately begin feeling ashamed of myself and wait for Edwin to chastise me, but all he says is, "Wow, mate, I wish I took a photo of that."

I've bicycled through a hundred mountain ranges, and usually the summits were hidden from view, and it appeared as if I were bicycling up endless rolling hills and switchbacks. Not so now. The tan walls of the valley are immense, occupying my entire field of vision, and the road seems to slope up forever. The sky, which at this altitude isn't graduated from the horizon to the zenith, is devoid of detail and makes my vision go blurry, dazzle and pop. After several hours of grunting, Edwin and I round the corner to view Mount Everest—*Qomolangma*—rearing its mass above the valley, like the cobra I encountered in Nepal, both a warning and a beautiful temptation swaying hypnotically. We're only 18 KM from the summit as the bird flies, and have already climbed 5180 meters, yet its remaining 3668 meters are still taller than almost all the peaks in the Rocky Mountains. I stop and hold my breath so not a sound but my beating heart and the blood rushing through my ears separates me from the surroundings: the wind whoosh-whooshing around the cliff; the tinkle of dust sculpting the mountains; the gurgle of a river gouging the valleys.

The atmosphere condenses on the eastside of Everest and appears like a great set of fluttering wings on the west. The form is a beautiful pyramid of blue rock and shimmering ice—the shape any sculptor would give the tallest most massive mountain in the world. As the sun progresses, like a great spotlight, it illuminates Everest in tantalizing sections. And like a masterpiece, it inspires me to want to walk around and admire all sides to see how the pieces fit. Even the name Everest, which happened to be the name of an English surveyor and could've been any name, perfectly suggests the peaks climbing evermore into the heavens and looming ever larger, no matter how close I approach. (I would've ridden as far as possible but the Chinese restrict everyone from going past Base Camp.) And the Tibetan name, *Qomolangma*, is equally provocative as my tongue trips up the word.

I understand why locals think of *Qomolangma* as a goddess, because she is so grand, she cannot be comprehended by a single person in a single lifetime. Sometimes she shrouds herself in a misty veil, other times she opens her arms and invites you to her peak, and just as easily, she can close her arms and snuff your life.

People often ask me what was my favorite place, but, as usual, I'm at a loss for a single or simple answer. Aren't all travelers supposed to say: "I loved the food and music. The scenery was breathtaking. And the people were absolutely fabulous." Call me shallow, but I've traveled through many bad places, and Tibet had its share of bad moments and places; nonetheless, for me, what comes to mind as the highlight of my trip, despite or because of the challenges, was the epitome of superlatives, Mount Everest, *Qomolangma*, the Tibetan mother goddess of the Earth, the mountain so high birds cannot fly over it. And, one of my deepest and dearest memories is when Edwin and I reached Base Camp, we met two climbers acclimatizing themselves for their attempt to summit the mountain. For a few moments, we all stood in awe of each other, "That's amazing. I could never do that," we all seemed to say.

As we left, I said, "Hey Edwin. Why couldn't we climb Everest?"

"Why not, mate?"

(Postscript: Many years later, I think the highlight of my trip wasn't so much Tibet, the people or the past achievement of climbing Everest, the highlight is what this place, this experience gave me to carry into my future—simply a sense of: "Why not?)

Scott cycling the road to Everest Base Camp. Mt. Everest in the distance. Note: I cheated and left my panniers in the truck with our guides. Photos courtesy of Edwin Tucker

39   What is your path?

I'm sitting on the balcony of an ashram. I watch the sunset over the Ganges River for 90 seconds. I count as a way of focusing my mind, otherwise my thoughts spin out of control, and I might as well sit in my room at the ashram and stare at the wall. I cannot simply let go of my ego-importance and be one with the moment. Wind is billowing down the Himalayas and through the river gorge, surfacing the water in feathery ripples. Chanting from the ashrams fades in and out with the gusts as do the gongs of bells from a nearby temple as pilgrims attract the attention of their gods. I'm drowning myself from the inside out with coffee. I have a migraine from my self-conflict, which I call spiritual questing. For the past few days, I have: climbed mountains to worship the gods; been smeared with ash and colored powders; been sprinkled in holy water; worn half a holy coconut like a hat; chanted for world peace; eaten dirty sacraments of sugar and puffed rice; bounced up and down until I bruised my insides; bent myself into yogic shapes that, formerly, were inconceivable and made me ache for days; floated boats of marigolds, roses and candles down the river; and I attempted to cleanse my sins by swimming across the Ganges. (I only managed a few meters in the near-freezing water. I'm not even sure the river was considered holy at this point, but it's clean compared to Varanasi where by Western standards it's 300,000 times more polluted than considered safe, not to mention the feces and half-burned corpses floating past.) And, of course, I've donated heaps of money to God's self-appointed representatives. All this in hopes of peace and enlightenment. But the only peace I found was stopping whatever torture—even sitting in silence—I was performing.

Dozens of times a day people ask where I'm going and how I'm getting there, essentially wondering which of all the infinite paths around the world will I choose and why? Westerners can be rather pedantic, but cycling is also a metaphor for life. As I penetrate further into the Far East and the second half of my journey, people ask me what is my chosen spiritual path through life, as if I must have a good answer because I've traveled too far to be fueled by simple coincidences, stubbornness or whims. Ironically, now that my egotism has faded somewhat, I avoid telling people what I'm doing because they seem to admire me and seek my counsel, when I often just choose my path with the flip of a coin.

One of the benefits of Hinduism and Buddhism is that you can't do anything wrong because you'll be reincarnated—millions of times if necessary—with another chance. (I've no recollection of past lives—I can't even remember where I was yesterday. However, I was told by a reputable psychic that in a former life I was Tesla's lab assistant and that I died in a fire. After some research, I discovered that most likely I died after an arsonist destroyed Tesla's lifework; in other words—I was murdered. That's some impressive karma.) Most religions consider the spiritual path in life as the most important; but, Hindus believe not everyone is meant to travel this path (someone has to stay home and bake the bread and protect the village from marauders), whereas, a famous Zen proverb says: "Before enlightenment chop wood carry water; after enlightenment, chop wood carry water." It's that in-between, nebulous, self-imposed confusion, seeking place on the road to enlightenment, where the meaning and actions of life are seemingly lost. Maybe it is wishful thinking, but I feel like my path is that of a bard; however, society seems to force me to be a drone, while religion suggests I should become the enlightened savior of the human race. Maybe my path is a combination of all three; but, mostly, I wish I didn't have to do anything. Perhaps, I should hang around for a few more lifetimes and earn more karmic bonus points.

I'm struck with an idea. I visit the ashram of a female Buddhist who's also a Hindu guru, Shanti Mayi. At the gate, I ask one of her shaven disciples, an American woman that reminds me of the butch dykes in San Francisco, for permission to visit.

"Everyone wants to see Shanti. There are disciples who've been waiting years to speak with her." Her clipped tone and succinct phrases suggest she was an aggressive businesswoman in her previous incarnation in America.

"So what can we do?" I say humbly, feeling at the mercy of her goodwill.

"Why do you want to see Shanti?"

I summon an eloquent explanation, "I've cycled twenty-eight-thousand kilometers around the world on a spiritual quest. I've done everything possible and I still feel empty, unfulfilled or, perhaps, full of self-importance and its ironic twin self-doubt. I've always felt a desire to contribute something to world; to realize my greatest potential, which seems to mean enlightenment—becoming at-one with God. But, I don't have enough faith to invest years of my life in what seems a gamble.... I've already wasted years of my life with my head in the clouds and my heart in the material world. Perhaps, my path isn't a spiritual one. I just want to live, to be human—to enjoy my life. I was hoping Shanti—being enlightened—can see through my emotional baggage or just ask God where my path lies."

She looks very serious and checks Shanti's schedule. "I don't like to disturb her, but I've never heard of anyone riding a bike around the world. I don't like this, but I'll ask."

"Thank you. I don't know what else to do."

The guru is busy, presumably meditating on more important matters, like world peace, to guide one lost soul, so I go back to my perch above the Ganges for more coffee, and watch three teams of men with donkeys hauling glittering gray sand off the picturesque beach and churning it into concrete. This is Lakshman Jhula, a suburb of Rishikesh, the self-acclaimed Yoga Capitol of the World made famous by the Beatles and Donovan (I regard Donovan as a guru of music), where the streets and river are swimming with all manners of holy people: swamis, sris, gurus, yogis, sadhus, monks saying things like, "Osho is a mosquito." (Osho was the most famous guru of recent times, and disciples use the present tense even if their guru is dead.)

"I am Osho's disciple. So, what does that make me? I've seen people fly. I'm not impressed by someone who can fly or walk on water. So what? So you will be shot down by jealous people who don't understand. What impresses me is giving—giving your heart, giving kindness."

Unwilling to endure the pain of cycling, I take a break for a few days, until I'm approached by another female monk with a shaved head. "Are you the man cycling around the world?" I agree. "We've been looking for you. Shanti would like to see you."

I rehearse my questions all day and arrive at the gate of her ashram a polite five minutes early. I'm told to wait until the exact minute of my appointment. Then I'm led into a bright glass room with several low wide chairs and a loom. I'm told to kneel on a cushion in front of one chair and wait. The sun is blinding me, and Shanti greets me before I'm aware she's in the room. She rearranges the chairs, invites me to sit in one, shuts the curtains and arranges some flowers before settling into her chair. One of my ten minutes is gone already. We sit face to face, like equals, unlike the monks in the ashram that kneel on concrete and bow and kiss her robe. I'm surprised that Shanti Mayi (meaning *Peace Mother*) resembles my mother, a handsome, middle-aged, Midwestern women, except, as you would expect, Shanti has an extraordinarily peaceful countenance and friendly, penetrating eyes. My eyes, I imagine, are curious and half-blind with problems. After a few more breaths to settle, studying each other, I ask, "Shall I begin?"

"Please."

I'm feeling foolish, because when I was rejected the first time, I had mistaken a whim for intuition and decided to forget God and spiritual matters. I take a breath and restart my quest, "In short, I don't know which path to travel through life." I avoid saying spiritual because I'm convinced she'll tell me my path, according to the Hindu caste system, is that of a warrior, merchant or peasant. Worse, I'm scared that I'll never see my bicycle again if she says I must join the temple and live an ascetic life of love and devotion devoid of any suffering or ill-will, much like a Buddhist monk I met whose purpose in life was chanting for world peace in his monastery, but who had never seen the world. "Shall I elaborate?" I ask, mindful of the time.

"Please."

"I've been riding my bicycle around the world—"

"I've heard. I think that's wonderful."

"Thank you. I wish everyone could see the things I see." I pause with the weight of all these memories on my tongue. "I feel obligated to live the best life I know how—"

"It's important you realize this. So often I try to express this idea to people, but I lack the words."

"I think of life as a gift; it would be a shame to waste it."

"Yes, that's it—a gift."

"I've come to believe that the spiritual path through life is the most important—"

"I agree. There is no other way."

To make my point, I must erase the nervousness from tongue and summarize my life's dilemma into a sound bite. "I've asked—and answered—many questions, but I feel I've reached the point of diminishing returns. I've been on a spiritual quest—for happiness, you could say, but I've come to believe that 'happily ever after' is a pipe dream, a modern myth, the devil's bargain. I mean, suffering is a fact of life—we all get sick and die; and, if the meaning of your life is to be happy, it makes the other half meaningless. But, I don't want to suffer through my ignorance to learn my lessons. There's gotta be a better way." I pause, convinced that I'm about to be recruited and feel I've trapped myself in her power to promise salvation. "I think my life must have some purpose I haven't discovered yet. But I'm stuck. I don't think I can even achieve a peaceful mind. Nor do I have enough faith to invest years of my life becoming at-one. I don't think I can become enlightened."

"It's not that you can't become enlightened: everyone is already enlightened they just haven't realized it."

"How do I realize it?"

"Enlightenment is not a plateau: there is always room to grow in awareness, to evolve spiritually."

"What do I do? I was thinking of taking the *vipassanâ* meditation course, but I don't want to be locked in a room for nine days forbidden to speak. I already go for weeks without speaking." (I'm more worried about going nine days without coffee.) "And I don't want to join an ashram. I hate singing for one thing. I'd feel like I was wasting my life."

She simply responds, "It is not for everyone." I'm flabbergasted that we agree on so many things, and I'm beginning to suspect that I am a wee bit enlightened.

"The last thing I want to be is a sadhu. I don't want to renounce the world. If they're so holy why don't they share their wisdom? Why do the rest of us have to suffer to pay their alms?"

"Sadhus do lack much fuel for life."

"I was hoping you'd say my path isn't a spiritual one. That'd be a lot easier."

"Any path can be spiritual."

"I like the challenge of cycling up a mountain: breathing hard, my body burning, and the feeling of peace when I reach the top: sweat being whisked away by the wind, watching the lizards scuttle, listening to the birds sing, sitting on a rock, the whole world spinning beneath me. That's what I enjoy most in life. I want to walk through the world barefoot, as if I were a child again, letting the leaves of grass tickle my toes even if my feet get dirty."

"Yes, that's it exactly. I couldn't have described it better myself." She pauses to straighten her clothes. Her eyes reflect dwelling upon my dilemma. "I agree an ashram isn't for you. I think you'll be okay whatever you do as long as your intellect comes from your heart." She pauses again as if her words need time to be digested. "The path of the heart is the way of the warrior. That makes you the Warrior of the Heart."

Her peace and warmth are contagious and I feel, more than know, that I'm not only on the right path, but I'm very well traveled. I remember when the idea of cycling round the world first popped into my head, I thought, "This is crazy. Am I trying to get myself killed?" But I knew, despite my fear, I must follow my heart. "I like that—the Warrior of the Heart."

"I want to tell you something and don't ever forget it," Shanti says with piercing eyes and intent. "Every time you open your eyes, the first thing you see is God."

(Unbeknownst to me for many years, Shanti had just informally initiated me as a sadhu. When I discovered this I laughed and knew it was true, simply because I disliked the sadhus so much, that I realized they represented a part of my shadow-self that I was denying.)

The following months, I cycle through the mightiest mountains of them all—the Himalayas. Somehow, as if Shanti imparted her peace and wisdom directly, as I've heard is possible, I grow stronger and more peaceful. I feel relieved of my imagined penance in the ashram, spending years in contemplation cut off from the real world.

I raise my gaze from the dusty gravel road. Several Indian children are playing a game in the dirt with sticks and stones. I ring my bell, and they giggle and chase me, barefoot and dressed in dirty rags, up the hill and around the corner.

Resting in the Himalayas. **Previous:** Elephant blessing.

40 · Did you find peace?

It was a wavy ride to Zanzibar. I sat in a plastic chair that skittered side to side across the diamond plate deck, while the ocean sloshed through the broken doors and over my feet and bicycle wheels, but the sun was crisp and the breeze fresh. Dhows, fishing vessels unchanged since Mohammed ascended to heaven, trolled for fish, and a pod of dolphins surfed in our wake. On Zanzibar, I enjoyed the hospitality and food of the Muslim culture (some of the best in Africa), toured the slave caves and spice plantations, and mostly slept in a hammock for six days. Like Zanzibar's turquoise water and white sand beaches, my vacation should've been idyllic, but I was unable to find peace because my mind kept raking the muck of problems that separated me from Cape Town, and the overwhelming task of zigzagging between the coups, famines and pestilence of Africa. I feel as if I'm trying to outrun the Horsemen of the Apocalypse on a bicycle.

My plan was to save 20 dollars by taking the night ferry back to the mainland and another ten on accommodation by being rocked to sleep on the deck in the cool sea breeze. I hog a bench on the top deck beside the bug-eyed first mate. My bike is below in the prow of the boat covered in plastic, hopefully sheltered from the sea spray. An old man tries to weasel into my corner seat by sitting on my head and when I move another man is quick to steal my space by lying down and falling asleep. Porters begin boxing in the passengers with odd-shaped boxes wrapped in brown paper and cinched in twine. They stumble like drunks and their eyes appear to be melting out of their heads. Alcohol is too expensive for the average African and generally unavailable in Muslim cultures. I suspect they're concocting a homebrew that contains methanol, the byproduct of fermenting fruit.

The fluorescent lights are flickering, making my eyes melt too, and the television emits a horrible wailing, like an out-of-pitch Hindu song in a tin box. Diesel fumes bellow over the boat for hours until all the passengers are boxed into a makeshift warehouse. When the ferry chugs out to sea—we're late, of course—I'm already nauseous and a sinus headache thickens my tongue. To my dismay we anchor a few hundred meters in front of Stone Town and wallow in the ocean for three hours, foiling my hopes of a slow peaceful cruise to Dar es Salaam.

At two in the morning, the engines power full steam ahead. The seas are stormy as we fight the same wind that I've been fighting on my bike and that pushed the boatloads of slaves to Arabia. The ocean is swelling 2–3 meters, not much, but our ferry leaps over the waves and plunges deep into the troughs. Only two men look comfortable: an old man that is so fat he rests his head on his cheek like a pillow, and a man who once was probably black as an eggplant, but is now pallid gray with a flush of blood in his cheeks. The edges of his bones stretch his thin skin like a sail, and lesions cover half his skull, making his ear appear as if it may slough off. He's a "walking skeleton," an AIDS victim. He can't have but one gram of life in him, yet he boarded erect and leisurely as if on a Sunday stroll, and seems unfazed by the lurching ship. (I would stop to talk to a gravedigger in Botswana. He buried 50 people that day, and told me, "People die very fast now. It is sad, but I have good business.")

A man is retching on the floor. I smell it first, then my eyes swim into focus on gobs of vomit and drool hanging from his face like snot. It makes me nauseous and I kneel on my bench and hang over the railing. The first mate offers me a plastic barf bag again. When we first boarded, I was impressed thinking these were garbage bags; normally passengers just throw everything overboard. (There must be a reef of beer cans below us.) "No. Thanks. I'm fine," I utter hoping it'll become true. I anchor my eyes on a distant ship, but the boat—my world—is in a drunken bed spin with a symphony of cats coughing hairballs into plastic bags. Vomit splattering on the rusted deck causes hot waves of nausea to wash over me. "I'm gonna be sick," I think. "No, I can't afford to throw up my water. I have nothing to drink. Just relax. Don't think." After 15 minutes of drooling into the ocean, I feel peaceful enough to sleep. Fortunately, two seasick passengers have sprawled on the floor leaving me half a bench.

I awake in a panic feeling warm vomit pouring over my arm—someone is heaving into a plastic bag draped over my arm. Simultaneously, a woman beneath my bench is retching, and a man in the corner is drooling like a waterfall onto the floor. He smiles sickly when he sees me watching. The fat man, his head resting on his cheek, awakes in a gurgling fit of retching. The majority of passengers have turned an avocado color.

Even the first mate looks ill. The walking skeleton is either the calmest man on the ship or dead. Nausea overwhelms me again and I hang over the rail like the bars of a prison, drooling into the ocean. I'm feverish and shaking from head to toe. Every pore on my body is spewing sweat. I stand to take the boat's lurching in my knees and steady my head on the horizon, but I can't fix a point in the darkness. My whole body is being shoved up into the air 3-5 meters, then falling, weightless for a second, until it appears I'll be swallowed by the black sea.

Cycling around the world is living the dream of a lifetime—although it's the worst night of my life—but even in good times, I'm plagued with the question: "If I can't be peaceful here and now, then where and when?" At this late stage in my trip, many people ask me if I found peace. I'm sure most are reflecting my own questioning; nonetheless, they seem to want to know what is the payoff for riding around the world, as if enjoying the journey was not enough. It occurs to me that my mind is like a ship on the sea—mostly a stormy sea. I struggle to keep an even keel, but my anchors, like pride and lust, drag me down, and my engines send me hurtling full-throttle into the storm, overworking and over-consuming, perhaps a form of denial or a misguided attempt to latch onto society's will-o'-wisps of happiness. Even during the doldrums, I seem obsessed with watching the horizon for the next tempest. Most of my life I've felt lost at sea, desperately trying not to run ashore and fearful of staring into the churning ocean depths, increasingly denying and distracting myself from the storm by putting the ship on autopilot and going below deck for a gin and tonic.

It isn't the pitch of the boat as much as the yaw that makes me sick. Up, up, up. Right, right, right. Down, down, down. Left, left, left. The stars zip into the invisible black hole of the ocean and back out in a big bang—Boom! The boat bottoms out in a trough every fourth or fifth wave. My head snaps forward catching a spray of foam, popping my vertebrae, and knocking my brain against my skull. My seasickness is compounded by the acrid smell of vomit and sour armpits. There's an ocean of acid rolling in my stomach, splashing into my mouth and churning out gasses. I clench my jaws to hold everything down, and drool so much it's like drinking a glass of water.

"I'm never putting a toe in the ocean again. I'm not going to puke. I'm not going to puke...." My lifeboat is a forced meditation. I still suspect the Hindu and Buddhist aesthetics, sitting in a cave or an ashram and chanting, *"Om mani padme hum,"* are missing the point of life, like a fair-weather saint who has locked himself safe and snug in a self-imposed prison. I wonder if a true test of achieving atonement is keeping an even keel while the world is falling apart. "I'm an island in a stormy sea. A reed in the wind," I chant to channel my passion to retch into calming my mind. But my mind is untrained and out of shape. Finally, I accept my fate, hang my head over the rail, staring into the black churning depths, and succumb to my urge to vomit; and, suddenly, the feeling is washed away in cool tingles. Paradoxically, as soon as I stopped fighting and resisting myself, my mind and body suddenly find peace. I climb down from the railing and offer a smile and a plastic bag to my neighbor. I lay down on the wooden bench, and as I drift off to sleep as the boat continues its roller-coaster ride to Tanzania, I wonder, "What if I just looked into the black, churning depths of my mind, illuminated the shadows of my spirit, and looked all my demons in the eye?"

We dock in Dar as the sun rises. I hop over the railing onto the pier ahead of everyone crammed in front of the gangplank. I rinse my bike with sweet water. In just one night the saltwater ate through the touch-up paint and rusted my black bike spotty-orange like a leopard. The Africans disembark full of smiles. I never heard one person complain. "I must've been spoiled by my American lifestyle," I think. When I taught school for a day in Bagamoyo, Tanzania I asked the teacher why there were so few students. He said most parents couldn't afford tuition (1.75 USD per month) and nobody could afford books. Whereas in America, according to the African newspapers, a father bought his daughter breast implants (7000 USD) as a high school graduation present. I theorize Americans have too much money, too much self-importance and too little time; somehow, this translates to a land of plenty and a mind of little. In other words, our culture has trained us to cast anchors hither thither and rev our engines, meanwhile our stormy minds rage unhindered, fighting themselves and the tide of society.

I mount my bicycle, point her prow towards the Cape, test the winds, measure the sea, draw anchor, set sail and breath deeply to calm the waters. Life is like riding a bicycle: if your thoughts and intentions get distracted, you might run off the road; if you carry too much emotional baggage, you might never reach your destination; and if you stop pedaling, you won't move forwards, sometimes coast backwards and eventually you'll fall off the ride.

41   Did you fall in love?

The sand bogs down my wheels and I slide to a stop in the withered shade of a eucalyptus tree. In Darwin, Australia, I overheard a woman who bought a packaged tour to Kakadu National Park say, "I accidentally signed up for the extreme adventure. I just wanted the regular adventure." Immediately, I had decided to go on a real adventure, a solo bicycle-about in the Aussie bush, which I'm starting to regret.

Despite having escaped the heat and humidity of South East Asia (averaging over 90% humidity and 90° F/32° C everyday), the Australian sun is much more intense. It washes the color out of the foliage and erases the shadows. The sky is an eye-bugging blue. In the background, I hear a low roar rise and fall, perhaps from the distant bush fire that mars the western sky, causing flurries of ashen eucalyptus leaves; in the foreground, I hear the ear-splitting buzz of hundreds of flies and the rustle of the leaves from gusts of hot air. I'm surrounded by sparse and stunted foliage punctuated with termite mounds three meters tall. My feet are sunk five centimeters into the sand. I estimate that my wheels have ploughed several tons of sand a few centimeters to the right and several tons a few centimeters to the left. In the valleys, I feel rooted to the ground, but atop the hills I can see for miles over the ocean of gum trees, palms and ferns all tinted kangaroo red from the dust. I'm over 25 KM from the nearest bitumen road. Aside from the tire tracks in the sand, there's no sign of humanity. My world has been turned upside down, and given one shake I'd fall into the never-never. This is the Australian Outback. Locals say that when you're in the back o' beyond you can see clear into next week. But Aussies love to exaggerate; I can only see into tomorrow, maybe the day after.

As the dirt road descends into a small valley, my feet scoop powdery sand with each pedal stroke until I bog down. Four-wheel-drive trucks have gouged two trenches into the sand. I walk hunched over on the plateau in the middle where the vehicles scrapped bottom and push my bicycle down one trench, the wheels sinking into the sand, panniers knocking the wall and my feet slipping. I follow the tracks of dingoes, wallabies and snakes. I see a dozen kinds of birds and bugs, and a baby brown snake, the second most venomous snake in the world. (In Thailand, I had a frightening moment when I was nearly bitten when I ran over a cobra that zagged across the road like black lightening. Fortunately, the cobra was even more frightened and stunned than I was.)

When the road ascends a hill of rocky sandstone and quartzite, I begin pedaling again until I reach my third river. A mysterious sign reads: "Warning. Snorkel advised for river crossing." Another sign reads: "Saltwater crocodiles have been known to enter this area undetected." Before I left, I asked a park ranger if there were any crocodiles in the rivers. "Aw, just some freshies. You'll be all right."

"Can I get my bicycle down that road?"

"Aw, that pushbike of yours is just a bloody lazy way o' walking." His gravelly voice, typical of the Aussies, revs into a laugh. "No worries, mate."

Saltwater crocodiles, or salties, are the dangerous kind. I visited a crocodile farm a few days ago. First, I fed on a crocodile burger—"I'm going to get one before it gets me," I laughed—then I watched the crocodiles being fed. The lagoon was foaming with fighting salties and the air filled with their prehistoric roars. With shocking speed and agility, one dominant male chased a weaker male up and over a small wall. Meanwhile another crocodile snuck ashore to feed on chickens tossed by two men. In one chomp and gulp, the crocodile crushed the chicken's bones and swallowed it whole, leaving blood trickling down its perpetual toothy grin. Still hungry after three chickens, the croc advanced on the men as they repeatedly clubbed its snout. Normally, crocodiles are stealthy hunters. From a bridge over a river in Nepal, I watched some crocodiles slide off the riverbank, disappear under a few inches of water and reappear without a ripple. And on the crocodile farm, I walked past a crocodile covered in slime and dust. He was only one meter away and I didn't notice him until he turned, tracking my movement, calculating how to get through the fence.

The reason saltwater crocodiles are dangerous is because they'll hunt humans. The tour guide at the farm said, "Once I saw a crocodile lunge out of the water and grab a fisherman by the head and drag him under. Like a true Aussie, the last thing he did was throw his beer can at that old saltie. Saltwater crocodiles can't eat more than an arm or leg at a time, so he probably stuffed him under a log where his rotting body attracted crabs and fish, which the salties like to eat."

"Sounds like a saltie smorgasbord," I said.

I walk down the ravine and peer in both directions. The creek has dug itself into the sand and is overgrown with grass and ferns. I can't see any need for a snorkel or any crocodiles, but I can't be sure there isn't a crocodile lurking in the reeds or mud on the opposite side. I walk up the bank, mount my bike and brace myself to slingshot down the bank, through the creek and up the other side, minimizing any opportunities for the salties. I zip down the hill. Hit the creek with a lurch. For a moment, plumes of water wash over my body and bicycle then suddenly disappear as my front panniers submerge. During moments like these, rather than those annoying thoughts that justify my existence, my mind thinks in bursts of images and feelings, a moment of clarity, I could call it, best translated into words as: "Too deep. Soft spot. Foot stuck. Damn. I hope there isn't a croc in here. I should've signed up for the regular adventure." Splashdown! Strangely, I'm not frightened or regretful; I even chuckle. "If I had a beer can, I'd toss it. *C'est la vie.* I had to try. I wonder if my panniers are still waterproof." (They're not.)

After a nano-lifetime in the creek and I'm still alive, I figure I'd better put some effort into staying alive. I push my bike up and off me, stand and dash out of the creek, up the bank and around the corner. I don't turn around because if there's a crocodile I know I'll panic and fall.

The sun dries my clothes quickly as I continue up the rocky hills and down the sandy valleys until I reach my goal, Surprise Creek. I need to camp beside the creek so that I'll have a full supply of water for tomorrow's 105-KM trek to the next water hole.

I thought the "surprise" in Surprise Creek was a reference to crocodiles, but the surprise is millions of flies. I climb the rocks to the top of the stagnant cascades and find a trickle of fresh water. I begin filtering the 20 liters I'll need for tomorrow. Swarmed by hundreds of flies. I look like a Dalmatian. Just one fly is enough to make me crazy: buzzing my ears, landing on my lips, walking up my nose, in my eyes, crawling over my glasses, tickling my skin, inhaling them, choking on them and eating them. Now, it's a constant buzz and tickle. While cycling as fast as 27 KPH, flies still buzz circles around my head. I can't shake them, if it gets too windy or I go too fast they simply hunker down on my panniers and wait. They even sleep there following me for days. Bug repellent only lasts a few minutes. The fly's only weakness is that it's extremely skittish. The only effective thing to do is buy a swagman's hat which has pieces of cork tied to strings that hang in front of your face and scare away the flies. "If you don't have a hat," an Aussie was teaching me, "what you do is put your thumb on your nose—c'mon, follow along—now wiggle your fingers. That's the traditional bush wave, mate."

According to the farmers, these are the worst flies in eight years. They say that because of the drought the dung beetles have died, leaving piles of dung where the flies lay their eggs. I asked a lady at a roadhouse the names of the different flies. "Oh, you know," she said, "those-little-annoying flies, those-blow-you-know-poof-poof flies, and the ones-that-sting-you-ouch! flies." The Australian bush fly is the most annoying creature I've ever encountered.

It's too hot and the shade too sparse to hide in my tent, so for hours I endure flies crawling over my skin and play a game of snatching flies out of the air with my hand (my record is four at once), and eat the lemon-flavored green ants, an ancient aboriginal food source. The flies are driving me mad; my skin feels like it is going to get up and walk away. I make offerings of water, bread and peanut butter but they aren't interested. I even sit next to a pile of kangaroo dung thinking, like Dennis said, "There's gotta be a more attractive pile of shit around here than me." Since I've covered my hat and face with mosquito netting, they're especially interested in my crotch. I must have a cult of flies worshiping my groin, "Hail the god of the Two Wheels from which springs forth the waters of life." Once I asked an Australian woman, "What do you think of all the flies?"

"I guess we just take 'em for granted."

After fighting them and irritating myself even further because there's no escape, I remove all my clothes scrub off in the stream and let the flies swarm me, tickling my skin, sucking my sweat and wounds, until I feel on fire, and my body seems as large as the swarm of flies. I marvel at how I can't distinguish between where my skin ends and the atmosphere begins. I can feel the whole weight of the sky flowing through me into the ground. I thrill at the push and pull, like a seagull in the surf. I feel everything at once: the air flowing over me, grasses waving to the side of me; the sun arcing through the sky, disappearing behind clouds and silhouetting hills; flocks of cockatoos screeching, the rustle and squeak of gum trees; dust settling on my skin. My senses seem over-stimulated and uncomfortable, but if I were comfortable I'd be asleep, or in my tent, or in a motel—I'd be numb to my surroundings.

The last of the flies flit away with drops of my blood and sweat, and mosquitoes arrive for the night shift. It feels as if my essence has been spread in a huge cloud of insects. Is my blood still busy conducting its business unaware that it has been kidnapped? Likewise, are humans cells that churn about endlessly unaware of the bigger picture?

I rise to pitch camp, cook and continue my philosophizing. I've been digesting a quote by Oscar Wilde that I read in an Irish pub, "To love oneself is the beginning of a lifelong romance." Meister Eckhart, the Christian mystic said, "If you love yourself, you love everybody else as you do yourself. As long as you love another person less than you love yourself, you will not truly succeed in loving yourself, but if you love all alike, including yourself, you will love them as one person and that person is both God and man." Judging by the amount of failed relationships in the world, people aren't doing a very good job of loving themselves.

When people ask me if I fell in love, they're wondering: if not, how I can bear being alone, and if so, how can I continue? I've had enough requited and unrequited romances to realize that the love I was missing was simply love for self or love for life, and that I was using lust or romantic love like an emotional supplement for my own being.

What is love anyway? I think the word "love" in English has been diluted. *Merriam-Webster's* dictionary defines love to mean anything from "strong affection" to "object of attachment" to "an amorous episode" even "a score of zero." I thought the Romance languages, such as Spanish had many more useful expressions for love, and therefore, the Romance people, had a better understanding of love, until I met Jose in a *super-mercado*, "Yes, we have many words for love," he confirmed, "Sometimes they work. Sometimes not." Seems expressing love is a problem all over the world.

The sun sets behind the smoke of a bush fire, lighting the sky and snowy ash emanating surreal colors. Meteorites stripe the starry sky. I eat my tuna casserole while watching the wallabies hop through the woods. Normally a day as hard as this would've worn down my morale and made me whinge and wonder, "Why bother?" But today I actually enjoyed conquering the hardship—I mean *challenges*—and savored the beautiful moments along the way.

In my opinion, love breaks down the wall between two people, creating a sense of at-one-ment, which opens a door to realizing your connection to all things, and creates a pattern, like a seed, that grows and perpetuates itself into the future. Certainly, I have a long road to travel, before this theory becomes a reality; however I think, "He who loves himself, loves life. And, I have developed a certain affection for crocodiles and flies."

Termite hill in Australia's Outback.

42   Are you happy?

"I want to be Coca-Cola this time. Sprite is unlucky." Some ragged and robust Zambians are teaching me to play draughts (checkers) at a bus stop. We're using bottle caps as checkers on a sheet metal board. The only indication that this is a bus stop is a path through the woods to the village and a gigantic *mancala* board made from a fallen tree. The object of *mancala* is to sow your beans around the board and capture your opponent's beans. I've played one variation called *bao* with 32 compartments; the game can last an hour and end in stalemate. The board we're using as a table has about 200 compartments, which indicates how long it takes for the bus to arrive.

"Jump backwards," a bystander instructs.

"Thanks. I keep forgetting." They've changed the rules so that any piece may jump backwards, which forces many errors because I play too much from habit.

"Don't worry, my friend. We feed you spoon, like baby."

"Tell me about America." My opponent makes a wise request, rather than the usual mundane questions, like: How many kilometers do you ride per day? (80-120 KM.) How many flat tires have you had? (Over 100.) How many gears do you have?

(Not enough.)

"It's a good country, but like all countries it has problems."

"You mean it has poor people like us?"

"Even more poor than you."

"But you see how we suffer." Everyone thinks they're suffering in Africa. There are hundreds of missions to alleviate the suffering, sucking billions of dollars out of the world economy; yet, the old-timers say Africa is worse now than 50 years ago. Discussing the cause of poverty is a major pastime among tourists in Africa.

"No, I don't see."

"Hello. Gimme bicycle," a boy pants. He has sprinted here as if this is his once-in-a-lifetime opportunity to have all his wishes granted.

"If you can ride it, you can have it," I say.

My opponent continues his sales pitch, "I am very poor. I have nothing."

"Do you have a family?"

"That is a bad move," he says.

I take back my move and he jumps three checkers. "You tricked me."

"I am teaching you," he chuckles.

"Do you have a family—a wife?" I ask.

"Yes."

"How many?"

"Only one, sir."

"How many girlfriends?"

"Only one, sir. Look, this is much better."

The crowd assures me this is a better move. I take back my move again. My opponent jumps back and forth and kings his piece. "You tricked me," I accuse the bystanders. "You're not even playing."

"Yes. We tricked you," they appear proud. I used to play speed chess on the streets of San Francisco, and a person's method of play always reflected their personality. Some were greedy and cheated for the instant gratification of winning, others were honorable and offered help to increase the enjoyment of the game.

"Do you have children?" I ask.

"I have seven children." Children are called *African jewels* or *gifts from God*, but, in my opinion, they're more like a retirement plan: the boys will work in the fields and the daughters sold to future husbands.

"Where are your children?"

"They watch my animals. Play faster. Like this. It is more fun." The bottle caps rasp over the board double-speed, and my strategy falters trying to match his pace. I feel he wants to impress his friends.

"You're trying to trick me again."

"You learn very fast, sir."

"You're a farmer—a businessman. I see you have clothes and shoes." It's cotton harvest now. There's so much cotton blowing in the wind on the roadside that I could weave several wardrobes; however, I've never seen or heard of a Zambian weaving. He's wearing a mass-produced Beckham football jersey that an English humanitarian donated when it went out of fashion. "You have clean air to breathe and clean water to drink." The bottle caps slow their march. The boy has gotten his leg over my bike, but he's too small to balance the weight. I watch the clouds morph for a moment, something I haven't been able to appreciate for years. "Plenty of sunshine today." I poke him in the ribs playfully. "You have too much food to eat. And, you have time to play draughts all day with your friends." He acknowledges everything I say with a glimmering grin. "I have no wife, no girlfriend, no children, no job, no house. All I have is a bicycle and enough money to go to Cape Town. You see how I suffer," I wince theatrically.

Everyone laughs and my opponent says, "You are very strong man. I can never do this." In fact, he's rippling with muscles, whereas I feel like jelly melting in the sun.

"You could if you wanted. It is all in the mind." Which brings me to my point, "Are you happy?" People often ask me if I'm happy. Perhaps they want to know my secret, or perhaps I look half-dead, and they're wondering whether I'm masochistic or insane. In countries lacking the Calvinistic work ethic of being depraved and deprived that has seeped into America's culture, the general attitude seems rather obvious: if you're not happy doing what you're doing, then why are you doing it?

"I am very happy," he smiles, Africans have the biggest, whitest smiles in the world. I've noticed that unlike Americans, Africans don't analyze whether they are happy. Certainly, the more I intellectualize something, the more detached from it I become, like having sex and thinking, "Am I happy now? Am I going to have an orgasm too fast or not at all? Is this love?"

"You see, you suffer terribly." Everyone laughs.

"The problem, sir, is money."

"If you're hungry, you need food. Everyone must eat. If it is cold, you need clothes. If it is raining, you need a house. If you want children, you need a wife. You can't make babies by yourself." While everyone laughs at my joke, I wonder if I'm preaching too much, and if I'm "walking the walk" enough to be able to give advice, and if he'll understand. "Can I tell you a secret?" He agrees eagerly. "If you have all these things, money won't make you happy. You will spend all day worrying about your money and you will have no time to play draughts. Do you know the number one rule in life?" His ears perk. "Life is full of suffering. It is the same everywhere, even in America. I think we are the unhappiest people in the world because we have no time for draughts."

"Can you invite me to America?" He wants me to write him a letter of recommendation for his visa, if not pay for his passage like so many others.

"It's too late for you. You must stay here and feed your family."

"But I want to see America very much."

"Then you must divorce your wife, and leave your children and girlfriend, stop drinking beer, stop smoking cigarettes and stop chewing *khat*. You must work everyday, save all your money, and maybe in eight years, like me, you can go."

"It is true," his friend says. "You have to save money. You think *mzungus* are rich, but they know how to plan for the future." I've stumbled upon some very thoughtful Zambians.

I met a Peace Corp volunteer who had been stationed in Malawi for two years. Once he asked some villagers if they'd like to learn how to farm. One man replied, matter of fact, "Why should we learn how to farm? You already do the farming." After much observation and ruminating, I've concluded that Africa has a much bigger problem than AIDS, malaria, famine, drought, war or monetary poverty. I do believe lack of education, unstable governments and over-population are parts of the fundamental problem, but Africa's biggest problem is poverty of spirit. I met a group of students who studied animal management for years and came to Kenya to apply their academics. They reminded me of Zim and Zam's "elephant problem" or the "kangaroo plague" in Australia, and were displeased when I said, "Animal management isn't the problem, you should've gone to school for human management." I believe greedy dictators and do-good missionaries perpetuate the poverty of spirit. Several Africans have even said to me, "We can't do anything without the help of foreigners." So, I believe that the missionary's main lessons aren't health, education or agriculture, but an unfortunate byproduct of taking away the people's responsibility—teaching them to feel poor and helpless.

I prepare to depart. I won half my games, besides the kid is starting to roll my bike to his village. "Believe me. It won't be easy for you in America. You have everything you need here. Don't worry. *Hakuna matata*. Enjoy your life. And, remember the number two rule of life: God made suffering to teach you a lesson." I no longer believe in a personified God or hell or penance—I believe suffering is a consequence of being alive and provides lessons and motivation for change, but that it's only half the formula, the other half being joy—but, I'm phrasing my concept in a manner that he'll understand and hope he'll redirect his energies into something he finds more productive.

I'm about to leave, but after a second thought I hold up a checker, "Do you know which man is the most important?"

They consult each other and agree, "The king."

"No, they are all the same—every man can become a king."

43　　Do you believe in magic?

Someone stole my thermometer, but I know it's hot—too hot! Yesterday, I suffered a minor case of salt depletion and heat exhaustion. I also had an itsy-bitsy confrontation with the Tanzanian army that ended with having a roll of film confiscated. And today, I had an embarrassing moment when I helped myself to a soda. I grabbed the reservoir for bottle caps, thinking it was the handle, and ripped it off the machine. Bottle caps tinkled on the ground like aluminum raindrops. Locals laugh endlessly at my faux pas.

The tropical plants have evaporated in the heat, and again Africa looks like what I thought Africa would look like: sweeping plains full of thorny acacia trees dwarfed by monumental skies. I saw two troops of baboons on the side of the road. One couple made sweet monkey love twice. Until today, I hadn't seen any animals in Tanzania (except for some interesting roadkill, including an antelope-eating rock python and several large cats). The locals guarantee there will be lions lying on the road as I pass through Mikumi National Park.

Bicyclists are prohibited in almost all parks. (I find it odd that the untamed wilds are now called parks.) The animals in Africa are the biggest and most dangerous in the world. On the ground, the Cape buffalo is considered to be the most dangerous, charging anything that moves; and in the water, hippopotamuses kill more people than crocodiles. In my opinion, the most dangerous animal is the lion. Only the lion will actively hunt people for food day and night. (Crocodiles are opportunistic predators and it's easy enough to avoid rivers.) Adding to my concern, I'm told there are lion cubs nearby, a lioness won't hesitate to protect her cubs.

I'm honored to be a friend of Simanga, a Maasai warrior. His presence was so peaceful that twice, I walked past him leaning against a palm tree in his traditional blood-red robes without noticing him until he chuckled, "I am here, brother." I met him in Zanzibar where he was making jewelry for the tourists. When he earns enough he'll go back to his tribe and buy a herd of cattle to exchange for a bride (about 15-20 cows at 100,000 shillings or 85 USD each). He'll probably marry a Maasai woman but says, "I don't choose the color or the tribe. That is the wish of God." Simanga has hunted lions that preyed on his family's cattle. He told me, "Lions have much magic. They know what you are thinking." So tomorrow, I plan to bicycle thinking happy thoughts.

At sunrise, I leave my hotel, which had turned into a brothel in the middle of the night. I cycle 70 KM, stopping only once for food and water, in order to position myself on the edge of Mikumi National Park. I hope to have enough time and energy to pedal 50 more kilometers before the sun sets and the animals wake. In Africa, most animals sleep in the heat of the day and are awake all night. A sign reads. "Danger Wild Animals," in both English and Swahili. Many Africans concur, "Mikumi is dangerous. Very dangerous." Then they ask me another question common all over the world, "Do you have a gun?" I've been asked this enough to consider buying one, but I feel that making a decision to resort to force is somehow a self-fulfilling prophecy. I've been discovering that "like attracts like" seems to be one of the laws of the universe.

I always reply, "Don't worry. Lions don't like white meat."

And the standard response is laugher: "White meat is their favorite."

I've been told that I only survived Africa due to my blissfully ignorant lack of fear. Once, I was greeted by a group of boxers that in my memory appeared two meters tall and one meter wide. The leader said, after feinting a punch, "Do you know why we would never fight you? You must be a very brave man—a very strong man—a very crazy man to ride your bike here. I am African, and I would never do this." And all his friends agreed. Little did they know, I hardly had enough strength to wield my machete.

I rationalize animals will: A) not bother me if I don't bother them, B) shy away from the noise and pollution of the road, C) be conditioned to ignore vehicles, D) won't recognize humans as a food source, and E) are scared of humans from millennia of being either eaten or beaten whenever they intrude on crops or cattle. I readjust my machete so the haft is within reach and practice a few toots on my whistle until my ears ring.

Supposedly, it's illegal for me to enter the park on a bicycle, but no one is there to stop me. The road is lined with a variety of flowering thorn trees with feathery com pound leaves. The ground is covered with an impenetrable thicket of bramble and tall grass that slice my legs and leaves burrs in my clothing. My visibility is limited to a few meters on either side. I check my mirror frequently, not to make sure trucks are giving me a wide berth, but to check for a lion's surprise attack. I give a few toots. Nothing moves. I tell myself, "Relax. Breathe. Remember Simanga's advice: "Do not be afraid like prey, or aggressive like a hunter. Think peaceful thoughts." That sounds simple and obvious. I've had many life-changing realizations throughout my trip, but my emotions still roller-coaster due to years of bad habits and the fact that I always challenge myself, digging deeper and revealing more character, yet excavating more garbage.

I see hundreds of baboons. They lurk in the woods and run to the road when a bus passes to fight over the orange rinds and banana peels that the great apes toss out the windows. This disproves almost all my theories on animal behavior, and I redouble my efforts to scan the grasses for any signs of lions.

I reaffirm myself, "If you get eaten, you get eaten. There's no use worrying about it. You're only going to make it worse." I pat my seat post for good luck where I've hidden my lucky charms.

The irony of cycling around the world is that I hate being alone, because I don't have anything to distract me from facing my own insecurities and angst. While my feet are spending long hours spinning in circles, my mind is spending long hours spinning, flip-flopping, wriggling and wrangling, seemingly trying to make sense out of everything "wrong" with my life, but really just caught in a self-justification loop. Ever since college when I graduated into the "real world" and realized that I didn't learn anything useful about how life actually works, I've been having an existential crisis. Combine this with a predisposition for depression and I've wasted decades of my life obsessed with what's wrong with my life, rehashing and relabeling my problems and 99 times out of 100, I just feel worse at the end of the day.

In Belgium, I went to see a dentist because I had a bad toothache for months. My checkup was flawless, and the next day my toothache was gone. I realized I had a psychosomatic cavity, and feasibly my depression is psychosomatic simply because that's what I think about. Depression isn't a logical disease; it's more like getting caught in an emotional reaction that spirals into oblivion. Ever since then I've been trying to starve my negative thoughts to death, but with limited success. Thirty-two years of being a pessimist—a "depressimist" would be more accurate—is a challenging habit to break. I suspect that I actually enjoy being depressed. Ironically, there's a benefit to depression—it makes me feel self-important, as if I'm so unique the universe has singled me out to make miserable, and gives me reason to avoid my life. I like to dwell on my problems seeking an answer that will "solve" my life; and, I like to punish myself as if I'm paying penance, and that if I do it long enough and painful enough, I'll stop. I've also mastered denial, drowning myself in senseless distractions, such as alcohol or lust. Ironically, even though I'm occasionally forced to face myself on this trip, one of the benefits, is that there are moments, like now, where I'm too busy surviving to indulge my favorite hobby of feeling sorry for myself.

I've been told, "Getting a life is a moment by moment endeavor to focus on what you want. How can you ever expect to find a solution if all you do is focus on the problem? All solutions are a matter of a new perspective. Pay attention to what you're doing. Your thoughts and emotions are what create your reality; and, if your thoughts and emotions are at crossed purposes, you create self-conflict, distortions and chaos." I think I've proven from my tens of thousands of hours of worry— the best way to be unhappy is to think unhappy thoughts, such as analyzing a bad feeling. On the other side of the coin, when I thought of my trip, I knew I wanted it with all my heart. The idea became alive, grabbed hold of me and has propelled me around the world ever since.

I travel halfway through the park seeing nothing but baboons and bramble; the park seems rather ordinary except there are no humans. The midday heat is making my head ache. Nothing is hunting me but tsetse flies. I curse my 36th set of speed bumps (I've become obsessed with counting things). Just as I fail my serenity test, I hear: thrash, Thrash, THRASH. An elephant materializes out of thin air less than 20 meters away and is charging in my direction. An African elephant's tusks can grow to be three meters long and weigh hundreds of kilos; this one's tusks are nine meters long and weigh a metric ton.

I come to a precarious perch atop a speed bump. I don't have the peace of mind to remember my Nepali guide's advice to run, weaving through the trees. (An elephant could pluck you out of a tree like an apple or just knock the tree down.) The elephant parts the grass like a ship in a stormy sea, trunk raised, trumpeting an alarm. Thrash. 17 meters. Thrash. 15 meters. Ten meters. Five. Seemingly inches away, it veers in a wide arc and disappears behind some bushes.

The elephant regroups with another adult and a juvenile. They are only about 50 meters away. I can barely discern their backs through the tall grass. Another adult is facing me, snuffling and waggling his ears.

I position my bicycle between us and freeze. My heartbeat crashes through my ear-drums, as if an elephant is still charging me. Soon the elephants drift away and resume grazing, as if they played a good joke to snap me out of my doldrums, just like every time I have grease on my hands my nose tickles. I laugh. Only I could miss a six-ton animal on the side of the road, due to the sixty-ton animal lurking in my mind.

I continue slowly, ringing my bell so as not to sneak up on any more elephants hidden in the grass. The bramble disappears revealing a savanna and dozens of elephants, and hundreds of buffalo and antelopes. For miles, the grass is clipped short and the bottoms of the trees are pruned straight by nature's gardeners.

I approach another troop of baboons, and just over the edge of the road a herd of impalas graze. The baboons fail to voice alarm and the impalas don't notice me until I'm in the midst of their herd. One impala sees me, freezes for a second before leaping over his neighbor, and suddenly the herd of impalas flows away like a torrent of golden water, spreading their legs like wings and flying over baboons, boulders and bushes; and, the baboons tumble through the trees and knuckle the ground, fleeing in opposing directions to the impalas—an African traffic jam, resembling my emotions.

When they disappear, I turn and on the opposite side of the road, shimmering in the late afternoon sun, five giraffes, dressed in regal puzzle shapes, heralds of the animal kingdom, puzzle whether I'm a friend or foe. When I swing my camera into view, they gallop away, tails swinging, muscles rippling, awkward yet gallant.

I see many more animals: zebras, steenboks, a bucking wildebeest (certainly, bitten by a tsetse fly). And in the dust beside me are the footprints of the king of magicians, *simba* the lion, lurking nearby, watching me, reading my mind and knowing that, for a few hours, Africa's magic vanished my self-importance and allowed me to simply be me in the moment. I've been told that the trick to being a magician of life is to be amazed by the trick of your life—and I'm certainly amazed at myself for bicycling through Africa unscathed.

Once upon a time, I could quote scriptures from various religions, and site numerous medical and psychological reasons for depression, though I sounded intelligent, I never found God or cured my depression, rarely even enjoying the moment. The bottom-line of life is not what you pretend to want or can theorize, but what you can actually demonstrate and exemplify, even if it's avoiding being trampled by negative thoughts, and converting emotional lions into a moment of peace, and a foundation to grow upon. You could say, I need to stop lion to myself.

Elephant and lion tracks.

44 · Did your trip change you?

I have a new trick. I wind rope around my handlebars, like reins, lean back and pedal. I wear my safari hat, as opposed to my helmet. And to amuse myself, I've taken up smoking. I'm temporarily adopting all the bad habits I can find. It's part of my depression therapy. I figure if I can't get out, I might as well get into it and wear it out. I also have a new bell, which I love hearing jingle down the bumpy cobblestone roads.

I've been following the Rhine River in Germany. I've given up my map, and just keep the river on my right and spin through the cities and woods. I've gotten lost numerous times, but I've never had such a sense of freedom, simply following any trail or road that appears nice, and generally heading southeast. For three days, I've followed my whims: pitched my tent among the bushes on the shore, opposite cities and hills capped in castles and cathedrals; sunbathed in the plazas, lollygagged in cafes; flirted with *Fräuleins*; and drank and ate and smoked whatever I desired.

I've seen more bicycle tourers in one hour than I've seen during my entire trip. Anyone you can imagine seems to be riding down the Rhine River with the wind. Of course, I go the opposite direction, but compared to riding over the Appalachians chased by hound dogs, life couldn't be easier. When I put my legs into it, I can pedal 50 KPH. I remember days in Bolivia where 50 KM would take twelve hours of strenuous pedaling. I can easily outpace the barges and tourist boats. Today, I passed the same boat four times as I kept stopping to talk to people. By the third time, many tourists ran to the port side, as if I were a dolphin, and waved. Some even took pictures of me, the crazy "German."

I enjoy being able to blend amongst the indigenous Germans. Even my bicycle appears German with its industrial black paint job, Ortlieb panniers and Schwalbe tires. "What kind of bike do you ride?" is a common question. I had a basic steel frame made in Waterford, Wisconsin and built the rest part by part off the shelf, fine tuning everything down to the millimeter; and I've been constantly tinkering, rebuilding and repairing my bike ever since it was born. I've worn out six rims, twenty tires, five drive trains, four seats, four derailleurs, six pedals, and much more. My bike is composed of parts from at least 20 countries, and all my gear combined must have come from over 50 countries, not including miscellaneous items that I've picked up along the way. Consider my Australian rim: The raw materials and fuel used to build it were scraped together from all over Australia and probably Asia. (That's not including the equipment used during manufacture, or the resources to support the employees, including, I'm sure, a few schooners of beer.) Then, most likely, this rim was shipped from Sydney to Los Angeles aboard a freighter. From there it traveled by train and truck to Waukesha, Wisconsin where the hub was installed and spokes laced. Then from Waukesha my brother shipped the rim via several connecting flights to San Jose, Costa Rica. Where I, after a long bus ride, carried it on my head for three kilometers, like an African, to my hostel to replace my damaged rim. Now I'm cycling the rim back to Australia.

My bike has literally been scrapped together from all across the globe—a bicycle of the world. It boggles my mind to think of the amount of energy, knowledge and people required to do this.

The only parts that are still the same are the frame, forks and handlebars, and even these I've had welded and painted numerous times. Philosophically speaking, is it even the same bike?

That night, camped on the edge of a forest beside a cornfield, I admire how I've sculpted muscles out of lumps of fat, and adapted myself to riding a bicycle. Cycling has also increased my awareness and reflexes. At a *biergarten*, someone knocked their beer off the table and I snatched it out of midair, shocking everyone. I wonder if I'm even the same person. Everyday I feed my body about 12 liters of water and two kilograms of food (between 6000-8000 calories) from all over the world. My body must have replaced certain parts dozens if not hundreds of times, like my skin, eyes, blood, muscles, bones, molecules, atoms.... Supposedly some of the cells in the eye regenerate every two days, which means so far on this trip I've gone through 2700 pairs of eyes. Nonetheless, even if I did replace my brain in part or whole, I still seem to be thinking and feeling the same depressing thoughts.

Nearby there's an anthill twice the size of my tent. I thought the anthill was a pile of sawdust. My tent is surrounded by hundreds of ants. A dozen inspect my shoes. I'm concerned they will find some cookie crumbs and alert their million closest relatives. I stand on the edge of the hill examining their habits. They don't appear to be building roads, but millions of ants have eroded paths like superhighways in the dirt. They drag pine needles and small twigs down thousands of holes. Each ant appears to have his own hole and sometimes they play tug of war with the pine needles and twigs. In the center is a small pine tree that is being undermined by the ants. A dozen meters away another anthill had destroyed itself by toppling a tree and uprooting the nest.

I still haven't solved the dilemma of how my head and heart disagree? Why do I think my bike trip is the adventure of a lifetime, yet just want to sit on the beach? Why do random thoughts bubble out of my mind, demanding attention and solutions? Why don't I admit that it isn't my intellect that drives me, but my emotions? Perhaps years of letting my mind wander untrained through its imagination is like a million ants eroding gullies and building highways of bad habits and negativity in my brain, making my self-image a residual effect of my past thoughts, feelings and actions. I could list possible reasons and make excuses for my nature and nurture malfunctions—but does it matter? The bottom-line is that I'm the only one responsible for the outcome of my life.

Perhaps my mind is like two ants playing tug of war with a twig; going two directions simultaneously; expending 99% of my energy fighting myself and struggling against the world. (Once when an Australian asked me where I was going, and I told him Melbourne, he said, "That's the entirely wrong direction. If you were going to Darwin, all you'd need is a bed sheet and you could sail all the way there.")

I retire in my tent and think, "If I'm not the ever-changing reflection in the mirror, then I'm not who I was yesterday, or who I'll be tomorrow. I'm not my past mistakes or future accomplishments, or vice versa. Perhaps I'm not my angst-ridden thoughts anymore than I am the water I drink? Maybe I can break the repeating pattern."

Half asleep I realize I've adopted many artificial perspectives throughout my life, like believing I'm helpless, which leads to depression. Fortunately my travels seem to be exposing them one by one and they fall alongside the road. It occurs to me that my trip is like forging metal in a furnace until it's white hot, my suffering burning out the impurities in my spirit. I remember the Mexicans used to call my bicycle, *"El caballo de acero."* (The Steel Horse.) And, my haze of depression lifts when I realize that makes me *"El caballero de acero."* (The Steel Cowboy.)

In one nanosecond, I'm wide-awake, thinking, "Oh! Fuck! I've just wasted my entire life feeling sorry for myself. I've even been wasting my trip, telling myself I can go home when I learn to love life, as if torturing myself were a solution, and missing the point of living."

Too excited to sleep, I crawl out of my tent. A cool breeze scented from the cornfield, where my bicycle hides, enlivens my skin. The trees wave rustling leaves. The glow of distant cottages warms the night. The stars wink, promising new worlds and wishes come true. I think, "It's time to stop fighting myself, stop being a mental hypochondriac, stop living in my imagination—trying to fix the past and fearing the future. I must focus my energies on living in the moment and align my thoughts, emotions and actions, like putting a bed sheet on my bicycle and traveling with the wind, down the river, towards my goal."

The next morning, my mind and body seem to have disappeared, and cycling is as effortless and exhilarating as flying over rooftops in my dreams. I reach a fork in the road, woe am I that I can't travel both paths. I flip a coin and go left. The sky is blue and the atmosphere crisp. Apple trees grow so close to the side of the road that I can pick them as I ride past. Everyone waves and smiles, even the Germans, and I feel like a light bulb illuminated by the electricity of life.

Proust said, "The real voyage of discovery consists not in seeking new landscapes but in having new eyes," and I wonder if he knew his statement was more than a simple metaphor.

Giant anthill undermining a tree. My tent and bicycle in the background.
Opposite: Sunflowers and a church spire in Germany.

Photo courtesy of Dennis Snader.

45 Did you make a difference?

The record-breaking rains and floods have followed us to Greece. In the midst of a torrential thunderstorm, the spokes on Dennis' rear wheel begin to rip out of the rim until it pops into a potato-chip shape and jams against the brakes. Frustrated, Dennis dumps his bike against a bus stop shelter and hides from the storm. I join him, and we eat cookies while watching the cascading rain turn the streets into foam. The tin shack begins leaking on Dennis' foot, and he doesn't bother to move. The lightening flashes and nearly simultaneously thunder cracks. I survey the sheet metal shack nervously and contemplate running across the street to hide in a concrete shrine to the Virgin Mary.

People bandy the phrase "make a difference" to the point it has become a nebulous rule: to live a meaningful life one must make a difference, revolutionize the world and leave a legacy. Most people's herd instinct entices them to join the bandwagon as if the popular opinion is correct and will increase their probability of survival. I'm only halfway around the world and I've fallen off the bandwagon. I wanted to contribute some boon to society, but it's presumptuous to impose a new set of values upon people, as if there's one right way of doing things, and turning the world into a homogenous soup. Besides, people's first inclination is to reject change even if it's beneficial, because they defend an idea (a synaptic pathway) as if it's an arm or leg or even their life that is being jeopardized.

Maybe people don't notice the difference they make. If I eat a cookie, I'm changing the world albeit in a very small way. From a quantum physics perspective if I observe a cookie I'm changing the world. And from a spiritual perspective, if I simply think about a cookie, I'm changing the world.

I believe what people actually mean when they say that they want to make a difference is that they want to see that they have an influence upon life. I've been told that in order to change the world, one must be willing to have their world changed.

As the shack springs more leaks and wondering if I have enough cookies to occupy my stomach until tomorrow, I doubt my trip has made a significant impact—or, should I say that I doubt I've allowed my trip to significantly impact me?

The fire department passes us several times with large vehicles to remove a fallen tree from atop two cars. The fourth time, the fire truck full of statuesque Greeks stops in front of our shack. "The chief ordered us to rescue you," they say. Soon, Dennis and I are sitting in front of the fire department's stove with our clothes steaming in the heat and shivering, numb hands wrapped around steaming coffees. They offer us a ride to Ioánina where there's a bicycle store and cheap hotel. When we arrive at the hotel and they're satisfied that we're warm and dry, their hospitality expands again to include a tour of the city and a dinner invitation. After talking about the politics of Cyprus with one fireman in the station—politics are often the litmus test for friendship—he bragged that Greece has the best food, wine, music and women in the world. (I agree with him, though I seem to think the same of every country.) Indeed, the beauty of classical Greek sculpture is still alive in the people. Golias, the fire chief, has the strongest nose I've seen, as if it's carved out of marble. With such a nose, a man must be destined to lead. His wife Maria is no less than a personification of Aphrodite with long, curly tresses like a Botticelli painting and eyes full of love for Golias. Their children, twin Cupids, are the cutest kids in the world, and when one notices me observing her, takes a cookie out of her mouth and offers it to me. Something of the spirit that inspired the Greeks to personify Dionysus, a god of feasts and wine, still presides over our banquet. Dishes are served until they go uneaten, which is an enormous amount of food for two cyclists that usually consume 3–4 times the average: marinated lambs tongue, spicy beef, rubbery octopus, several gooey cheese dishes, bread, wine, ouzo (a liqueur which tastes like anise and burns my sinuses), and baklava that squirts honey over my hands and face.

Upon parting, Golias, who is an inspiration to all, beats me to the good-byes and thank-yous. "You are very brave men."

"No, we have done nothing." I don't feel brave. I was run off the road today and nearly crashed into a barbwire fence at 35 KPH. Often I feel like a fool for being so reckless with my life. What's the difference between a fool and a brave man? "It is you who we should thank," I continue. "If it weren't for people like you, we would never know the beauty of Greece."

"We might not even have survived the thunderstorm," Dennis adds.

"No, no, no," Golias says vehemently. "You have brought the world to us. Thank you. What you are doing is a great thing, not only for you but everyone you meet."

"You're welcome," I say, wishing I could better express my gratitude.

"I hope to see you again, my friends," Dennis says.

I think, "Yes, that's it, Dennis—friends." I'm amazed that while traveling, sometimes in a matter of minutes, how many kindred spirits that I meet and am honored to call a friend, and how ironic that back home in cities full of millions, that people I saw everyday were mere acquaintances.

The next morning two of our rescuers return. Ladas, like Mercury the messenger, christens our bicycles with bottles of homemade, fruity wine. "Bon voyage," he says and shoves us off with two Greek proverbs: "Starting is half the journey," and "Go slow and you will arrive faster." And alluring Rania, who struck me with Cupid's arrow, says, "Keep bicycling, make your dreams real, give your hurt to the roads, and don't lose your crazy never because it's you."

I like to think that I inspired the thousands of children that I met. Many days I would say hello so many times my voice went hoarse. Is it a coincidence that they are standing on a bicycle tire?

46   Do you have any regrets?

At five in the morning, a booming gong carried on the dense monsoon air, passes through my body, more palpable to my skin than ears, it sets my nerves a tingle and the monastery dogs a howl. Due to exhaustion, my body feels as if it's floating in a void like a singular planetoid and a chorus of dogs seem like a sphere of stars chiming a celestial fantasia. The gong tolls twice more and I feel it vibrate the planks of the rectory floor, approaching like a wave and washing through me. I flop on my stomach and drag my shirt over my eyes and pad my ears.

Yesterday, a Thai family that invited me to dinner was concerned that I wouldn't sleep well in the temple. "Ghosts," they said. Thai people build spirit houses, elaborate miniature shrines containing offerings of food, bottled water, flowers, incense, and candles, intended to lure the troublesome spirits away from the residence of humans. Many times I've seen the spirits take the shape of cats, rats, ants or flies to accept the offerings. Last night, while the monks sat watching game shows, unmolested by mosquitoes in their cloud of cigarette smoke, a spirit was reincarnating as the same mosquito over and over to feast on my sweet *farang* flesh, and I smashed it into oblivion over and over—the Wheel of Life. Was I reducing the karmic debt of an unfortunate soul or increasing my own?

A smaller gong tolls, painful to my ears, like a snooze alarm. I prop myself up on the floor beside the dozens of golden statues of Buddha and underneath the portraits of the benevolent protectorates, the king and queen of Thailand.

Several monks approach. They are very excited. "Buddha. Buddha."

"Buddha? Where?" I wonder if they're talking about ghosts or statues.

They nod excitedly grabbing their robes and pantomiming photography. I grab my camera. No, no, they hold up three fingers. This is how they communicate, "Eight o'clock."

As the morning aches leave my body and mind, I remember that any enlightened individual can be referred to as a buddha. Still I'm uncertain of the Thai's version of Buddhism. Later, a wiry man who has grown stronger with age like a withered stalk, explains in better English, "Do you see the buddha this morning? He walk past you." I shake my head sideways in a combination of disagreement and disbelief. "He come again later."

"Where is he now?"

"In the village with his family. He come eight o'clock. Turn into buddha. You wait. Take picture. Okay."

"He turns into the buddha at eight o'clock." A smirk curls my lips. "How does he do that?"

"He changes from the white robes to the yellow robes."

"What is he now?"

"Human." I can't get a more specific answer as to why this entity transmogrifies between man and god (in this case, he will be a god for three months) other than his obligations are balanced between his family and community. I had hoped enlightenment was a one-way road.

"Where did you learn to speak English?" I ask while we wait.

"I flew in helicopters with the Americans in Vietnam." He pantomimes firing a rifle.

"You were a Thai soldier in the Vietnam War?" He agrees. "And now you're a monk?" He smiles, giving me the impression that he finds his monastic life a humorous quirk as opposed to a penance.

On schedule, a parade of dancers escort a handsome, young man adorned in white silk robes embroidered with flowers, and shaded by a large, lavish umbrella with patterns and fringe. "Do you dance?" the veteran asks me.

"No, I don't dance."

Five minutes later, I'm manhandled to the front of the parade, wedged between two Thais with bottles of Thai rice whiskey. "Drink, drink."

"No, thanks. I have to drive bicycle."

"Try, try. Buddha." Fearing to offend the local customs I imbibe the noxious brew once per revolution. Luckily, we circumambulate the lotus-like temple only five times, drinking whisky, throwing flowers, wiggling hands in the air and bobbing up and down. I feel as if the whole universe is watching, but it's only one small village and the-buddha-to-be, who glances furtively at me every time I pass, as if he's breaking deity protocol acknowledging the bacchanals.

The-buddha-to-be bows before a stone monolith in front of the doors of the temple and repeats verbatim from an elder man kneeling beside him what I imagine are the incantations meant to transform him to godhead. Then he rises and begins throwing gifts of origami lotus flowers to the revelers. The first fistful strikes me like throwing stars in my face and shoulders. The Thai villagers swarm to scoop up the presents. "Money," they inform. The-buddha-to-be, seeing I didn't get any, chucks another handful, pricking and jarring my skull. But, I forgive him; he's still only human at this point.

The-buddha-to-be and the monks enter the temple and close the doors. Everyone disperses and I refuse two invitations to breakfast (the monks have already fed me rice and chicken) and two invitations to more bottles of whiskey. "I must go. I have one-hundred kilometers to ride today."

I'm left alone to repack my belongings, which are drying in the sun. The monks are hanging out the windows of the temple smoking cigarettes watching me. Becoming the buddha takes about three hours and, apparently, is a tedious process. I want to get a photo of them lollygagging—monks love to have their photos taken—but as soon as they see a camera they hide their cigarettes and smiles and turn into religious automatons.

During the ceremony, they invite me into the temple for more photographs. The-buddha-to-be seems as disinterested as any young man would be with raging hormones and a vow of celibacy and, consequently, confirms my suspicion that this is only a figurative ceremony. The monks ask me to stay, "You can talk. Ask questions. Buddha sleep same place you."

"I must go to Laos today." Each syllable drops from my mouth heavier than the last while I simultaneously think, "I should stay." My visas are stacked like dominoes, and the monsoons are sweeping north; if I don't accomplish my scheduled mileage, I will have to pack my bicycle on a bus. I've already skipped past nearly all the national parks, waterfalls, caves and historical sites and drop exhausted at the end of the day. The veteran monk invites me to return. I say it could be many years.

"Mâi pen rai. [No worries.] We will wait."

I leave the sanctuary of the monastery, chug past the villagers, wave goodbye, decline more invitations to breakfast and whiskey, and turn north onto the highway hazy with humidity and fumes, riding around the urban sprawl sprawling onto the road. Only one kilometer down the road, swarmed by tuk-tuks and scooters, like flies in the Outback. I regret my actions—how pointless to travel the world and see nothing. Nonetheless, I continue chugging forward telling myself I don't have any extra days, and remind myself that I set the goal of bicycling around the world eight years ago, and I'm not going to ruin my chance to finish for a whim.

In another few kilometers, after chastising myself, I realize the amazing feat I've just accomplished: I wasn't inspired to play my game of Twenty Questions with the buddha, like I did with the guru in India. My questions are endless, but they all seem to share the basic theme: "What the hell is wrong with me that I can't enjoy the simple pleasures of life?" (Which is a self-defeating question, because my mind begins creating lists of al my problems, making me feel worse.)

Since India, some of the answers seem so obvious (or, perhaps, the questions irrelevant) that I feel like the dumbest person in half the world (I haven't seen the other half yet) seeking the secret of life, while excluding enjoying my life. Feasibly, I have found *the* answer to life, and that is, there is no answer to life. There are no right answers, but I do have the right answers for me right now; and, I believe, the beautiful and mysterious and creative nature of life allows for the questions and answers to evolve, just as me, life, the universe and, even, God evolve. As the guru said, there is no spiritual plateau. I'm almost amused thinking of all my past existential squirming: Who? What? When? Where? Why? How?

Many people seem to think my biggest regret would be losing my career, squandering all my money and opportunity to build a home, or wasting my youth and never being able to have a family because by the time I return most of the women my age will already have husbands and children.

My biggest regret is all the time I wasted cycling around the world while spinning circles in my head. If I could change one thing, it would be to turn back and ask the buddha some questions: "How are you? What is it like to be a buddha? Are you happy? Don't you get tired of people asking you questions all the time? Is there somewhere around here we can get a beer?"

A monk hiding his smile and cigarette
while posing stoically for a photo

47   What next?

Once Shaka Zulu, famous king and warrior who expanded the Zulu territory far across Southern Africa, walked up the Drakensberg Mountains, probably through rain and snow and strong winds, and certainly short of breath, attempting to assail Moshoeshoe's "unassailable mountain fortress". When he reached the top, I imagine he said to his warriors, "I don't know about you guys, but they can have this place." And thus, the Mountain Kingdom of Lesotho survived the Zulu and in a similar manner survived Rhodes, the ruthless entrepreneur, the British Empire, immigrants, Apartheid, and the current invasion of tourism, nearly including my own assault. I ask many people if it's feasible to climb Sani Pass in early spring. Most locals say: "I don't think it's possible. You'll be stuck in a blizzard and just slide back down the pass—that is, if you're lucky. If you're not lucky…." The most sage advice comes from the old-timers: "Course it's possible, just depends how much you want it. It may be sunny. It may be rainy. You'll just have to go see for yourself."

The Drakensbergs (Dragon Mountains) are aptly named: the escarpment is like an ancient corpulent dragon too fat to fly, green scales flaking off to reveal black flesh, with a peach and gray fin along the back, like a dimetrodon, and puffs of clouds, like dragon smoke, condensing atop the mountain. I ride up the dragon's flanks hoping to break its back at Sani Pass. The last few kilometers is an astonishing, nearly unassailable, 33–36% grade on a gravel road loosely anchored to the knolls of the dragon's bones. It's like cycling a staircase. I can't maintain enough momentum to bounce over obstacles, and get stuck on a golf-ball sized stone. I appear immobile, but inside muscles levering titanically against bone, try to move me. Feet locked into the pedals, almost tipping, I dismount quickly and lose grip of my brakes. My bike coasts towards my groin. I jog backwards to avoid being crushed. I can't reach the brakes without getting tangled and dumping my bike, and I'm too off balance to jump clear; out of control, I run backwards down the mountain until I crash into the wall where the switchback switches.

With zero forward inertia, my wheels spin in the grit but don't bite. So I walk slipping backwards. Eight times backwards, nine times forwards. Even just resting with the brakes engaged is challenging, because if my wheels aren't wedged against a rock, I slide backwards. I struggle like this for hours, with my odometer reading zero. Nearing the top, I have energy in my blood but no strength in my muscles, making my knee joints grind like dry gears and a worn chain.

I can see for more than 50 KM over the tops of the foothills the dragon kicked up. In a few hours, the burning African sun has clouded over and icy winds numb my joints. I strain with all my might, snaking up the dragon's switchback like a snail, racing the storm front pouring off the ocean and being knocked out of the air by the Drakensbergs. Gargantuan forces formed these mountains so massive they not only change the weather patterns, they create them. As I crest the summit, fog envelopes the pass and I can barely see the stone wall around the chalet, my night's accommodation, perched on the edge of the escarpment.

Overnight the fog turns to mist to rain to ice to snow. Early in the morning, East Coast Radio calls our lodge and broadcasts a fellow lodger's, weather report: "Everything's white. White white white. Visibility is thirty to fifty meters. The pipes are frozen. You can't flush the toilets," says Steve. A few years back, Steve cycled 12,000 KM from Cape Town to Nairobi skipping some sections due to malaria. Later, I tag along Steve and Graham's *recky* (reconnaissance) of Black Mountain. They have a car full of gadgets, including a GPS that tracks our route so if a whiteout occurs we can drive back blind. The two men check everything: braking through the slush and snow, sliding, steering, Steve even drives through the river, rather than using the bridge, to see if there's ice. Sani Pass is too steep and slippery even in a dusting of snow for their Land Rover and caravan and, since the other side of Black Mountain is warmer, they'll attempt driving in a semicircle north around Lesotho and back south to Durban. Of course they offer me a ride. Hitchhiking around the world would've been relatively easy, yet adventurous and a good way to meet fascinating people.

Steve and Graham drop me off at the lodge, hook up their trailer and begin their trek over Black Mountain, while an Aussie and Yank begin a foot trek down Sani Pass. There's three inches of snow now, even if the sun comes out tomorrow the roads will be slush and mud. I'm stuck here alone except for the staff of locals, and wondering where to go to the bathroom. I've discovered the pipes are above ground, so they have frozen. I thought Steve was exaggerating. In Wisconsin, pipes would not freeze at these temperatures.

I sit by the fire and ruminate. I feel frozen in space if not time. For almost four years I haven't seen grass grow or people age, because I've averaged only 2.4 days in one spot. Time seems to be playing tricks on me now. I remember in New Zealand, the Earth stood still for a moment and then reversed; brown leaves picked themselves off the ground and fluttered back into the branches of their poplar tree. My glucose-depleted brain was tricked by a flock of hedge sparrows roosting. At Victoria Falls, I stood at the edge of a cliff. Raindrops hovered before me on the updraft of the falls. Some flattened into convex shapes like flying saucers. For a moment—or was it an eternity?—I thought I was dreaming or that time had stopped until I reached out and I poked a raindrop, restarting time, and all the drops rained to the ground. Once, I was caught in a swarm of bees, moving in my exact speed and direction, also appearing frozen in space, as if the world was rotating past us. Along the Stuart Highway in Australia thousands of dead kangaroos decay, each like a still frame from a movie: the fresh kill with a trickle of blood at the mouth and tears in its eyes; the next bloated like a balloon and rigormortis pointing the feet towards the sky; another deflated, swarmed by flies, gnawed by predators; a corpse with maggots reanimating the flesh, spilling out the holes like foam from a rabid mouth; then a wrinkled skin covering haphazard bones; and finally bones being crushed by tires, weakened by the sun, and blown away by the wind. I feel like a forensic scientist studying time-lapse photography and circumstantial evidence. "Aha, time does exist. Life is short." But it's my shocking countenance in a mirror once every month that provides the most evidence: my skin is a bit more wrinkly and freckled from the elements; my flesh sags a bit more under gravity's relentless pull and jiggle of the bicycle; my teeth are yellow and worn, my hair thinning and graying; and I have an arse like a baboon from all the cycling—reminders of life's ticking clock counting down the days. Perhaps, I'm being melodramatic, but it's dramatic to me, and death seems a bittersweet reminder that I've a time limit to earthly delights and tribulations.

For years, people often accused me of lying about cycling round the world; suddenly, despite being a month away from finishing in Cape Town and unimaginably further from home, people are asking: "What are you going to do next?" I pace the lodge to warm my blood and ponder: "What's bigger and better than riding a bike around the world?" It seems like a trap to always seek bigger and better. Like Dennis, I feel I've reached the point of diminishing returns. I dream of silly things I never would've imagined, like planting some basil, oregano and tomato seeds and nursing day by day the miracle of fragrant herbs and a plump, red, juicy tomato hanging on a vine like a concentrated drop of sunlight; I dream of making tomato sauce as I dream of meeting a woman and sharing a new adventure, watching the wrinkles unfold on our faces, like a roadmap of our lives together. And possibly the adventure of children, who will stand on my shoulders and see farther than I can see. As my Australian friend, Matt, said, I'm getting clucky in my "old" age.

The snow is up to my knees now. A tour group arrived a few hours ago. As prophesized, they drove blind using GPS. They passed Steve and Graham going the opposite direction and laughed, "Did you see all the snow on their vehicles?" But if they had been thinking, they should've turned around and followed Steve and the storm north out of Lesotho. Now we're all stuck here with two days of firewood, little water, food reduced from a ten-day supply to two days and a dysfunctional loo. (Traveling around the world, I've been amazed that a simple thing like a toilet can rule your life.) Jonathon, the owner realizing we'd be stranded has just arrived; he had to abandon his vehicle halfway up Sani Pass and walk. "Look, I don't want to alarm anyone here," says Jonathan, "but we're not playing. It's not a matter of whether you can walk down tomorrow—you're going to walk down. Look everyone's happy enough now, but wait until tomorrow when the shitter is piled high and we're running out of food and firewood. It's not cold out. In July, this happened and it was too cold to walk out. The roads were closed for ten days. There are no snowplows in Lesotho—you wait for the snow to melt. After four days, the chopper came and picked up the guests and dropped off food for the staff. It was a good excuse for a military exercise, but in this weather, they can't fly even if they want to. No, it's going to get uncomfortable. I'm telling you we're going to have to walk out."

After I announce that I will follow Steve over Black Mountain to the dry valley beyond, Jonathon says, "If you ride up that pass and decide not to move another yard, you'll die. There's no one else—you're on your own out there." My mind gets stuck on the peculiar phrase "decide not to move." South Africa has a strong pioneering spirit that I imagine the States used to have, so he amends, "You can do what you want. I just came to tell you the facts. Tomorrow, I'm walking down with or without you."

I discover the kitchen, with its eternal pots of boiling food, is the warmest room in the house, and the staff are very cheerful compared to the panicking tourists. The tour guide, Frank, is panicking about losing money on his tour and whether one of his group will drop dead walking down the pass: the oldest man is 75, another woman has angina. Ironically, I'm the strongest, yet the most willing to stay and eat mealy maize three times a day until the snow melts. The staff says we could survive for weeks. In the kitchen we sing and dance songs in Zulu and Basotho. One of the maids, Thombi, volunteers to show me how the Basotho stay warm at night.

Outside a herd of sheep is stuck in the snow in a line, unable to flock together for warmth. I'm shaking even by the fire. My feet are wet. The tour leader, with jug ears, is laughing and taunting the elements while smoking cigarettes lost in his glove compartment for a year and drinking a whisky with a snowball stuffed in the glass. If the situation is as grim as everyone behaves, I think he'll regret being cold and hungover, like Samuel's dad, regretted throwing half a sandwich out the train window on the way to the concentration camps. He thought about that sandwich for two years in the camps. Actually, it's been over 60 years and he still talks about that sandwich. The owner's face is weathered, cracked and dry like the Drakensbergs, yet cheerful looking, but I can see moments when his eyes glaze as he ponders the situation. He has turned on the generator, stoked the fires and served a thanksgiving-style dinner to boost morale, even though he has further depleted our food reserves.

During dinner one of the guides asks me, "How are you ever going be happy going back home? I can't ever sit in a cubicle again." I've noticed people have the idea that you're only entitled to one dream, one purpose in life, and once you've done that, there's nothing left to do, except to roll over and go to sleep.

"How could I ever be happy traveling all the time?"

"What are you going to do next?"

"Fly to England. Bring the woman I love back to America. Write a prize-winning book. And live happily ever after."

Mr. Snowball-in-his-whiskey guffaws, "Good luck. Mate."

Jonathon says solemnly, "You must have dreams."

And the guide says, "But if you can bicycle around the world, you must know you could do anything you set your mind to."

"People say that a lot. It's more a matter of heart than mind." I'm reminded of Jasmine's most recent email. "If you want to tell me you love me, just say so. P.S. I love you." I tell the guide, "What I miss most are my friends. I want to be part of a community again. I'm tired of just passing through, just looking, just consuming. I want to build something lasting."

After dinner the others retire in the main house. I'm alone in the dorm. Someone, perhaps Thombi, has lit a fire for me, though it seems we should be saving the wood for cooking. I stand in the blue-black night, the warm yellow light flooding out the windows, and watch the snowfall. It's so peaceful that I can hear the snow tinkle when it hits the ground. I never thought I'd see snow in Africa. I never thought I'd miss snow. It has been eight years, but it feels like just yesterday, I was home watching a peaceful snowstorm in Wisconsin. I long to have a home again where it doesn't matter where I'm going, or what I'm doing, and my friends and family are a short bicycle ride away.

I awake to a day as beautiful as possible. The sun is on full strength. Down the pass, where yesterday it was dry and barren, today it's only snow—thousands of square kilometers of scintillating snow-capped mountains. The lodge looks like Santa's workshop.

Tensions are melting fast. Snowmen, snowballs and icicle sword fights ensue. We're stuck at least one more day but it's pleasant. Helicopters are on standby if there are any problems. Ironically, as we're all trying to get down, all the S'afers (South Africans) are trying to get up to see the snow.

Another day passes waiting for the snow to melt. This is my third day of eating and drinking snowmelt. The Italians left, *"Arrivederci! Sie matto pazzo! Buona fortuna."* (Goodbye. You are crazy. Good luck.) I've learned this phrase in several languages. They made it down safely with minor trouble and will be on the beach in a few hours. Trucks are beginning to climb Black Mountain pass and creating a trail of packed snow. To test the roads, I switch my slick tires to knobbies and hike and bike two kilometers to the general store. It's cold, wet and windy, and my feet go numb. I buy some food, gumboots and two pairs of socks. The return trip with gumboots builds up a lot of steam and I decide to risk Black Mountain Pass tomorrow.

The following day my strategy to wait for the trucks to clear the snow almost worked, but they've churned the roads into mud. The first 14 KM takes three hours. Cycling in gumboots and four layers of clothes is like swimming fully clothed. At the summit, there are soppy mountains covered in scrub and snow as far as I can see. Mud erodes my rims and brake pads, and bitter winds chill my sweat. I won't be able to control my descent and my sweat will freeze. I consider turning back, but I'll have the same problem.

I roll forward and leave behind the "real world," a place where time claimed my grandpa, my sister engaged someone I've never met, other friends and ex-girlfriends have married and divorced and bore children. Bypassed by the hiccupping civilization of South Africa, I enter the timeless bubble of The Mountain Kingdom of Lesotho, where villagers ride horses, raise sheep, wear earth-colored clothes, live in straw and stone huts and huddle around dung fires, where no mirrors exist to remind me of time's relentless march. I leave the place of "What next?" and enter the "What now?"

And the now is enjoying my dream, and daydreaming about a new dream.

48 How does it feel to cycle round the world?

I jinxed myself. South Africa's prevailing winds do not prevail: my panniers function more like parachutes than parasails. I push myself past millions of stalks of wheat, thousands of ostriches and roll down the rolling coast. It rains for days at a time and once a flooding river nearly washes away my tent with me inside. I'm very strong, but the weather has weakened my knees so that I can't even step up to the urinal, just lying down stretches my muscles, and when I awake, I moan and claw my way out of my tent, feeling as if I have rigormortis. Breakfast in-cludes doping two thick cups of coffee that make my teeth tingle, two ibuprofen to loosen my joints, and a handful of sugar to turbo-boost my blood stream.

In Hermanus, the weather calms long enough for me to watch the southern right whales. They've traveled from Antarctica to mate or calve in Walker Bay. I spy dozens of whales spyhopping, sailing, breaching, spouting, splashing and, generally lollygagging and sunning their flippers. It's also the season for great white sharks. I pay a stranger to ship me out to sea, chum the waters with shark livers and fish guts, wrap several kilos of lead around my neck and submerge me in a cage. I'm hoping for a glimpse of a ten-meter shark named Submarine. Several passengers are too frightened or too cold to go into the water, and one man spends the trip chumming the water with his breakfast, so I'm the first one in the cage and the last one out. While sitting atop the cage to keep warm, I see the dorsal and tail fin of a four-meter shark slice the sea towards the bait and towards me. "Dive! Dive!" the dive master commands. (It's safer to be inside the cage.) I go down struggling to keep by my rubber suit from bobbing me to the surface. I position my head in the porthole of the cage, occasionally hanging a bit outside because of the rocking sea and the tendency of my rubber suit to float to the surface. The dive master is pulling the bait towards me luring the shark closer. A torpedo-shaped shadow emerges. The school of mullet, called shark toothpicks by the local fisherman, scatter. The shadow gathers particles of the murky sea together and a great white shark materializes before me. The lips pull back from the gaping mouth exposing rows of serrated teeth. A shark's nose-length from my face—Chomp!—the shark attacks the bait. The great white shark turns, revealing the scars on his flank and his great white belly, and—Bang!—his tail thumps the cage. I swallow one of the Seven Seas and surface with a case of the hiccups frightened into me, choking and gasp, "That was awesome!"

It hurts to swing my leg and worn out joints over the saddle the next day. The sky is brilliantly blue, dappled in puffs of white. The spring flowers appear illuminated from the inside out. The ocean is red during the day and glows phosphorescent blue at night from the annual tide of red algae. I cycle down the infamous Garden Route for days and by the time I reach the Cape Peninsula, the scenery is world-class. Soon, however, the weather turns against me. I trundle into the famous southeasterly wind, known as the Cape Doctor. I pass large tortoises, penguins, whales, seals, shipwrecks (cursed winds), 1200 species of the fynbos flora kingdom endemic only to the tip of South Africa, past the Cape of Good Hope to Cape Point, the intersection of the Atlantic and Indian Oceans and, according to my brochure, the most southwesterly point of Africa.

The winds push me effortlessly at 40 KPH up the other side of the peninsula. I pause at a curio stand and top off my panniers with rocks carved into African motifs. I haven't seen my family in years, and I figure they'll disinherit me if I don't bring presents for their efforts to manage my mundane affairs back home and bail me out of trouble abroad. The wind and my legs stall in Kommetjie. I pitch camp and walk down to the beach for a sundowner, minus the beer and cigarettes. The clouds glow like the coals of a *braai* (a South African wood-fire barbecue) and I watch the sun set on my last full day. I was born in Milwaukee on the edge of the Great Lake Michigan; most people don't realize that Milwaukee, even though it's in the middle of the North American continent, is a seaport connected to the Atlantic by a series of lakes, rivers and locks. While grandpa was fighting on the

European frontlines in World War II, grandma was building submarine destroyers in Sturgeon Bay, Wisconsin. I dip my toes in the ocean. If I had enough energy, I could swim all the way home. It's not far now.

As I watch the sea gently swell, its colors shifting between lavender and magenta, a frightening monster materializes from the murky deep blue haze of my mind. I never believed that my knees were strong enough or my self-esteem great enough to succeed. And I thought I had better-than-average chances of being killed by over-exposure, crushed by a truck, murdered for my wallet or riddled with disease. I had made a will, giving my mother, who had brought me into this world, the legal right to remove me. Yet, I'd risked traveling because my previous life hardly seemed worth living. Chuckles and snorts rattle out of my lungs, and tears gush from my eyes. "Damn, I'm still alive!" Angst, my loyal fear, materializes like a shark in the ocean of my mind. "Now, what to do with my life?"

After surprising myself at how good it feels to cry, I realize I'm sure to disturb my mind if I chum the waters. I massage my puffy eyes and meander through the beached kelp to my tent. I've weathered the trip well. I'm ever grateful for being healthier, stronger, more peaceful and wiser. I'm grateful for my opportunity, my family, my friends and the kindness of strangers. I'm proud of all the experiences I've collected. Experiences are like diamonds, which are relatively common stones in Africa. No matter how a diamond is cut, it could be better or worse or simply different; some feel the most beautiful crystals are the ones nature sculpted, and some people's diamonds are lumps of coal; in any case, what makes a diamond special is the quality of light cast upon it in such a way the diamond catches, refracts and reflects the light back. Now that I've survived, and can laugh at my frustrations, I'm most grateful for my uncut diamonds buried in the muck that I've since polished and held in the sunshine, in the light of my mind, en-light-en-mental. A grand paradox of life is that one must suffer to enjoy it. As my eyelids close the curtain on my last day, I vow to break my limbo and go to Cape Town tomorrow rain or shine.

The next day, during a peaceful drizzle on a quiet road snaking along the cliffs, I spy a lonely whale, smooth as an innertube except for occasional barnacles, bobbing in the waves in time with my heartbeat. A few minutes pass and the whale bobs closer. "I should go before the weather worsens," I think, "Stop procrastinating. Let's finish this and start a new life." When the whale rolls his head out of the water, stopping when his black eye, big as a bowling ball, focuses on me. We look at each other for a minute, and then he submerges, his tail waving goodbye, symbolizing the end of my trip. The tempest blows again, washing they sky gray. I've learned that even sharks prefer calm waters and whales prefer sunshine; yet, if worst comes to worst, animals, even cows stick their arses in the face of the storm, aligning themselves like iron fillings in a magnetic field, and go about their business of enjoying sweet grass and the warmth of leaning against a friend.

It rains so much that the sewers overflow and the manhole lids float away. I hardly notice the storm or hills as I go about the business of enjoying life. I descend a hump of Table Mountain and the water causes my brakes to fail. My life—or is it my death?—flashes before my eyes one last time. I barely control my descent by hunkering down low, pumping the brakes, swerving side to side to decelerate, and grinding my cleat into the pavement. I screech to a halt hundreds of meters later, relieved and impressed. At the beginning of my trip, I wouldn't have had the strength, agility or peace of mind to have done this.

Physically, I've accomplished my goal; literally, it's the end of the road: I've cycled the circumference of the planet (nearly four times the circumference of the moon) through 50 countries and six continents. If I include my 10,000-KM warm-up across the United States and all the preparation, it has taken me 9 years to accomplish my dream.

I still find it interesting that people spontaneously ask me the same questions everywhere I go. Now that I've arrived, everyone wants to know: "How does it feel? Are you a different person?" Conceivably, they're asking themselves: "Was it worthwhile? Should I try to live my dream?"

I believe the conception that traveling destroys prejudices is true; however, there's also a popular misconception among travelers: that traveling will make you a different person, meaning a better person, that the longer and harder your travels, the more different you'll become. I think it's the opposite: the more difficult your travels, the more you separate the chaff of your mind and body from the wheat of your soul—the more you become who you are.

Perhaps this is also the answer to *what next?* I don't think life is like climbing a ladder, each rung bigger and better than the last; I think my bike trip was about as big as possible. Does that mean that I should retire my bike or my self?

No. It seems that the next adventure in life is *not* about turning my gaze towards cycling around the moon (as many people jokingly suggest), but turning my gaze inward towards my true self and towards the details in daily life and seeing the miracles that have always surrounded me.

As for how it feels: I arrive at a hostel stuffed—as usual—with Germans and English. There's no yellow tape at the finish line, no journalists, no friends or family, no woman of my dreams waiting to wrap her arms around me. I tell the receptionist, "I just rode my bicycle around the world," words I'd envisioned would be a magic spell transforming the Wisconsin frog into a prince of the universe.

Nothing happens. I don't feel anything. I don't feel like the Vasco da Gama of cyclists. I wonder, "Did I do something wrong? Have I worn out my emotions?"

Nonplussed the receptionist responds, "We get a lot of cyclists here." Ironically, a nearby sign reads: "Our deepest fear is not that we are inadequate. Our deepest fear is that we are powerful beyond measure.... And as we let our own light shine, we unconsciously give other people confirmation to do the same. As we are liberated from our own fear, our presence automatically liberates others. ~ Nelson Mandela."

Her comment chums the waters of my mind, and the postpartum bicycle blues begin to surface. For two weeks, I'm in shock: weeping at silly things and laughing at serious things. I feel wise and naïve. I feel proud and humble; and, my ego desperately tries to interpret my life as a prince.

My friend, Jesus (pronounced "hey Zeus") and I are taking a cappuccino—what a luxury this steamy foamy milk!—in the hostel café with a view of Table Mountain through the windows. A rose-colored pigeon that's accustomed to taking his breakfast from the crumbs on the floor is caught inside when the doors and windows are shut during a squall. The pigeon flutters into the window, cracking his head. The fat, short, lumpy bartender says in a gravelly voice, "Wait a minute. Oh no. Don't hurt yourself. I'll open the door for you. Come this way. Oh, poor thing." She flaps her arms herding the pigeon towards the door.

"I used to think she was an old hag," Jesus says while I sip my cappuccino. "By the way, she's dying of cancer—but did you see her talk to that pigeon? To talk to a pigeon, you have to think like a pigeon. Part of your mind has to be a pigeon. For a moment, she was divine. Watching her, we forgot we existed, and we empathized with that pigeon. When we sympathize with something, we become that thing for a moment. Isn't she wonderful?"

A few days later, I ask the bartender how she feels. "Fine," she replies, a stock answer.

"I brought you a book. Do you know Lance Armstrong? He survived testicular and brain cancer and then won the Tour de France seven times in a row." I've never spoken to her before, but I've often heard her yelling at the young hostelers working in the bar, and I expect she'll be offended that I know her secret and yell at me.

"Oh," she says, sounding like a slow leak in a tire, and seems to deflate in stature. She gingerly slides the book towards her. "Thank you. I like to read anything that may help." Her eyes flood with tears, "Thank you so much. It is so scary sometimes," her voice warbles, "but I'm surviving."

My eyes flood and my voice warbles, "I hope it helps."

"I'm sure it will."

I realize this is what it feels like to cycle around the world; and, I realize that I found what I'm looking for—not an answer to a question—but a feeling of being more alive—and that I didn't have to ride all the way around the world to find it... or did I? The irony makes me laugh and cry at the same time, which I didn't know was possible.

Now, I'm free to be whatever I may be—I can be the frog or the prince, or both, or neither, or something never imagined before. I can feel the panicking of a pigeon, or the fear and hope of a woman dying of cancer.

I imagine myself a whale, and I feel the sun on my tail as I wave goodbye-hello.

Epilogue

A hero ventures forth from the world of common day into a region of supernatural wonder: fabulous forces are there encountered and a decisive victory won: the hero comes back from this mysterious adventure with the power to bestow boons on his fellow man.

~ Joseph Campbell

The Hero with a Thousand Faces. Princeton: Princeton University Press, 1949. Page 30.

49 ○ What's it like to return to the "real world"?

I've left the world where everyday is Sunday and returned home. I was amazed simply to drive a car effortlessly up hills, and walk through grocery stores where the average citizen has more options than all the ancient kings and queens combined. My friends had endless supplies of ice-cold beer. My mother and sister seemed to material-ize food in the kitchen (without having to chase a chicken around the backyard). I was mesmerized by my brother in-law's gigantic, wide-screen television promising to ship hap-piness to my doorstep, including pills to get me up and pills to put me down, and cures to dozens of new societal ills. Women I'd never met wrote to tell me how adventurous and handsome I was, and that they always wanted to meet someone like me. I had numerous job offers from a wide variety of fields simply because employers thought I was a fascinat-ing and capable person. Even my father was proud. It seemed I'd earned the keys to the doors of opportunity in a country full of resources to make any dream a reality.

However, after my four-year hiatus, returning to a culture that claims to be a modern life of convenience and freedom, that has adapted the environment to suit every whim, yet requires a minimum of 13 years of schooling just to learn how to survive in its synthetic habitat, visiting foreigners were having their retinas scanned in the airport, old women forced to dump their water and perfumes in the garbage, and I was told to remove my worn-out flip-flops so they may x-ray them for security risks, I made a seemingly obvious observation—"What the hell happened to America while I was gone?"—and was told by the Homeland Security Officer, "If you don't like it, you can go back to where you came from. We don't need people like you here!" and I realized that America is the strangest, most foreign country I've ever visited.

I've moved three times, and my wanderlust is compelling me to move again. People often ask, before my trip even began, "How are you going to ever be happy back in the real world?" It baffles me that people who've never left the country knew it would be so challenging to return. Conceivably, they realize on an instinctive level that the "real world" is *not* the real world, but more like the artificial culture. People also enjoy saying, "You've had your fun. Now it's time to get down to business," meaning: restart my career, climb the corporate ladder, and earn my fortune so I can buy a house, attract a mate, provide for a family, retire as soon as possible, and live happily ever after (meanwhile, taking two weeks of vacation per year). These people seem to view me as a maverick; and, I hypothesize, they'd prefer I join their game of climbing the cultural ladder, so that it justifies and supports their own existence, rather than consider the frightening possibility of: "What have I done with my life?" which might lead to a more frightening possibility: "Now what?"

Traveling, it was easy to see through people's cultural baggage, thinking I was the normal one, and everyone else was curiously abnormal, but submersed in my own culture again is like being in a funhouse, seeing hundreds of reflections of myself in the warped mirrors; therefore, my major realization—more like an obvious fact that I can no longer runaway from—is that I've been programmed, culturally conditioned, brainwashed by my parents, teachers, pastors, friends, enemies, officials, professionals, books, televisions—every aspect of society, most being well-intentioned people that have no idea they are running on automatic pilot. I've even programmed myself to adapt to a manufactured environment and justify my self-worth in a society that constantly portrays we're inadequate at best if not worthless sinners. (While we may not be more significant than the swirling eddy of a butterfly's wings in an infinite universe, we are not insignificant; society ignores and denies that we're as special, unique and important as anything else.) In other words, I've been sucked into the culture's game of trying to prove myself more special than everyone else at the expense of everyone else. In one of my favorite books, which fueled my trip, *Walden*, Thoreau said the worst overseers are men who are slave-drivers of themselves: "...slave and prisoner of his own opinion of himself." Thoreau elaborated upon the pitfall, "What a man thinks of himself, that it is which determines, or rather indicates, his fate." And concluded in a famous quote, "The mass of men lead lives of quiet desperation."

Since I've returned strange words and phrases are bandied in daily conversations, like: *anti-terror, weapons of mass destruction, war for freedom and democracy, axis of evil, time of crisis, shared disaster*—endless mantras (*blamestorming*) of America versus the world. Yet,

I'd just returned from a world full of happiness and kindness, where everybody and every-thing was a cause of exploration and surprise. I'm disheartened to discover the American culture is even more isolated (less than 10% of the citizens have traveled abroad), ego-centric and fearful than when I left. I feel caught in an Orwellian universe ruled by the *doublespeak* slogans: "War is Peace. Freedom is Slavery. Ignorance is Strength." Not only have Orwell's fictional words—*doublespeak, doublethink, newspeak, thoughtcrime*—be-come incorporated into the English language, but they have also have become day-to-day concepts to *spin* reality.

I had no doubt that most of my cultural beliefs were lies consciously propagated by the media, governments, religions, corporations, and maybe even the *illuminati* (another new word I've learned). The benefit (there's a benefit to everything) is that cultural lies (myths, beliefs, illusions) contain a grain of truth: they help quell fear, give a sense of hope and faith, protect people who can't or don't want to understand, channel the ener-gies of the masses into beneficial endeavors; but the cost is that myths can also distract people from what is meaningful by hiding the truth (preventing corrupt people from becoming powerful or keeping corrupt people in power) effectively teaching victimiza-tion and turning ordinary citizens into fearful, mindless slaves. (Possibly the dozens of recent zombie movies are a subliminal rebellion against this mentality.) Consequently, almost everyone spends their lives trying to mold themselves to the expectations of the outside world, or trying to mold the world to their expectations, so that they can confirm their self-worth in an infinite self-justification loop.

If this is the real world, my trip was feeling like the surreal world. Joseph Campbell's books are some of the rare books that altered the course of my life; however, I've had my adventure, been called a hero, but where is my "power to bestow boons"? Where's my Holy Grail. My Golden Fleece? Did I even win a "decisive victory"? For a few months, I thought so, but now.... There's a plaque on a bus stop near my apartment that I've walked past almost every day for a year, "A good traveler is one who does not know where he is going to, and a perfect traveler does not know where he came from—Lin Yutang." I don't feel like a perfect traveler, but after discovering how the world really works and what it means to be human (opposed to a cultural zombie), I feel I've turned myself inside out and upside down, and must reevaluate my life, disadapt and readapt; yet, I keep thinking, "I'll still be stuck in an artificial culture. Doesn't anybody else see that life doesn't have to be this complicated or cutthroat?"

Samuel, my housemate from DC, who had visited me in Thailand, calls to see how I'm readjusting. In the three years since I've returned, I've also had several I-can't-live-without-you relationships, and a dozen jobs ranging from artist to Balinese art importer; I even had a job offer to be a househusband and father. Samuel asks, "I would really like to know your thought process. Why do you continue to willingly and knowingly plant seeds in rocky dry soil that will never produce beautiful flowers or delicious fruit?"

"I don't want to play the victim, but I have to confess it's a lot harder to fit back into our society than I ever imagined."

"Why? After what you've done; this should be easy."

"I thought anything would be easy compared to cycling around the world, but I underestimated how exhausted my body would be. And, maybe I got lazy, or lost my motivation to run the rat race... but what I really think happened is that I lost my identity."

"Your identity?"

"My self-concept, reality, culture, personal myths, belief system, philosophy, fantasy— whatever you want to call it—has been shattered. I just don't fit in America anymore."

Samuel says, "I've been observing you for a long time to see if you're any better off because of your bike trip, and I haven't been able to find any evidence; in fact, I think you might've ruined yourself. You're like a war vet whose risked his life and seen his friends killed. Now you've come home and realized that the whole system is bullshit."

"It *is* bullshit. After traveling the world and seeing the most beautiful people and places, it seems ridiculous to sit in a cubicle doing graphic design and advertising, trading my life for electronic dollars. There were advertisements stamped on the eggs I just bought. I don't want to be part of that mentality anymore." I sigh, "You're not the only one analyzing me; seems everyone I know is seeking evidence that I'm a better person, and discovering that I'm more dysfunctional than ever. Dennis made a prophetic remark years ago when he resigned in Turkey, 'The real test of whether we have grown on this trip is what kind of life we create for ourselves when we return to the same environment.'"

"From what I know, it's not uncommon for people who've achieved a monumental goal to become depressed afterwards. My theory is: unless they actually enjoyed the journey, they realize they've traded their life for the gold at the end of the rainbow, and that gold can't buy a life of experiences, a personality, friends or happiness. I also think people get burnt out and aren't happy with the little things anymore."

"I don't think I'm ruined. It's natural to always want to experience new things. I just haven't found a new dream. I must've fell for the cultural belief that there aren't supposed to be Monday mornings in life, that we're supposed to be hooked by life, dragged along, constantly entertained; and, I've been waiting for something to find me, rather than create something. I feel trapped between two worlds—the mundane and the magical."

"You have to do something. Be a squirrel. Store some nuts. One day you'll be old and you won't have anything. Our days of carousing are over. What do you need to do to put closure on your trip? The clock is ticking. You have to stop running away."

"I can't go back to being blissfully ignorant, but I don't know how to go forward."

Several weeks after our phone conversation, Samuel flies to Arizona to help me recover from culture shock. As we get reacquainted, we simultaneously drink beer, surf porn and take some intelligence quotient exams on the Internet. I surprise myself by consistently scoring in the top 1% of the population. Then I take several emotional intelligence exams, and shock myself by consistently scoring in the bottom 1%. "I'm an emotional moron," I say.

"That explains a lot doesn't it," Samuel says. "It's amazing you survived your trip. Really, I mean that. What kind of idiot walks into a bar in Africa and announces he's trying to find the man who robbed him?"

The following day, we hike Camelback Mountain. It's my favorite thing to do, because it burns off my angst so I can sit peacefully at the top of the mountain looking down at the sprawling humanity, small and seemingly insignificant. As we climb a steep boulder staircase, we discuss life. "Have you already forgotten how good you have it? In Wisconsin, it's minus five degrees; here, oranges are falling off the tree."

"I know. I just feel like I'm living in an illusion."

"What do you mean?"

"I mean, I think we've all put ourselves inside a tiny box, and that box is our safe comfortable version of reality." I expound on my theories of cultural conditioning, essentially saying: We're all born into a system, and I don't mean whether we drive on the right or left side of the road; I mean all the societal rules about good and bad, impossible and possible, that design the fabric of our minds and drive our self-image. I've discovered hundreds of cultural rules and beliefs. I've been told, and I'm beginning to understand, everything our culture teaches us is a lie—and there's nothing more dangerous than to believe your own lies.

Sam says in his overly-pragmatic manner, "I don't know if all that spiritual philosophical stuff improves anybody's life. It doesn't put food in people's mouths. I understand what you're saying, but I don't think anyone else cares that society is living a lie as long as they have their creature comforts."

"I still love America and think it's full of opportunities. My opinions aren't fixed; I'm just attempting to put things in perspective. But it seems we're on the brink of disaster. Imagine what happens if we run out of oil even for one day. People have to wake up, before our society consumes itself."

"I hate to break the news to you, it's not the rest of the world that's the problem, it's you," Samuel says. "Besides all this ranting, what're you going to do to actually improve your life?"

"There's nothing wrong with ranting if it leads to some positive change. One of my favorite quotes is by Nietzsche: 'One must still have chaos in oneself to be able to give birth to a dancing star.' I know I sound hopeless, but without yin there's no yang, without pain there's no catalyst for change. I just wonder how much more pain I'll have to endure—if my trip around the world didn't force me to change myself, what will?"

Samuel pauses on the edge of a cliff overlooking the Phoenix megapolis, cupped by a mountainous bowlful of misty smog. "Are you okay?" I ask.

"I'm fine, but we gotta figure this out before we reach the top of the mountain. You're almost forty," Samuel says, "and I might not always be around to help you." He rests near a monumental saguaro. "It just occurred to me, people are like a cactus. They're soft on the inside, and as they grow they get a thick skin full of thorns. And if you took the cactus to the arctic, it would still be a cactus, because that's all they know how to be."

"And it would freeze to death before it could adapt. But," I reflect, "some people are like lotus flowers. They sprout in the bottom of mucky ponds, reaching towards the light, eventually breaking through the surface to blossom and reveal their inner beauty. I feel I'm on the edge of a great discovery, but I'm afraid to jump into the unknown," I say as I teeter on the edge of the cliff. I have no fear of heights; in fact, I find it thrilling to lean over the edge, just to the point of losing my balance. Why can't I do this with my emotions?

"So, you explained the problem. What's the solution? What did you learn?"

I summarize in rambling puzzle-piece fashion, essentially saying: I've discovered there are an infinite amount of answers or cultural perspectives and traditions. In almost every culture, for example, success fundamentally means surviving first and thriving second. In the Aborigine culture, their values stem from dreamtime (which to them is objective reality, as opposed to day-to-day life) including their traditions to ensure a successful life. Christians believe a successful life is rewarded in the hereafter; whereas, Hindus believe success is being reincarnated on a higher plane in the next lifetime. Success in China doesn't revolve around the self as much as the family and future generations. The American Dream believes individuals can create their own definition of success; contrarily, it bears mentioning again, many Americans believe success is related to status—feeling important compared to the rest of society, even relishing other people's failures, look at all the tabloids. Each culture's definition of success has both a grain of truth and a grain of lie. Furthermore, every individual within a culture has a slightly different definition of success. The common denominator is the desire for success; the difference is the definition.

There are many common denominators. I've concluded from the questions people asked during my journey, that, more or less in order of importance, we all have this in common: We're needing to survive, afraid of dying, even more afraid of not having an influence in life, wanting to thrive and grow, and love and be loved, gently accepting the unknown with a sense of hope and faith, questioning if there's something more, dreaming of realizing our fullest potential, and, occasionally, living life beyond our wildest imaginations.

I find it comforting knowing that if I've experienced an emotion, someone somewhere shares that emotion with me. The reasons may differ, but we all feel fear and joy and everything in between in infinite variations. The most powerful emotion that drives most people is fear—fear of physical survival but more often fear of emotional survival. Consequently most people are struggling to prove their self-worth, while hiding and denying their fears, especially from themselves, and distracting (supplementing) their egos with their favorite obsession (the most popular being: food, sex, gossip, money and drugs)—a behavior pattern that devolves into an infinite variety of psychological dysfunctions which results in physical dis-ease. That is the human pitfall. The second most common group of people are creatures of habit, stuck in neutral, conditioned to reactively deny both their fear and their joy. And the most uncommon common denominator are people that drive their life with the desire for joy—the desire to turn dreams into reality, creating bigger, better, faster and more joyfully (meaning *full-of-joy* or *full-of-love*).

Despite a few melodramatic moments, almost everyone everywhere that I've met with an open heart and open mind, has been kind and generous, valuing their friends and family almost more than anything, and wanting to leave a legacy for their children, if not humanity. I believe people always make the best decision for themselves, with some unfortunate, unforeseeable consequences if they're being reactive, meaning fearful. Fear (pain of loss) is almost always imagined, a residue from cultural and emotional baggage. Often fear grows into anger (resistance to change) and sometimes anger grows into violence (forcing the outer world to cooperate with your inner world). I'm not sure I've ever encountered someone trying to harm me as much as protect themselves. I think if I truly understood someone else's point of view, I wouldn't be able to blame them for anything; therefore, I remind myself to have compassion for my fellow human beings, because other people's answers to life work perfectly for them (otherwise they wouldn't feel a need to do them) and are often better than mine, and whenever we've combined our views, we've discovered an even better answer. Of course, there were some hard people and hard lessons, but I learned something from everyone. Viewing my trip from the safety and comfort of my home, I can truly say that I've enjoyed mutually beneficial encounters with every single person I've ever met. My only regret is the people I didn't meet.

I can also say with certainty—not because it's a belief or myth, but because I experienced it to be true—everyone loves somebody and something, and everyone feels safe because they love and are loved. And as a whole people are far more capable of creatively changing for their benefit than they give themselves credit.

As for everything else, I realized that I cannot intellectually digest the world based upon facts—it's far too complex and constantly evolving—it's also far more mysterious and awesome than I imagined, and I've only scratched the surface of the adventures possible. But if you want a bottom-line, there's no right way or right answer, just a right answer for right now. In fact, maybe the answers are irrelevant, maybe it's simply the questioning, questing and mysteries of life that are the answers. Actually, maybe it's not as much of a factor of discovering as it is creating.

I conclude my lessons learned with my favorite expression, "Like they used to tell us in Thailand: 'People are same, same but different.'"

"Sounds like you might have fallen in the trap you spoke about. Why don't you exemplify everything you talk about?" Samuel says. "Why not combine what you learned with your passion and create something new? It doesn't matter what you do, but you gotta do something."

"Sometimes I wonder if I subconsciously intentionally jumped into the pitfall just to see what it is, and discover how to escape. On my trip, and even now, I've never felt so alive, yet there are times as if I feel like I'm literally dying, as if I'm going through labor pains, about to be born again. Anyhow, you're right. It doesn't matter what I choose, provided that I'm passionate about it."

I'm reminded of a story I heard during my journey: Before the Wright Brothers invented the airplane they were bicycle and kite designers. One day while riding a bicycle with a kite tied to the handlebars, the front end of the bicycle lifted slightly, and the brothers realized that if they could bicycle fast enough or design a kite big enough, they could fly. And eventually they turned that dream of flying into a reality.

We arrive at the hump of Camelback, with a 360° view of urban sprawl. It's ironic that from an emotional perspective, my trip started and ended with Samuel, and I've circled back to the same dilemma-opportunity as 13 years ago when alone on the couch in our DC apartment. Since I've returned, I haven't had the courage to ask myself one simple question because I'm afraid of the answer. It's almost the same question I asked myself 13 years ago, "If I can ride around the world, I could do anything I can imagine; and if I could do anything, what would I do?"

I've always wanted to be an example to people that they could do anything; ironically, I realize it's the lesson I've always been trying to teach myself. The irony of my trip is that I went around the world thinking that if I tortured myself to learn the meaning of life it would solve all my problems and *then* I could live my life; when, actually, if I would just live my life, that would give it meaning and all my problems would be resolved or appear as simple stepping stones to my goal. In other words, I had the whole equation of life backwards. I understand a simple quote for the first time: "There is no way to happiness. Happiness is the way."

There's a big difference between intellectually understanding a concept and having an emotional understanding of an experience and realizing it on a deep heartfelt level that reshapes the foundation of who you are.

When I returned I did have a heartfelt experience that cracked my foundation and began this culture shock: while I traveled, I often dreamed of a tomato garden, to me it symbolized a successful trip, finding a new home and watching my influence nourish the community. Months after I returned, my landlord was inspecting the property and said, "Did you see this tomato plant back here? I've never been able to get tomatoes to grow, and all of sudden this one's sprung up like crazy. You'd better keep an eye on this; you've gotta lot of tomatoes that need to be eaten."

As I explained this coincidence to a very wise friend, I realized all the other dreams and fears my mind must have turned into reality, and came to the shocking conclusion that I must be careful what I think. He said, "Congratulations! You're a beginner," meaning after all these years of cycling around the world, I've only taken the first step down the spiritual path, because I've finally had a heartfelt realization that my emotions, thoughts and intentions not only influence reality, but can create reality. Ever since then it seems my life has been a chaotic cause and effect of my thoughts colliding with my emotions; but, finally, I seem to be gaining hope—if I can wish a tomato into existence, what else can I do?

Now I realize that the true adventure lies inward, and I get to begin a magical, mystery journey, from child to adult, from zombie to magician, seeking to discover the truth of myself. Taming my emotions until I can play them like a musical instrument, savouring their flavors like a gourmet meal. Restructuring my hard drive. Rewriting my rules. Dropping my box. Centering myself and setting a new reference point to reality. Finding the hope that life is full of infinite adventures and joys waiting to be discovered, and not only can I choose my adventure, but I can create my adventure. I think it begins by being honest about who I am, where I'm actually going versus where I truly want to go, and then jettisoning all the emotional baggage from my bike so that I can arrive in this lifetime, and taking responsibility that I am the only one who can engineer my destiny.

I look down at the grid pattern of Phoenix. "Look at all those roads, all those possibilities," I say to Samuel. "I come up here every week and look at all these roads, and still I travel the same way everyday. Wouldn't it be interesting if we had this perspective on our own life?"

I reached the limits of my physical body during my trip many times; on the other hand, I never came close to reaching the potential of my mind, and I suspect that my mind's potential is unlimited, and that if I were skilled enough, if I could break out of my box, if I could master being a human being—I could fly. People used to laugh at me when I told them I wanted to cycle around the world. What will they say now if I tell them I want to learn to fly with my mind and to do and create things that are unimaginable and impossible? Would they still laugh? And if they laughed, maybe I would simply say, "If you could do anything, what would you do?"

"I think I know what I need to do."

"Are you sure, do you want to talk about it?"

"It's a little hard to explain now. I'll tell you someday, but thanks for your help. If it weren't for friends like you…. We'll, let's just say life wouldn't be so fulfilling."

"Why don't we climb a different mountain tomorrow?" Samuel asks.

"Why don't we?"

50 Did you find what you were looking for?

Ironically, it isn't until I return home, and due to a chain of improbable events going back seven years, if not my whole life, that, as an ancient Buddhist proverb says, "When the student is ready, the teacher will appear."

— Buddha: You may. You have many questings.
— **Scott: May I refer to you as the Buddha?**
— You may. What you may also say is not *The Buddha* but *a Buddha*, meaning in the heart of each of you is God. The Buddha is more a philosophy of existence than it is a God to be worshipped. It is a life to be lived rather than a solution. Think of it this way: as you were riding and as you were thinking, you were not only riding away from something, but you were riding to something with every pedal stroke. On the way, there were things that you were observing, but the whole thing was done in solitude, isolating you so the trails that you went across and over were little changed by your passage; but you were changed by your passage, as well as others were changed that came in contact with you. To some of them, the sheer insanity of what you were doing elevated you to a level of almost god-like proportions in their mindset. That you had traveled to

places, you had done things, it made you for a moment be the center of their attention. And there was part of you that had the thought process: "This is what I want," and another part of you that said: "Wait, I'm not getting everything out of doing this that I wanted."

— Getting what exactly?

— What do you perceive you were searching for when you started your trip?

— Peace, happiness, enlightenment....

— And all of those other nebulous, external things, which you can make part of your life anywhere, moment by moment, as long as you're willing to pay attention to: *It's peaceful. It's joyful. It's beneficial.* By recognizing the outside world as a thing that isn't going to go away, you can then start pedaling to absorb the very thing that you think you're searching for.

— What is enlightenment?

— En-*lighten*-ment is where you shine the light of consciousness on the inner depths of your own inner self and you en-*lighten* that inner depth. It doesn't mean giving up pieces of your self. It means, don't live in the shadows of your self. Shine the light on your inner self. None of it is good. None of it is bad. It all serves a useful purpose. Ultimately, enlightenment is seeing the light of consciousness en-*lighten* everything.

— What happens when I experience a moment of enlightenment?

— In that one brief moment, you lose the need to defend the body. Your mind detaches from the self-defense posturing and can actually travel upward and outward to envelope as much of the universe as it is that your mind will allow itself to do.

— Is enlightenment the same as a peak experience?

— No. Enlightenment is seeing everything as a peak experience in it's own solitude.

— How many peak experiences have I had in my life?

— Literally millions.

— Is this normal? [Disbelief.]

— It is normal to have them; it is just not necessarily normal to realize them. Most of the time people's peak experiences pass them by.

— How many peak experiences does the average person have?

— There is no average. Concept: When you have a peak experience. It's merely a peak. Then you have another peak experience that's bigger than this peak or different from this peak. And every moment of every day is actually to a certain extent a peak of something. Do you have pivotal experiences in life? Yes. Do you have few of those? Comparatively few, yes.

— How many peak experiences did I realize, did I observe?

— About four.

— Four? [Disappointment.]

— Yes.

— How can I have a peak experience at will?

— You deconstruct your ability to doubt at will.

— How can I become enlightened?

— Actually, you already are enlightened.

— What? [Shock.]

— You dreamed of your trip—this is enlightenment. You started your trip—this is enlightenment. You kept pedaling—this is enlightenment. You proved you could do something big when you felt little—this is enlightenment.

— How did I become unenlightened?

— Because you could. Because the world wasn't requiring it of you anymore. Because one of the mysteries of humans is that they forget they are as magical as anything could possibly be.

— Are people good or bad?

— Both, and it is human beings that make the determination of good and evil. The world is not that threatening of a place if you are not an antagonist. For the most part, you did not example yourself to the world as a target or a targeter. People viewed you as an emissary, not as a foreigner. Consequently, the world was open to allowing you to pass through unmolested. Here's concept: you were never hunted by lions. Your bicycle was, but you were never in danger of being eaten. However, you were watched. They saw you pass, and in their mind, as an animal, they were looking at you to know whether you were food, or whether you were a predator more powerful than they. Now had you stopped and done some constructive grazing then started again, you would have attracted their attention. Had you seen the lion, and tried to make yourself go a lot faster, the lions would have then thought that you were responding as food would respond. They might have attacked. But you observed with a state of wonder; and, therefore, they did not sense within you this state of fear that food might get, nor the state of attack that a predator might give. Consequently, you were invisible on their scale of experiences and an unknown, and they simply ignored you, lest you were a threat to their existence.

— How do people find peace?

— By eliminating the sense of lack, however that gets eliminated. It can be eliminated internally, and it can be eliminated externally. And just because you happen to have a lot of money does not mean you've eliminated the sense of lack. The other half is, you give peace by not projecting what somebody else *should* be and becoming angry when they aren't.

— How do people find love?

— They accept it, rather than find it. They accept that the definition of love is a discernment quality. They value the differences and they value the samenesses, and they value every moment, and that by valuing love, they actually increase its value.

— How can people be happy, in other words, enjoy the moment?

— By recognizing that the moment is part of a larger whole, and the larger whole is what you are going to live, but what you are going to experience is the moment; and that means your lives are not about the goal as much as they are about the process. When you rode your bicycle, you inhaled where you just came from, and to an extent you inhaled a sense of self, and moved on with a sense of purpose for the next place. The more places you passed, the more times you discerned there was something new you were going to experience.

— What is the meaning of suffering?

— It is a way of perceiving that you are actually doing something. Here's thought: What was it you were thinking when you were pedaling up the biggest mountain?

— How much it hurt, but that I didn't want to live with the regret of quitting.

— So, essentially you were making a sacrifice of your body and your body's energies for the feeling of success at reaching the top. You could have at any point in time said, "It's not worth it." But you didn't. Why?

— Because I wanted the experience—the emotions.

— Yes. So, you kept going. At any moment, you could have quit. At any moment, you may not have been able to continue. But you accepted those things as part of what it was, and you didn't make the projection that somehow you as a person were going to be a better person after having done this. You instead stayed focused upon your sense of accomplishment as what you were looking for.

— Did I find what I was looking for on my trip?

— You found moments of it.

— Am I still looking for it?

— Yes. You won't always be looking for it; but you won't ever find it.

— I'll never find it? [Worry.]

— No.

— Is that the same for everyone?

— To a lesser or greater extent, yes. Some look for it so hard that they kill themselves. The answer is: you won't find it if you are looking for it, you'll find it when you stumble across it. You'll know it for what it is, and once you know it, it doesn't need to be repeated, and you get to discover the next new thing.

— Is it beneficial for me to stop looking for it?

— Yes.

— But you say I'll never find it?

— You won't. It is not a conundrum kind of riddle although it may seem like that. *You will always* be driven by that feeling, that sense of complete euphoric detachment from all threats in life, that one moment when it is you didn't need to think about living or dying or creating, but just focusing on the thing you were doing right then. It is always going to be a part of you along with that other-existence feeling that you got, that spaciness that for a brief moment allowed you to connect to the ten-dimensional universe with your three-dimensional emotional mind.

— You mean a moment of enlightenment?

— Yes.

— This feeling is what drove me around the world?

— Yes. The creative force that is the Is-ness seeks change—new creations in everything. What you might say is: the Isness abhors boredom; and, because you are part of the Isness, you also abhor boredom. Your search has been driven by the thought process that if you find just the right place then you'll get to be happy. But in the nature that you've found that anytime you do a thing because you choose to do it, it tends to be a happier event for you.

— So, should I change what I am looking for?

— Maybe changing *why* you're looking for it is better. The *why* can be anything, but if you don't know the *why* or you don't sense the *why* you get a crossed purpose very easily.

— Should I choose to look for what gives me joy as opposed to what I feel I *have* to do?

— Yes, the other part is, in everything you do there is an element of joy to begin with. The other problem is, it becomes less than joyful when you start seeing the bad parts. And you see the bad parts because you discern and define that they are bad parts, not because they inherently are. Why not discern the difference between what you think you are, what you think you *should* be, and what you are actually willing to be? Another way is this: intellectual responsibility for emotional laziness.

— Am I emotionally lazy?

— [Blank expression.]

— [Laugh.] Okay, I'll assume that's a yes. Why can't I just find love in the way I am?

— In part, because the same thing that caused you to ride a bicycle around the world—a projection that there is some grand huge truth that if you just know it you can be safe and productive.

— **But there is no big grand truth.**

— There is. The big grand truth is that there is no big grand truth, that you make that big grand truth by your own participation.

— **Can I make a new one?**

— Yes. Every minute of every day and you must. Another way to think about it would be this: ask *why* rather than make defenses. Here's thought: why would it be necessary to ride around the world on your bicycle? Why not just ride around your neighborhood everyday?

— **Because this would be nothing new.**

— In part, but also because you have many emotional things like *should be, should do, should know,* things you learned about what you are supposed to be if you are doing it right. These are imaginary lions, and it doesn't matter whether you outrun them or not, or whether they scratch you or not, the reality is you are going to live, but they can create a sense of anxiety, a sense of fear. In part, you found a useful thing in your fear, and so by riding around the world no one could look and say, "Gee, that's a silly pastime."

— **So, why did I ride my bicycle around the world?**

— Because of the way that you thought about yourself regarding your education and teachings and responsibilities, and the way that you were dictated to by your father about how you should feel about yourself, and because of the way you interpreted your mother's interpretation of the world. Effectively, you were fed and believed that as a human being you're supposed to contribute what someone else might want. Because you didn't want to have to answer the reason why you didn't want to do anything else except ride around on your bicycle. And, it had a sense of adventure. It had a sense of uncertainty, a sense of intrinsic value and you played with it, because you didn't exactly have any-thing right at that moment that was a thing you could join with in the way that you thought the world might want you to join. So, you rode around the world instead of falling into the sense of being someone else's answer for what they needed done. You were taking advantage of being the adventurer in your own life. For half of the trip, you were running away. The other half you were realizing.

— **What was my trip's intrinsic value?**

— The intrinsic value is this: *you* did the bicycle trip and every new person you passed, every new person that you talked to, every new person that you ate dinner with was an added thing to your life; and you were an added thing to their life. No moments of the day were expended in wasted life moments. So, another thought would be this: how many minutes of your life are you willing to commit to anything? You're trading a moment of your life that has some inherent value. Are you trading it good?

— **Does the world care if I am doing something that I think is valuable for it?**

— Human beings, the world, the Isness, doesn't even register that you are doing something for it. But you do; so, therefore, the universe does register it, it just doesn't register it outside of you. Will it appreciate what you've done? It may. But then again it may not even notice you did it.

— **How did my bicycle trip change the world?**

— Doing the apparently not useful thing and doing it in a very big way, gave a lot of people a sense of hope and a state of wonder of why it is that someone would travel so far from their home for nothing more than to simply see the sites. Having done this some of the people that you interacted with grew a sense of faith that it's possible. In the scope of world events, it was an event not unlike events that have occurred before. What made it special is—you did it. How did it affect the world? As anything that human endeavors have ever done for a state of passion and a state of curiosity, very highly. Did it bring world peace? No. Did governments look at it with a sense of *this is the power of a man?* No. But the people that you interacted with will remember, and they will tell stories to their children and their children's children of the day you passed through their village. In some places, yours is a legend to tell children, "Conquer the world." And in other places, it's a legend to say, "What a silly thing to do. Why would anyone wish to go more than ten miles?" Once you are gone, what you will have lent to the world is simply a sense of "it can be" and hope.

— **How did my bicycle trip change me?**

— It left you with many hours of self-indulgent pedaling and isolation from other people interspersed with true participation. And part of the enhancing element of when you met people and you did things was because of the long hours that you had nothing but your own sense of concept. And because you were traveling in places that were very different and you were doing things that were very different, these added a heightened state of awareness for you. What you might say is you became super aware. Also, the long hours of using the body and exhausting the sugars and exhausting the waters altered the way that your brain pattern thinks as well as the way that your body works. In one way to speed up your conceptual mind, in another way to slow down your absoluteness; and the shortening of the eventual length of your life by a little bit.

— What's a little bit?

— Approximately five years.

— Oh... Ah... You mean I wore out my body? [Fear.]

— Yes.

— **What can I do now that will give me the greatest joy in my life?**

— Do not disregard the large portion of why you rode around the world is the reason why you can't find doing something different.

— **I don't understand.**

— As each country passed you by, you left it behind and embarked on a new thing. As each person that you talked to was left behind, you could remember the interchange, they could remember the interchange, but effectively they required nothing more of you than simply to be there and to ride on. Consequently, you didn't have to plan very much other than, "Where's the road?" and "When do I eat?" The rest of it was just keep pedaling. Very clearly defined. And as long as you did it, you could have adventures along the way and go back to that clearly defined path. So, it was safe. It was safer riding around the world then it would have been to do any other thing that you possibly could have done at that point. So there's an element of safety that you were looking for. An escape from something that you perceived you had to do.

— **Because I was afraid?**

— And that's also part of your strength of character—you tend to take challenges to your abilities, and face them directly increasing your abilities as much as possible. Here's another thought: you don't have to make great huge things occur. It's doing the little things that makes those big huge things occur. How did you ride your bicycle around the world? One pedal push at a time. One revolution of the wheel at a time. You just happened to have the dedication to keep making the pedals go around until you finished the test.

— **The test?**

— Yes. A test of your own character.

— **What is the meaning of life?**

— Almost the same as the meaning of the Isness. The Isness is really the thing you are looking at and claiming to be God. Most of your sense of God is a subset of the Isness. For most humans, God is a useful justification of their behavior patterns as an external justifier of whatever it is they choose to do. The Isness is all things plus one more thing. It has no prejudice against any creation. It accepts all creations, all endeavors, with *equal* sense. As far as the Isness is concerned, for you to pick up a small puppy and feel a sense of joy is just as important a creation as the star that sits within your solar system drawing in enough materials that it creates another planet. To the Isness, they are both equal. Neither is more powerful, neither is bigger, neither one is absolute in that regard. You as human beings like to think that your life has a big special purpose. Everything you do as a human has a special purpose and intention. There is no one thing. The meaning of life is to be committed to living it, and not be vested in living it exactly a certain way. Have the passion to live, and have the purpose to know it is yours. How many cultures did you go through and discover that the meaning of life for each person was individual?

— **Every country. Every person.**

— And doesn't that meaning of life for them have to do with their sense of participation with their life? Their ownership of their life?

— **[Nodding agreement.] What is my soul's purpose?**

— To give you the answer crosses free will because it gives you the path out of it without you taking the steps of creativity. It would give you an easy way that you didn't actually learn, that you couldn't use the next time. It's still the same fundamental purpose, though, as every other soul, and that is to co-create.

— **What is the secret of life?**

— To a large extent you might say there is no secret. The bigger question is: Why are the lies of life so necessary? The secret is to understand that whatever you think another person is that's only part of them. The secret is to give yourself the grace to know that no matter what you experience it is still only part of you, that you, like the Isness, are everything you have been plus one more thing. The *one more thing* is whatever creation you endeavor, whatever thought you have, whatever emotion you experience. And that is the added thing to the wholeness of what you have been, and added to the whole of the Isness. And the secret is to focus on what you enjoy rather than what you don't.

— **How come I feel I must have already known these things we are talking about?**

— Because you have. What you haven't, you might say is, the faith in self. Not yet.

— **Uh. Okay. Thank you. [Disappointment.]**

— Don't thank me thank yourself for taking the step of action to participate.

— **After everything I've done and everything I've learned, why do I feel I'm missing something... lacking faith?**

— Part of it is: understanding something and living something are two different things. Another part is: that you realize that you never need to create the same thing twice. You never need to ride your bicycle down the same path twice. And you have not yet decided what to create next.

— Is there something I can do now that will be like riding around the world, that will give me the greatest sense of creativity in my life?

— Concept: There's an infinite amount of opportunities that you may come into contact with wherever you are. If you allow yourself to be the explorer instead of the expecter, if you are willing to walk uncharted territories, if you realize that it will not save you from anything including yourself, then you don't need to know the name of what to do next, you will discover the name. Here's hint: the biggest muse you can have in life is to be amused by life.

— **What is the probability that I will have an adventure bigger and better than my bike trip?**

— One-hundred percent.

— **Wow! And what might that look like?**

— [Smile.]

Thanks again to everyone that helped make my trip possible. **Previous:** The Wheel of Life.

Appendix—Metric Conversion Table

I have decided to use the metric system in my book, because it's the standard everywhere except the USA, Mynamar, and Liberia. In addition, I find the metric system to be very beautiful and simple. Like my bicycle trip, the length of the metric meter was originally defined by the circumference of the planet. Specifically, the distance from the equator to the pole was measured and assigned to be 10,000,000 meters, which is a rather arbitrary number except that ten happens to the number of fingers that we have, and one meter made a convenient unit, similar to the empirical yard. One liter was defined as the volume of a cube of water ten centimeters squared, which also defined the weight of one kilogram. Temperature was defined according to the freezing (0°) and boiling point (100°) of water and also based on units of ten. The metric system made it very easy to plan my days, estimating such things as the inclination of roads, distances to the summit, how far I could I ride, and how much food and water I would need.

Conversion Table
1 Kilometer (KM) = 0.62 miles
1 Meter (M) = 1.09 yards
1 Liter (L) = 0.26 gallons or 1.05 quarts (2.2 pounds)
1 Kilogram (KG) = 2.2 pounds

1 mile = 1.60 kilometers
1 yard = 0.91 meters
1 gallon or 4 quarts = 3.78 liters
1 pound = 0.45 kilograms

Help prove one smile can ripple the world.

One of the main reasons I travel is to see my influence and be influenced by the world. I think that's what we all want. For my next book, I wish to showcase how the ripple of your passage can influence the world, maybe it can even flow all the way around the world, back to the source, elevating us all to the next level. Please share how Falling Uphill inspired you to live your "impossible" dream and how you passed the Olympic torch of inspiration on to your community. The best stories will be featured in the next book. More info: http://www.theArgonauts.com/success

Visit the website:

~ *More stories, photos and movies*
~ *Schedule Scott for speaking events*
~ *Download the audio book*
~ *Order additional copies of Falling Uphill signed by the author. (Bulk discounts available.)*
~ *And much more of course....*

Printed in the United States
151536LV00001B/2/P